Watching
Their Dance

Sherrie Crutcher-Marin

We can never lose HOPE...

ATTENTION, CORPORATIONS, UNIVERSITIES, AND
PROFESSIONAL ORGANIZATIONS: Quantity discounts are available on
bulk purchases of this book for educational purposes, sales premiums, or
fundraising. Special books or book excerpts can also be created to fit
specific needs. For quantity purchases of this book:

  NorCal Publishing Company
  Address: 6235 Barbara Lane
              Auburn, California 95602
  Email: theresecrutchermarin@gmail.com
  Phone: 530-906-8415

Publisher's Cataloging-in-Publication data

Name: Crutcher-Marin, Therese, author
Title: *Watching Their Dance: Three Sisters, a Genetic Disease and
Marrying Into a Family at Risk for Huntington's*

Description: Auburn, CA: NorCal Publishing Company, 2017
Identifiers:
ISBN 978-0-9984422-0-4 (print book)
978-0-9984422-1-1 (Kindle)
978-0-9984422-2-8 (ePub)

Subjects: LCSH Crutcher—Family. | Huntington's disease—Personal
narratives. | Huntington's disease—Genetic aspects. | Huntington's disease—
Patients—Family relationships. | Huntington's Chorea. | Sisters. | BISAC
BIOGRAPHY & AUTOBIOGRAPHY / Medical
Classification: LCC RC394.H85 C78 2017 | DDC 616.8/510092—dc23

First Printing 2017

Cover photo by the author
Author photo by Filmworks Photography
Edited by Pamela Feinsilber: pamelafeinsilber.com
Cover design/interior design: Jim Shubin, bookalchemist.net

Watching Their Dance

A MEMOIR

Three Sisters, a Genetic Disease and Marrying Into a Family at Risk for Huntington's

THERESE CRUTCHER-MARIN

NorCal Publishing Company

Author's Note

This is my story, a work of nonfiction, and I've told it as I remember it to the best of my ability. Everyone views the world through his or her own eyes, and I've done my best to write the truth as I see it. My intent is to share the story I lived and breathed. I have changed the names of some individuals and have occasionally omitted people and events, but only when that omission had no impact on either the truthfulness or the essence of the story.

100% of the profits from the book will be donated to the nonprofit organization Huntington's Disease Society of America.

Dedication

For the mother-in-law I never knew,
Phyllis Iva Cahoon Marin

And for my three beloved friends and sisters-in-law,
Loralee, Marcia Louise,
and Cynthia Ann

We can do no great things, only small things
with great love.
—Mother Teresa

Introduction

Forty years ago, a strong, cold wind blew into my life and upended everything.

I was in love with a man I planned to marry. He was extremely close to his three sisters, and I loved them as deeply as if they were my own family. I looked forward to one day having a beautiful wedding, bearing children, enjoying many good times with these women, growing old with this man.

Then we learned all four were at risk for Huntington's, a horrific neurological disease. Woody Guthrie, the great songwriter and singer, is still the most famous person to have suffered from this fatal genetic disorder, which causes the progressive breakdown of nerve cells in the brain—leading, eventually but inexorably, to the destruction of one's physical and mental abilities. It's been likened to having Parkinson's, Alzheimer's, and ALS at the same time. Every child with a parent who carries this mutated gene has a fifty percent chance of inheriting it.

The disease usually manifests when one is between thirty and forty-five years old. When Guthrie died, in 1967, there was no test to determine who carries the mutated gene, no treatment, and no cure. There's a blood test now, but still no treatment. And still no cure.

Because only seven to ten percent of those who might have inherited the gene decide to be tested, it's not known how many people are at risk worldwide. The highest frequencies of HD are found in Europe, Australia, and the United States (with one hundred cases per million people). The lowest documented frequencies of HD are in Africa, China, Japan, Finland (with six cases per million people), and Hong Kong (with 3.7 cases per million people).

But numbers mean nothing when the risk of developing this disease comes into your life, as it did mine. John and his sisters had not had a happy or nurturing childhood, and I admired them from the day we met for their ability to be positive, loyal, fun-loving, forgiving, and kind. What I learned from them could never be found in a book, a classroom, a religious setting, or a therapist's office. Forty years ago, I took the biggest gamble of my life by keeping these people in mine, and it has made me the person I am today.

Contents

1

*S*ome lives seem to move smoothly along a natural continuum, with one event or decision seeming to slide into the next. Such people seem to have faced no dramatic forks in the road, had few life-altering choices to make. Other lives, at least in hindsight, travel in a particular direction at one particular life-changing moment. That's what happened to me, when, at age twenty-two, I suddenly had to confront the most complicated decision of my life.

I met John Anthony Marin in 1976, when we were attending junior college in Contra Costa County, across San Francisco Bay on the far side of the Berkeley hills. I was twenty and he was one year older, with light brown hair and kind hazel eyes, tall, handsome, and athletic; I fell for him immediately. We felt so close so quickly, it wasn't long before we were a couple.

I quickly learned that being with John meant having his three older sisters in my life as well. The four had had a difficult upbringing and were exceptionally close. Their mother had been placed in a psychiatric hospital when John was just a baby. Their father, Big John Marin, would never tell them why their mother was gone and when she might come back. Of course, his life was difficult, too: In addition to having four children under age six and working full-time, he helped his elderly immigrant parents manage a five-acre ranch next to his home. Even so, he didn't seem to take much interest in his children, never showing them affection or encouragement, only criticism and negativity. He treated his oldest daughter, Lora, as a housekeeper, and the others just stayed out of his way.

When I met them, Lora was twenty-eight, a blond, striking woman with a creamy complexion, twinkling eyes, and a welcoming smile. Her generosity and bubbly personality drew people to her; I always felt a light radiated from Lora. By day, she was a secretary at an accounting firm in Sacramento; by night, a highly creative chef. I loved visiting her and her husband, Dave, a jokester and life-of-the-party kind of guy. He and Lora had become a couple when she was fourteen, and Dave had embraced John, then eight, like a big brother.

Marcia was twenty-six. She was shy but sophisticated, glowing with gentility—the first woman I knew who looked chic in jeans, maybe because she had them dry-cleaned. Her light brown curly hair and makeup were always impeccable. Neither sister had a college degree; after Marcia graduated from high school, she'd gone to work in San Francisco in the typing pool at Pacific Bell. But she was smart and ambitious, and ten years later, her title was Marketing Representative. She lived in an apartment in Walnut Creek, about fifteen miles east of Oakland. She'd been with Glenn, a local realtor, for several years.

By the time I began dating John, Cindy, two years older and his childhood buddy, was working as a dental assistant in Surrey, British Columbia, just above the Canadian border. She visited during the holidays, so I'd been with her a few times. John called her a "free spirit" and the positive force in their family. Like John, she had a wide smile and hazel eyes, and there was no denying their kinship.

Whenever I was around the sisters, I noticed how they doted on their little brother, who, at six-foot-three, towered over them. It had become clear to me how much they supported, protected, and defended one another, no matter what. We spent lots of time with Lora and Dave, Marcia and Glenn, playing softball, having barbecues and parties, camping, just hanging out.

At times, I envied the Marin siblings' relationship. Even though they'd had such a challenging childhood, John and his sisters were all positive, fun-loving, giving individuals, so different from my Catholic-ritual-driven, take-no-chances family. I'd grown up in a home where the first reaction to just about anything was negative, and I'd been taught never to draw outside the lines. Independence and self-esteem were never encouraged; instead, my parents used guilt, a good Catholic method of control, to motivate my sisters and me. How could I not feel guilty when I felt closer to Lora and Marcia than I did to my own sisters?

By 1978, my relationship with John had become a long-distance one—four hundred and eleven miles, to be exact—since he was at California State Polytechnic University (Cal Poly) in Pomona, and I was attending the California State University in Sacramento. John would drive the eight hours to see his sisters and me as often as possible, and whenever he was home, we stayed with Lora and Dave. We had so much fun during those visits, I never minded sharing him.

Our lives changed dramatically one Saturday afternoon in early November. Though Thanksgiving was just a few weeks away, John's sisters had asked him to come home that weekend and to bring me with him to Lora and Dave's house that afternoon.

Cindy was there, too, having flown in from Canada the previous week. I wondered why she, too, was there before Thanksgiving. John's sisters and Dave greeted us at the door with their usual smiles and hugs. John and I sat on the comfortable white couch as his sisters finished preparations for dinner and Dave took a phone call. I looked at Bubba and Cedrick, their Keeshond dogs, lying on the brown shag carpet in the sun; at the custom-made macramé hanging I'd always admired, above the brick fireplace; at the framed photographs of Dave and Lora, the Marin siblings, Lora holding Bubba with a huge smile, on the sand-colored walls. The fire roared in the hearth as soft music played on the stereo. This cozy room, always such a safe haven, now felt strangely cold and unfamiliar.

My apprehension grew as the sisters' whispers floated into the living room. Turning to John, I murmured, "Do you have any idea what they want to talk to us about?"

He shrugged. "It's something to do with our mom's side of the family, but other than that, I'm as clueless as you."

Just then, the three sisters entered the room. I felt the hair on the back of my neck stand up. Dave leaned against the doorframe as Marcia took a seat across the room, crossed her legs, and wrapped her hands around her knees, smiling vaguely, like a Cheshire cat, I thought. Lora sat next to John and began patting his thigh and nodding as if to say, "Everything's going to be all right." Cindy pulled up a footstool and sat down in front of us.

"The three of us visited Aunt Evelyn last week," she began. "It's been years since we'd seen her, and we decided it was time to reconnect." She looked at me. "She's our mother's younger sister; she lives about an hour south of Sacramento, in Galt. We learned from her that we have a genetic disease in our family, called Huntington's disease. Our mother, Phyllis, and three of her siblings had it." She paused a moment to let the words sink in. "We rarely saw our mother's siblings after she died, so we were unaware that they had suffered from it. It's an inherited disease that causes the progressive breakdown of nerve cells in the brain. It affects muscle coordination and leads to behavioral symptoms and, um, mental and physical decline."

"Aunt Evelyn was shocked that we didn't know about the disease in the family," Lora added. "Since Dave and I don't have any kids and Marcia and Cindy are single, she assumed we'd made these choices because of Huntington's."

My hands squeezed John's like a vise, and I moved so close, I was almost sitting on his lap. Otherwise, no one moved; it felt as if an icy despair had frozen everyone in the room. My eyes darted from sister to sister. The word *what* formed on my lips, but I couldn't make a sound.

The only thing I knew about Huntington's was that the great American singer and songwriter Woody Guthrie had died of this terrible wasting disease, and that his last years were even worse than they had to be. Slowly losing control of both muscles and cognition, he became increasingly erratic. At first, he was deemed an alcoholic and then diagnosed schizophrenic. Like John's mother, he lived in psychiatric hospitals for years until he died.

Cindy, always the fearless one when it came to dealing with their father, said, "After the visit, I called Dad and asked him if what Aunt Evelyn had told us was true. I pressed him for answers, but you know Dad. He got angry and never admitted that Mom had had Huntington's."

Coming out of her trance, Marcia said, "The good news is now we know what was wrong with Mom. But the bad news is we each have a fifty-fifty chance of inheriting this disease. And there is no test or cure."

Cindy went to the French doors and stared out at the piles of crimson leaves in the yard. Then she turned and faced us. "I'm tired of not knowing why things happened in our lives. Dad kept us in the dark, not just about Mom but about everything. It wasn't fair, because we deserve to know, especially about this."

Lora said, "We asked him for Mom's death certificate, and

he refused to show it to us. So Marcia went to the Contra Costa County recorder's office and got a copy, and sure enough, it said, 'Cause of death, strangulation,' with Huntington's disease as the underlying cause, because she'd had to be tied down in her bed."

The room grew silent again. Lora continued to pat John's thigh while watching me. "We're sorry to drop this on the two of you, but since you guys are talking about marriage, it's only fair you know about the family, Therese."

I blinked my eyes rapidly, trying to clear my head, and looked at John. He just smiled and squeezed my hand tighter. After a few moments, Lora said briskly, "Okay, who wants a drink?"

"I do," we all responded simultaneously.

As she and her sisters walked into the kitchen, I shouted, "Double shot of bourbon for me, please!" John sauntered across the room and began talking with Dave; Dave slapped John on the back, and they immediately started to laugh.

I leaned back on the couch and took a deep breath as I felt this compelling information slowly registering in my consciousness, alerting my senses to danger. A struggle began between my brain and body: As anxiety and doubt crept into my mind, a primal instinct screamed, *Run*, but my heart said, *Stay*. I felt as if I were being pulled one way and then another, back and forth, back and forth.

My body jolted to a stop when John sat down. "Here's your drink, Therese. Are you all right? Did I scare you? You jumped when I said your name."

"No, no, I'm fine, just…just a little chilly. Can you get my sweater, please?"

John returned with my sweater and wrapped it around me. "Are you warm enough now?" I nodded and took a gulp of my drink. When Dave turned on a football game, John's head snapped toward the TV, and he moved to the edge of the couch.

Stirring the ice with my finger, I stared at the russet liquid as my racing heart slowed down. I felt as if I had just watched a scene from a bad play and the curtain had come down with a thud. Needless to say, I was glad it was over and the actors back to their usual selves, but my anguish remained. I had no idea why the sisters had sought this information now. So many questions were popping up in my mind, and unfortunately, they would remain unanswered, because the final act of this play was unscripted, the starring actors unknown. Happy or tragic, the ending would play out only over time.

I looked at John and Dave, cheering for their team, and watched the sisters laughing in the kitchen. Were they trying to put on a good face for me? No, they'd chosen to ignore something they could do nothing about, at least for now. So I tried to change my frame of mind, too, and went into the kitchen. "Can I help?"

At dinner, Lora kept serving us her delicious lasagna, arugula salad with glazed walnuts and mandarin oranges, the world's best garlic bread; Dave never stopped pouring wine and telling funny stories, and we got through the meal. By the time we were devouring Lora's homemade apple pie with vanilla ice cream and Irish coffee, life seemed almost normal. For these four siblings, the new reality meant living at risk for a terrible disease, for how long, no one could predict. All they could do was push the thought aside for a while.

❧❧❧

The next morning, John and I said goodbye to his family and went back to my apartment. It was about a mile from campus, your usual two-bedroom student digs, with posters of Rod Stewart, Kiss, and Fleetwood Mac on the walls, a little balcony off the living room where we stored our bikes. We had it to ourselves, since my roommate, Mary, had gone home to Martinez for the weekend. John and his sisters had also grown up in Martinez, an oil town about fifteen miles west of Walnut Creek, on the south side of the Carquinez Strait. Martinez had been home to a Shell Oil refinery since 1915, and its tanks, buildings, smokestacks, and hundreds of miles of pipes covered a thousand acres of land. Every year, oil tankers docked in the Martinez marina unloaded thousands of gallons of crude oil and shipped out thousands of gallons of refined gasoline and other petroleum products. When you drove past the town on Interstate 80, the smell of oil permeated the air for miles. John and Mary had gone to high school together; in fact, she was the one who had introduced us, at a party in Martinez when we were all attending junior college.

As we studied, I wondered how John felt about the shocking family secret that could change his life, but I didn't know how to bring up the subject. There really wasn't enough time to talk anyway, and I wanted to enjoy the time we had left that weekend.

At one o'clock, John looked at his watch and closed his book. He had to get on the road, and in a few hours I had to start working in the men's department at Weinstock's, then "Sacramento's finest department store."

John gathered up his stuff, then stopped and leaned back in his chair. "I know we haven't talked about yesterday, and you must have a million questions. How about we talk about it over Christmas break? It'll give me time to discuss it with my sisters and get some of my questions answered. You probably have the same ones."

I reached across the table and took his hand. "That sounds good. And I'll try to find more information about the disease." In the parking lot, we stood next to his car, unwilling to say goodbye. As we hugged one another, I leaned my head on his chest. "Be careful on the freeway," I said. "I'll call you Friday night."

John drove out of the parking lot waving and honking his horn. As soon as he disappeared, the realization that my life would never be the same hit me. I stood there a few minutes more, tears rolling down my face.

2

The next morning, I didn't have a class until eleven, so I headed to the library, Marcia's words echoing in my brain. "We each have a fifty-fifty chance of inheriting this disease. And there is no test or cure." As I walked across the campus, the wind was blowing hard and leaves swirled around my feet. Then it began to rain, so I picked up my pace and ran through the library's automatic doors, right before Mother Nature unleashed a torrential downpour.

Searching for books and magazine articles on Huntington's disease was frustrating. I finally tracked down a medical-reference book, though it took me awhile to locate it. When I had the book in my hand, I slid onto the cold, dingy tiled floor and began reading the two paragraphs on the disease.

"Huntington's disease was first known as Huntington's chorea, as in choreography, the Greek word for dance. The term chorea describes how people affected with the disorder writhe, twist, and turn in a constant, uncontrollable dancelike motion. It is a hereditary, degenerative brain disorder for which there is no effective treatment or cure."

I could hardly breathe as I continued reading. "The disease causes certain areas of the brain to atrophy (break down) faster than normal, causing the gradual decline of a person's ability to walk, talk, and reason. Symptoms usually appear between the ages of thirty and forty-five."

The words on the page became fuzzy and my stomach began to hurt. I flung the book away, as if it were too hot to hold. The slam as it hit the floor drew stares from kids roaming the nearest aisle, but I didn't care. I didn't want the book anywhere near me, and I pushed it away with my foot.

When I noticed I'd begun panting like a dog, I started taking deep breaths and leaned my head against the bookshelf, trying to calm down, as bile threatened to crawl up my throat.

My thoughts quickly shifted to John. If he carries the mutated gene, he could conceivably show symptoms in less than ten years. And if he does have it and we have children, they will also be at risk. I could feel anxiety bubbling inside me like lava, tightening my chest and throat. Was this the way Phyllis had felt when she died? But an even more terrible, because more immediate, question came into my mind, and I dropped my head into my hands. Could I live with such uncertainty?

After several minutes, my body recovered, but my heart began to ache. When I stood up, the room began spinning, and the shelves seemed to close in on me. My mind was screaming, Breathe, Therese, and get out of this building as fast as you can!

Outside, the rain was still coming down in buckets, so I threw my backpack down on the nearest bench and followed it. I was protected from the rain, but the gale slapped my face and whipped my hair into my eyes. Thunder boomed, lightning flashed, and the storm intensified. Like this storm, breaking branches off trees, uprooting bushes, and mowing down plants, Huntington's was changing the landscape of my life.

❧❧❧

On the Tuesday before Thanksgiving, I completed my accounting test, handed it in, and left the classroom feeling pretty good. I was heading to the campus bookstore to sell back my accounting book when I remembered that the firm

Lora worked for was not far from campus. I'd been so busy the past few weeks, trying to stay focused and study for midterms, thoughts of how John's sisters were coping hadn't entered my mind.

That evening, I picked up the phone to call Lora, then hesitated and put it down again. When the sisters had given us the news, they'd made it clear that they didn't want to discuss Huntington's at any length or dwell on it at all. I considered waiting to call her, especially since I didn't know what was going to happen with John and me, but I quickly changed my mind, because she was my friend and I cared about her. As I dialed, my palms were sweaty and there was a metallic taste in my mouth, because I'd bitten my lip and it was bleeding.

The phone rang four times, and I was just about to hang up. "Hello," Lora said.

"Hi, Lora. It's Therese." I could hear the rustling of paper bags and the dogs barking.

"Hi, Therese. Sorry it took me so long to get to the phone. I just walked in from work. Can you hold on for a minute while I let the dogs in? They're really wound up tonight."

Once she was back on the line and we were done with the pleasantries, I said, "I'm sorry I haven't called and thanked you for the wonderful dinner." I grabbed the phone holder and walked the room with the cord dragging behind me. "How are you doing? I mean, with the news about your mom?"

"Oh, I'm fine, Therese, don't worry about me. How's school going? Are we going to see you on Thanksgiving?"

"School is fine. I had my first midterm yesterday, and I have two more tomorrow. And yes, I'll be over on Thanksgiving, later in the day after my family has finished with dinner. I'm really looking forward to it, because I'll get to see your brother and exams will be over."

"Well, great! I need to run. We'll see you later. Bye."

"Bye."

Lora was acting like the news was no big deal. But it was a big deal to me, and I wasn't even at risk for this horrible disease. I began to think that might be a normal reaction for the Marin siblings: ignoring a problem until they came face to face with it.

❧❧❧

The next day, after my marketing midterm, I packed my stuff and drove the roughly one hundred miles to my parents' home, arriving that evening. As I opened the front door, I dropped my laundry bag and backpack and shouted, "Mom, I'm home."

My parents, James and Rita, lived in Concord, about ten miles from Marcia's apartment. Our ranch-style house was on a cul-de-sac, with friendly neighbors who took as much care of their homes as my parents did ours. The pie-shaped property had an eight-foot-high concrete wall running the length of the backyard to cut down on the noise generated by traffic on Treat Boulevard. The previous owners had left treasures in that yard, though: orange, cherry, plum, and apple trees and a grape arbor with mature vines. Like most married women of that time, my mother was a homemaker. She loved to cook and bake, so I could always count on finding homemade jam or applesauce, fruit pies or coffee cake in the kitchen.

My mother also loved to hunt for old, discarded furniture and repair or restore it, so our house looked like an antique store. We had a 1900 Victrola phonograph in the living room, and a glass-topped, claw-foot spindle oak parlor table next to the antique couch my mom had reupholstered. In the dining room were an aged dining room table, creaking matching chairs, and a refinished china cabinet. The four bedrooms all had old headboards, footboards, and dressers.

My parents had married in a Catholic church in Kansas City, Missouri, in September 1952. My father worked with the U.S. Postal Service, and important decisions were always based on how they would affect him, not how they would affect the family. My older sister, Ellen, and two younger sisters and I started life in Shawnee Mission, Kansas, with lots of family—aunts, uncles, cousins, and both sets of grandparents—nearby. Our world revolved around St. Pius Catholic Parish and School. Until I was thirteen, we interacted only with Catholic Caucasian families like ours.

That year, my father got a big promotion. After working with the post office since he was twenty, he became a postal inspector and was transferred to Riverside, California (the birthplace of the California citrus industry), sixty miles east of Los Angeles. After years of Catholic school, my sisters and I were thrown into a public-school system, with students of varied backgrounds and cultures and nothing hip to wear, since we'd never worn anything but school uniforms. It was culture shock for all of us, particularly our parents, who could scarcely comprehend what was going on in California in 1969: demonstrations against the Vietnam War, unrest on college campuses, Flower Power, hippies....

Two years later, my father was transferred to Washington, D.C., another tough move for us. And in 1974, after I graduated from high school, my father was transferred again, to San Francisco. By then, Ellen had married, so she remained on the East Coast.

My old-fashioned parents saw no reason for a woman to attend college, so they had never encouraged my sisters and me to be anything other than homemakers, like our mom. After we moved to the Bay Area, I worked for a year in a "good government job," as my parents put it. Then I quit to attend college full-time. That paved the way for Amy, three years younger and a bookworm and introvert, to attend Diablo Valley College, as I had. Jennifer, eight years younger, was now a freshman in high school. My grandmother, Lena, was working as a companion to a woman in Rossmoor, a senior-living community in Walnut Creek. When I was still living at home, I used to pick up Grandma on Friday nights and drive her back to our house for the weekend. Amy had that duty now.

Our Thanksgiving dinner was as quiet and unexciting as usual. As my sisters and I cleared the table, Grandma sat at the breakfast bar, stripping the turkey carcass for soup stock. I was so happy when the telephone rang and John said he'd be over in half an hour to pick me up.

❧❧❧

John's upbringing had been completely different from mine. His father had grown up on a farm in Martinez, spent two years fighting in the Philippines during World War II, returned to his job as a planning technician for Contra Costa County, and soon married Phyllis Iva Cahoon. John's mother had already exhibited symptoms of Huntington's. They didn't know she had the disease, of course, but Big John's older brother, Jack, and his wife, Faye—as well as his three older sisters, Jessica, Christina, and Alice—had tried to persuade him not to marry her. They'd all noticed her irritability, lack of enthusiasm, occasional depression, and violent outbursts. She often seemed unable to focus on a conversation or initiate one; they'd even found her talking to someone no one else could see. But Big John didn't want to hear any of that nonsense. He'd made up his mind, and besides, Phyllis was pregnant.

John's parents married in late November 1947; Loralee was born the following July. Marcia Louise was born eighteen months later, and Cynthia Ann in 1952. After that, Phyllis began staying part-time in Napa State Hospital, about thirty miles away, where she could be observed and tests conducted. John was born on September 6, 1954, and not long after his birth, his mother was admitted to the hospital permanently, coming home only on rare occasions. Until John was about five, the four siblings visited their mother one Sunday each month or so. She died in the hospital on July 8, 1968, at age forty-five. By then, her uncontrolled movements were causing such violent flailing, the nurses had tied her limbs to the bed, and she'd gotten tangled in her bindings and strangled.

Once John and I were in the car, I slid close to him. It felt so right and comfortable to have this man with whom I was irrevocably in love wrap his arm around my shoulder. At some point, Big John had sold the home his children grew up in and now lived in the rolling hills above Martinez with their stepmother, Lucy. When we got to Martinez, John and I stopped at the waterfront to have a few more minutes alone. The air was crisp as we walked along the shore holding hands, looking out on Carquinez Strait and listening to the sea lions bark.

I was always a little reserved around Lucy and Big John, though I only saw them on holidays and at the annual Marin family picnics. I felt Lucy wasn't fond of John's sisters; I'd heard her make rude comments to them over the years, which they always ignored. And Big John talked nonstop, a know-it-all who was never wrong, as far as he was concerned. When he talked at me, his voice boomed and I felt cornered, unable to get away from him, so I usually stayed close to John or his sisters.

The front door was ajar, and John held the screen door open for me as we walked into a hallway lined with gold-speckled mirrors. In the living room, I paused as usual before two tall black display cabinets, whose special lighting enhanced the dozens of beautiful Japanese tea sets and figurines displayed on glass shelves. On the opposite wall were two prints of Japanese women with white-painted faces and wearing kimonos. (Lucy's first husband had been a pilot during World War II, and Lucy had lived in Japan.) A huge picture window looked into a well-manicured backyard and Big John's garden, in which he nurtured peas, tomatoes, grapes, peppers, pears, and apples.

When we walked into the family room, his sisters greeted us with their usual smiles and warm hugs. The positive atmosphere surprised me, since they had just discovered the secret their dad had kept from them and still would not acknowledge. I assumed they had forgiven him, because their behavior was nothing short of tender.

When John interacted with his father, however, which wasn't often, I saw a different side of him. He became sarcastic and angry; unlike his sisters, he wasn't looking for his father's attention or approval. Since Phyllis had been unable to care for her children by the time John was born, his Aunt Christina had taken him into her home, in Sacramento, and cared for him until he was two years old. Then his father moved him into his paternal grandparents' home, on the ranch next to Big John's house, and he lived with his Spanish-speaking grandparents for the next four years. His grandmother called him Yanni. He started kindergarten when he was four years old, and after school he helped her with chores and in the garden. On weekends, he played with his sisters.

Big John had met Lucy in 1960, just a year after John

joined his sisters in his father's home. She was from Texas, divorced and working at McClellan Air Force Base, in Sacramento. John had told me that six months into the relationship, his father had begun traveling to Sacramento every weekend, leaving on Friday nights after work and returning on Sundays after his children were in bed. "On Thursdays after school, each of us had a job to prepare him for his trip," he remembered. "Lora washed his clothes, Marcia ironed them, I polished his shoes, and Cindy packed his bag nice and neat. We were glad to get rid of him, because we could do whatever we wanted around the house. Plus, we had three nights free from sitting at the dinner table for hours listening to Dad rant and rave about work, bills, and all the other stress in his life."

Even so, John had felt abandoned by his only parent. "Dad didn't always make sure we had food in the house when he left, so we ate what we had. Saltine crackers with mayonnaise and Grandma's baked bread were our staples. My grandparents were in their seventies and eighties by then and didn't have a lot of money, so when Aunt Jessica and Uncle Jack visited them most weekends, they'd bring all of us a few groceries." John remembered the arguments his father had with his sisters, who tried to talk to him about leaving his kids the way he did.

After dinner, John's sisters and I cleaned up and put the leftovers in the refrigerator, while Lucy sat in a big chair with her granddaughter on her lap. Her son and daughter-in-law played on the floor with their son. As I watched them, I wondered if John's father ever thought about why his daughters had never had children.

When Big John and Lucy and her family retreated to the bedrooms, I read the relief on everyone's faces. Dave grabbed an album he'd brought with him and put the record on the turntable. It was comedian Richard Pryor's *Live in Concert*. "He uses the F-word a lot," Dave warned us. For the next half hour, I laughed so hard my sides hurt. Just when I thought I couldn't laugh any harder, Dave turned the record over.

When John drove me home late that night, he told me a little more about what had transpired when his dad married Lucy, the year after Phyllis died. "The four of us had only seen Lucy at family picnics and at Christmas. Once they married, Lucy moved into our ranch house, which was a hovel, with four teenagers and my dad around only half the time. She wasn't kind to my sisters, so Lora and Dave married quickly later that year. Dad had been notified by the State of California that the state was going to buy our ranch under the eminent domain law, so that Highway 4 could be built. That's when Dad and Lucy bought the house they're in now. We moved into it in early 1970. Marcia lived there only a few months before she moved in with some girlfriends.

"Unfortunately, Cindy and I were still in high school, so we had to stay. Lucy treated me fairly well—I think she got along better with men than with women—but Cindy wouldn't take any of her meanness, and they clashed a lot. After a couple of years, Cindy moved out, too. I finally figured out that Lucy must have been jealous of my sisters and wanted her husband's undivided attention, like she'd had for the past nine years."

I had always loved John's sisters, but that night, witnessing their unconditional love for their father and their kindness toward a woman who resented them, I felt my love deepen. And then I felt angry. How truly unfair it was for women like this to face such a precarious future.

3

With the help of their Aunt Evelyn, John's sisters had collected information on the Cahoon family. Evelyn had teared up when she told her nieces that only she and her older sister Louise had not shown any symptoms of the disease—so far, anyway. She believed that all her other siblings—Ben, Dennis, Betty, and, of course, Phyllis—had inherited Huntington's from their father. Growing up, the Marin siblings had rarely seen their uncles or Aunt Betty. Aunt Evelyn and her children had lived in Concord until they moved to Galt, after which the families lost touch. Now Betty, who had three children, and Ben, who didn't have any, were seriously ill. Dennis, who also had no children, had died four years earlier at age forty-nine.

In early December, John's sisters talked with a neurologist who specialized in genetics at the University of California at Davis Medical Center. The hospital provided clinical care for people with neuromuscular conditions and neurological disorders, such as Alzheimer's disease and other forms of dementia, epilepsy, dystonia, multiple sclerosis, Parkinson's, and Huntington's disease. Specialists in the department of neurology conducted basic and clinical research on the nervous system.

His sisters had suggested that John and I also speak with this doctor, and John made an appointment for December 22, the day after he arrived at Lora and Dave's for the Christmas holiday. That morning, I woke up with a terrible stomach ache.

In the waiting room, we saw several people in wheel-chairs; I watched as their loved ones cared for them and wondered if any of them had HD. I couldn't help fidgeting in the uncomfortable chair and practically jumped out of it when the nurse called John's name. In the doctor's little office, John sat quietly. I was too nervous to do anything but stand staring vacantly at a poster that displayed the right and left hemispheres of the brain and described the functions each half controlled.

As soon as the doctor entered the room, my heart started pounding. He wore black-rimmed glasses and a white lab coat with Dr. B. Jones NEUROLOGY embroidered in blue above the chest pocket. He shook our hands and asked us to sit. He seemed a kind man. He spoke very softly, choosing his words carefully, but they were tough to hear. He described a genetic disorder that, as we knew, causes the progressive breakdown of nerve cells in the brain, leading to the deterioration of one's physical and mental abilities, usually during the prime of life. It is known as the quintessential family disease, he told us, because of how strong the chances are that the child of a parent with HD will inherit it.

The next words out of his mouth were chilling. "The only sure way to stop the disease is not to have children. Since you don't know your gene status, John, not having children will ensure the disease will not affect another generation. It's the only way of annihilating it."

He picked up the Cahoon family-tree diagram that John's sisters had put together and showed us how Huntington's had moved through the family over four generations. "It looks as if the HD in your family originated from Ora Butler Cahoon, your mother's great-grandfather. He passed the gene on to his son, Wilbert D. Cahoon, your great-grandfather, who married Alice Finch in 1877. Wilbert passed it to his son, your grandfather, Charles Wilbur Cahoon, who married Iva Edith Crane in 1913.

"As you know, he and Iva had six children," he looked at the diagram again, "Ben, Louise, Betty, your mother, Evelyn, and Dennis. Only two of the six have not shown any symptoms." He paused, and I knew what he was going to say next. "Sixty-seven percent of your mother's generation had Huntington's disease."

With so many siblings in the previous generation inheriting the gene, my fear escalated, since it was clearly not a matter of if but of who. I left his office with a churning stomach and barely made it to the nearest restroom before heaving into a toilet. Back at my apartment, I grabbed a box of saltine crackers and lay on the couch while John made chicken soup and tea. I sat up when he brought me the tea, sat down, and put his arm around me.

"I know what the doctor said isn't good news, but we can get through this, Therese. Look at it this way. I could get killed walking across the street tomorrow. Nothing in life is for sure."

I really couldn't talk about it anymore, so I asked John about the internship he had just been awarded through the environmental design department at Cal Poly. I nodded as he spoke, acknowledging his words, but my mind kept shifting back to the doctor's remarks.

"It's a five-month internship with the City of Glendora," John said excitedly. "They want me to work one to five, Monday through Friday, with the redevelopment officer. This will look great on my resume, much better than working at the liquor store. And graduation is only seven months away," he reminded me happily. "Then we can be together."

That night as I lay in bed, I evaluated my strengths and weaknesses, ticking off the boxes one by one: hardworking, caring, compassionate, determined, empathetic, organized, responsible, honest, kind, deeply loving, a person of integrity. But I couldn't tick off one important adjective—brave—because I wasn't sure I could muster the courage to have Huntington's in my life.

When I thought of my weaknesses, having Obsessive-Compulsive Disorder, or OCD, said it all. None of us likes uncertainty, but in people with anxiety disorders, the least bit of uncertainty creates intrusive thoughts that cause uneasiness, apprehension, worry, and fear. It seemed to have ramped up in my family over the last three generations. I had wrestled with this demon for years, always needing to know what, when, what time, who with, for how long. To be able to move through life, I had developed a strategy for any situation: find out everything I could, always be prepared, and plan and plan again.

It was exhausting, but the alternative to being in control as much as possible was too frightening. Balancing my checkbook to the penny, mapping my route to every single place I drove or walked, outlining every facet of my college life, with a backup plan just in case—anticipating every possible outcome to anything is what kept my demons at bay.

This frightening new factor in my life was a far bigger challenge than not knowing how much I had left in my checking account. I saw three possible options for dealing with it: trying to control the possibility of Huntington's; removing the ambiguity from my life; or finding the courage to live with it. There was no way to control when the disease might manifest, and I doubted I could bear the uncertainty, especially since I had been conditioned to feel pessimistic before any positive emotion. I really saw just one option. I tried concentrating on the fact that John had a fifty percent chance of not inheriting the disease, but unlike the Marins, I couldn't find any comfort in that statistic.

The thought of turning my back on the man I loved because he might develop a horrific disease seemed selfish and cruel. But the fear was more than I could take, and hope was not enough to calm my terror.

❧ ❧ ❧

Before I knew it, a week had passed, and John was leaving the next day so that he could work at the liquor store for the rest of the break. When he dropped me off at Weinstock's that morning, he stroked my face and said, "I'll make us a nice dinner at your apartment. We'll celebrate the New Year a little early."

My throat constricted as I choked out the word *okay*. Even though we were busy with returns and exchanges, my eight-hour shift at the department store seemed endless.

That evening, my stomach was in knots and my palms were sweaty. The table was set for two, with a single rose in a vase and two red candles. John pulled out a chair for me, opened the wine, and poured it into a chilled glass. Then he lit the candles and said, "Now, you just relax. Dinner will be done in a few minutes."

The chicken smelled good, but my stomach was churning. As John filled my plate with chicken wings (my favorite part), fried zucchini, and Rice-A-Roni, I kept my gaze on the candles. When he sat down, I couldn't look at him; all I could do was nod, move the food around my plate, take small bites, and pray I wouldn't throw up.

After he finished eating, John leaned back in his chair and said, "Therese, are you okay? You hardly ate anything." He reached for my hand, but I pulled away and went into the living room. The Christmas tree was twinkling in the corner, and I stood close to it and stared at the lights. John tried to put his arms around me, but I pushed him away.

"What's wrong, Therese?"

I felt like such a coward when I couldn't even turn around to face him. The hurtful words I was about to say to this wonderful man were killing me, but I knew I had to say them.

John said, "I know this whole thing with Huntington's is so unfair, and I'm so sorry. If I could make it go away, I would. But I can't." He took a deep breath. "Come on, Therese. Nobody knows what's going to happen in the future. I could be killed walking down the street."

"I know, I know," I said faintly. "But I have to stop seeing you, John. I'm so frightened! I don't think I'm strong enough to live with this terrible disease hanging over our heads every day of our lives." I tried to wipe my tears on my sleeve. "I'm so confused. Why did this have to happen to us?" I covered my face with my hands and sobbed. "I'm sorry."

John turned me around and held me as my body shook with uncontrollable sorrow. "If you need time, I'm fine with that," he said gently. "Take as much time as you need. But don't cut me out of your life, Therese. We can work it out." He sighed. "Please, don't do this to us!"

I pulled away. "John, I'm so sorry. I can't see you anymore." I could hardly speak. "I have to do this. Please, just go!"

I heard the doorknob turn and the door close. Then I sat on the couch and stared at the Christmas tree lights for what seemed hours, hardly able to believe what I'd done. When Mary came home, she asked before she even closed the door, "What's the matter, Therese? Did you and John have a fight?"

I shook my head. "I wish it were that simple, but no. I broke up with him, because of the stupid disease in his family." I searched my friend's face. "What if he doesn't have the Huntington's gene? I could regret this decision for the rest of my life."

Mary was like the Marin siblings, never dwelling on the negative, always seeing the glass half full. I knew she wouldn't judge me, but she couldn't advise me, either. All she could do was shrug and say softly, "I don't know, Therese. Only you can answer that."

The next morning, after only a couple hours of sleep, I made my way to the kitchen and started making coffee. I sat at the kitchen table and opened my marketing book, but after reading the same paragraph three times, I closed the book and dropped my head onto it.

The phone rang, and I answered before thinking who would call so early. "Therese, it's John. I'm leaving in a few minutes, but I wanted to talk to you again. I understand you need time to figure this out, but if you need anything, anything at all, call me, even if you just want to talk. I promise not to put any pressure on you." He hesitated. "Please remember one thing, Therese. I love you."

The silence on my end was palpable. Finally, I whispered, "Okay. Drive safely."

4

The California State University semesters had not yet been reconfigured to end before Christmas break, which meant we took final exams after the holidays. I was glad the finals in two of my classes entailed group projects rather than written exams, because that kept me around friends who could distract me from despair. And Catherine, the men's-department manager at Weinstock's, allowed me to work as many hours as I wanted. Thanks to her, I was too busy to think about John and fell asleep as soon as my head hit the pillow. Unfortunately, I was helpless at keeping John out of my dreams.

Once our finals were done, Mary and I had a girls' night out, and over pizza and beer, she brought up a delicate topic. "What's going on with you and John? Have you decided what to do—if you really are not going to see him anymore?"

I burst into tears.

"I'm so sorry I brought him up, Therese. Please, don't cry." Mary filled my mug with beer and slid it in front of me.

"He hasn't contacted me, and I haven't called him." I grabbed the mug and took a big gulp. "I still don't know if I can handle living with this threat in our lives." I held my head and sobbed. "I'm such a horrible person! I'm such a coward! He's such a great guy, and I love him so much." I raised my head and looked at Mary. "How do I fall out of love with someone who hasn't hurt me?"

❧❧❧

Spring semester began, and I took a seat as my marketing-strategies professor began handing out the course syllabus, with required reading, projects, etc. Many of my friends were in this class and would graduate with me in a few months. With the thought of graduation came thoughts of John, and immediately I felt deflated. He was supposed to be in my life; we were going to celebrate my graduation together. I pictured him sitting with my family in the stands lining the school's football field, partying with his sisters afterward. I'm sure he pictured his graduation in much the same way.

Halfway through that semester, I was curled up on the couch studying when the phone rang. When I heard Mary say, "Hi, John. How are you?" I couldn't decide whether to talk to him or to bolt. Mary was waving her arms, trying to get my attention. Finally, she covered the mouthpiece with her hand and asked sternly, "Don't you want to talk to him?"

I nodded reluctantly and took the phone into the kitchen, leaning against the counter to steady myself. John would be visiting Lora and Dave on his quarter break, and he wanted to take me to dinner on Saturday. "Dinner? On Saturday?" I repeated like an idiot.

Mary tapped me on the shoulder and nodded several times. I gave in and agreed to go.

On Saturday, my heart pounded in my ears all day long. The men's department was inundated with spring merchandise, and it all had to be "on the floor" for a big sale the next day. Even so, I found myself looking at my watch every fifteen minutes, and every time, as if on cue, my stomach flip-flopped. My feelings were swinging like a pendulum, back and forth, from excited to petrified to excited again.

When the doorbell rang, Mary answered the door. She and John greeted each other like the old friends they were, but when I came into the living room, Mary quickly excused herself. John moved close and put his arms around me. I wanted to move away, but my legs felt like jelly.

"Do you want to go to Marie Callender's for dinner?" he asked.

I thought of the many fun times we'd had there with his sisters and shook my head. "Let's go to a little Chinese restaurant I know downtown. It's not far."

Once we'd ordered, John said, "Well, we're almost done—with school, that is." He paused and shifted in his seat. "Thanks for seeing me, Therese. Oh, yeah, Lora and Dave say hi, and they hope you're doing well."

I smiled and nodded. "Please tell them hello."

John played with his chopsticks and fidgeted. Then he took a deep breath and said, "I wanted to see you and find out how you're doing. I'm not trying to pressure you; I just want to know if you've had enough time to reconsider. If you need more time, that's fine." He leaned back and ran his hand through his hair. "I feel like a blubbering idiot. I'm just trying to see where I stand here."

For once, I didn't avoid his eyes. "I'm still not sure." My voice was ragged, and I blinked back emerging tears. "I need more time, John. Please be patient."

After that weekend, John didn't contact me again. Who could blame him?

❧❧❧

Over the next four months, I tried my best to forget John, or to make myself fall out of love with him, but it was impossible to oust him from my heart. The rest of the semester flew by as I completed classes, prepared for graduation, and interviewed for jobs. But John was always in the back of my mind. I wondered whether I would ever get over him, and more important, whether he could ever forgive me for being such a weak, selfish person.

On the advice of my roommate and a few friends, I did try dating again. I was president of the school's marketing club that year, and when a colleague asked me out, I said yes. I gave it the college try and dated him for a month. Unfortunately, I couldn't help comparing him to John, and once I did that, he didn't stand a chance. When he started pressuring me to go to bed with him, I broke things off.

At the beginning of May, I accepted a full-time position in Weinstock's management-training program. This hundred-year-old department store chain was sold to Broadway stores in the early '90s and later to Macy's, but at the time, the company had eight stores in the greater Sacramento area and others in and outside the state. Just ten trainees, from all over California, were hired. When I got the job offer, my immediate reaction was to call John. Instead, my parents were the first to hear the news.

Weinstock's was building an imposing new flagship store in the K Street Mall, in downtown Sacramento. It was just about complete, and all the merchandise buyers were moving into offices on the second floor. Five management trainees would work in the new store under a department manager, and the other five would become assistant buyers. By then, I'd been selling menswear at Weinstock's for a year and a half and had developed a good relationship with Jim, the men's dress shirt and accessories buyer, so I became his assistant. Since I didn't need to go through an orientation, he asked me to start as soon as possible. My professors agreed to let me miss the last week of class and take my finals early.

I exchanged my backpack for a brown-leather briefcase. On my first day in the buying office, I wore a stylish new Evan Picone wool and camel-hair suit, which I'd been drooling over for months, a silk blouse, and black pumps. Weinstock's men's slacks buyer was in the next office. His assistant was Heather, who had graduated from college the previous semester. She and her husband, Don, had been married for a year, but he traveled a lot for work, and she and I quickly became friends.

Much to my surprise and delight, after I'd been on the job just a week, Jim turned the necktie-buying business over to me. With his supervision, I would buy the ties all the stores would sell in spring 1980. Friday, May 25, the day before my graduation, was a busy one. My last appointment was with the Oscar de la Renta tie salesman, Jerry, a nice guy who was helping me navigate the world of men's fashion. Heather's husband had been in Chicago all week, and she was picking him up at the Sacramento airport that night. I'd invited her to have a drink with my friends and me to celebrate our graduation before she left for the airport.

Jerry began laying out beautiful silk neckties on my desk, describing those in each category: paisley, polka dot, foulard, sport and club, university and regimental. In less than half an hour, a hundred ties covered my desk. Around two, the phone rang, and I scrambled to find it under the pile of ties. "Men's buying office, Therese."

"Therese, it's Sue." Sue was a college friend who worked in the women's-accessories office. "Are you sitting down? This is terrible. You're not going to believe it."

"What? What happened?"

Between sobs, Sue said, "Heather's husband got on a plane in Chicago to come home from his business trip, and it crashed just after takeoff. He died."

My hand went over my mouth. "Oh, my God!" I rocked back in my chair, feeling as if I'd been punched in the stomach.

"Hello, hello. Are you still there, Therese?"

"Yes, yes, I'm here. Oh, how horrible!" Now I started to cry. "Poor Heather! They were such a happy couple. They had their whole life ahead of them!" My brow furrowed as I heard familiar words escaping my mouth. "I guess you never know what's going to happen in life."

As I groped in a drawer for a tissue, Jerry patted my shoulder, packed up his ties, and said he'd call me next week. The assistants quickly gathered in Sue's office, where she had a small TV. The newscaster said, "American Airlines Flight 191 took off from O'Hare International Airport in Chicago at eleven a.m., and moments later, it crashed. Two hundred and fifty-eight passengers died, along with thirteen crew-members and two people on the ground. An investigation by the FAA will begin tomorrow."

The rest of the afternoon was a blur. The whole buying office was quiet, with none of the buzz usually heard throughout the department. Trying to get some work done, I looked down at my desk pad and found *you never know what's going to happen in life* written all over it. The words stared back at me as I attempted to read the secret lying between the lines.

When I got home, I turned on the television right away. "It is the deadliest aviation accident to have occurred in the United States," the newscaster said. After a few minutes, I had to turn it off. When I called Heather, her mother answered and said she didn't want to talk to anyone. I asked her to please let her know I had called and to tell her that everyone at work was so sorry.

I went out with my friends that night as planned. We danced to Donna Summer, the Bee Gees, Boz Skaggs, and Fleetwood Mac until two a.m., and the words *you never know what's going to happen in life* never left my mind.

5

I hadn't expected that sitting in my cap and gown on the football field with my fellow students would feel like such a poignant moment. I shaded my eyes with my hand, searching the sea of people in the bleachers, but I couldn't find my family. About thirty minutes into the ceremony, the graduates of the School of Business marched one by one up the stairs and onto the stage to accept their diplomas from the dean of the business school. I turned the tassel on my cap to the other side, held the diploma close to my heart, and walked down the stairs grinning.

The path back to my chair afforded a view directly into the bleachers. John was sitting on the lowest bleacher seat, and when our eyes locked, I felt my heart jump in my chest. Oh, my God, I thought. I can't believe he showed up! I jerked my head back and quickly looked at the ground. The crowd was whistling and clapping, but the sound seemed to come from miles away.

After the ceremony, I scurried to locate my family, hoping to calm down and gather some strength. I tried to focus on my grandmother as I showed her my diploma. "This isn't the real one, Grandma. The official one will come in the mail in about a month." My heart was palpitating wildly. "Can I show you around the campus and Jenkins Hall, the dorm I lived in?"

"Therese," said my mom, "there's John. I'm surprised to see him. Did you invite him?" All heads turned in his direction, and my face grew hot.

"No, I didn't, but it's a nice surprise," I said, avoiding her eyes. My hands went to Jennifer's shoulders, and I turned her around. "Come on, Jen, stop staring at him. Why don't you guys wait for me in front of the library? There are benches at the entrance. I'll be there in a few minutes."

Learning about the Huntington's in John's family had terrified my parents, and they were so relieved when we broke up. But they knew I was heartbroken. Seeing John, Mom understood my dilemma and pushed everyone off. John approached with a big grin on his face, his hands behind his back. When he was about a foot away, he swung his hands forward and presented me with a bouquet of lavender roses, fuchsia carnations, purple lisianthus, white Asiatic lilies, and lush greens. "Surprise! Bet you didn't think you'd see me today, huh?"

"Ah, ah...you're right about that. You totally surprised me."

The fragrance of the flowers and his presence were intoxicating. "They're lovely. Thank you, John."

"Beautiful flowers for a beautiful lady."

I started walking to a shady spot on the lawn. I could hear my voice shaking as I said inanely, "Let's sit under the tree."

He took my hand to help me down and didn't let go of it until I was sitting next to him. My hands were sweating from the heat and my nerves. Finally, I was able to speak more intelligently. "It was very sweet of you to come, John."

"Well, we talked so much about this day, I couldn't miss it. I know how hard you worked. Congratulations! You did it, Therese!" He leaned back on his elbows and looked up at the sky. After a few minutes of silence, he added, "You know, your tenacity and strength inspired me." I felt his eyes penetrating the shield I'd created, but he didn't look away until I looked back. "No matter what happens between us, I want you to know how proud I am of you."

All I could think to say was "Thanks."

We sat quietly and I fidgeted with the hem of my dress. A soft breeze blew wisps of hair into my eyes. When he grasped a strand, his hand lingered on my face, and he turned it toward his. "I miss you, Therese."

John's hands were hot on my skin, and his hazel eyes were making me melt. The world seemed to tilt, so I leaned back on the lawn and took a deep breath. After a moment, I came up with "June ninth is your graduation, right?"

He nodded.

"You must really be busy with your projects, work, and studying for finals. It was nice of you to drive up to see me."

"Yes, I'm busy, but to tell you the truth, Lora and Dave gave me my graduation present early. They flew me up here to see you. I came in last night and will fly back late this afternoon." He shook his head. "It's hard to believe I'll be finished with college. Seven years is a long time."

"I'm so happy for you, John. You've worked hard, too."

Again he found my eyes and again I tried to pull away. "We're going to lunch," I said awkwardly. "Do you want to join us?"

"Thanks for the invitation, but I've got to get going." John stood up and brushed off his pants. "Tell your family hello, and give Grandma a hug for me."

I stood up, too, and wanted to move toward him, but I couldn't. I felt like such a weakling as I watched him walk away.

When I reached my family, Jen grabbed my bouquet. "You can have it," I said.

Mom put her arms around me. "Are you okay, sugar?"

I nodded. "Come on, Grandma. Let me show you the dorm I lived in."

My family took me to lunch, and my parents presented me with a check for five hundred dollars. "Your dad and I are proud of you, Therese," my mom said. But I had to struggle to stay upbeat. This day would have been so different, I kept thinking, if Huntington's hadn't entered my life.

~~❧~~❧~

That evening, as I opened a drawer to get my pajamas, my eyes fell on a picture atop the dresser: John and me lying on a beach, happy as can be. That night, I tossed and turned until I finally gave up and let my mind drift to John, and how hard he'd worked to finish college.

John was a junior in high school when Cindy moved out of their father's house. "The tension between Dad and me had always been pretty bad," John had told me, "but when I was the only one at home, he focused his fury on me."

Unlike his sisters, John was intent on getting a college degree. One morning at the beginning of his second semester at Diablo Valley College, his stomach hurt so much, he couldn't get out of bed. He called Cindy, who took one look at him and drove to the nearest emergency room. The doctors there thought he had the stomach flu and sent him home, but late that afternoon, his temperature spiked to a hundred and four degrees. Cindy and Lucy took him back to the hospital, where doctors immediately performed surgery on what they thought was a ruptured appendix. It turned out to be a perforated intestine. "I was septic," John said. "I was dying."

Lucy frantically called his father at work, but Big John never showed up, leaving Cindy and Lucy to make the decisions. "The doctors removed many feet of my large intestine and several inches of my small intestine. I woke up in ICU delirious with pain." More than three weeks later, John left the hospital thirty-one pounds lighter. He soon developed a fistula at the surgery site; when it wouldn't heal, he went back into the hospital and had corrective surgery. The final diagnosis was Crohn's disease, an inflammatory bowel disease. He lost the entire semester.

"The next fall, I started school again, got a job at the Bubble Machine car wash, and bought my first car. My goal was to work, save money, complete my A.A. degree, transfer to a four-year university, and get the hell out of the house. By then, Cindy had moved to Canada, and whenever we spoke, she said the same thing. 'Get out of that house as soon as you can, because it's not healthy living there. If your draft number comes up, head north to Canada and live with me.'

"Cindy," he reassured her, "I'm pretty sure Crohn's disease will keep me out of the military."

John studied hard for the next three years, working the whole time, and dreamed of transferring to the University of California at Berkeley in the fall of 1976. He was guaranteed acceptance, but not until the following fall. Some of his friends were already graduating with four-year degrees, and here he was, transferring schools with another three years ahead of him. He couldn't wait that additional year. Fortunately, he had also applied to Cal Poly.

"Even though I had never visited the campus, it was my ticket out," John said. He left for Pomona without telling his father goodbye.

❧❧❧

The day after we graduated, Mary moved in with her boyfriend, and I moved into a three-bedroom townhouse about three miles from downtown Sacramento. Kate, another friend from Martinez who had gone to high school with John, and Sue were my new roommates. I felt my career was off to a good start, and I tried to embrace this new chapter in my life. I wondered, though, if people could see my shattered spirit.

That evening, exhausted from the weekend of celebration and moving, I lay on my mattress, which was still on the floor, and stared out the window. The words I'd written on that desk pad continued to float around in my mind as I tried to make sense of Heather's tragedy. As I drifted off to sleep, I saw the phrase *you never know what's going to happen in life* swirling like a huge banner blown by a hurricane. I was running after it, yelling, "Come back, come back."

At three a.m., I woke with a jolt and sat up in bed. At that moment, my path became perfectly clear. Nobody knows what's going to happen in the future, I remember thinking as distinctly as if I'd said the words aloud. I'm not going to walk away from the love of my life because he *might* have a disease. I'm a strong woman. I will stand by his side, support him no matter what, and we'll get through this together.

Then I fell into a deep, peaceful sleep, the first I'd had in months. I woke up early, refreshed and full of energy, and wanted to wake Kate and Sue to tell them the news. But first, I had a phone call to make.

John was sharing a house in Ontario with four other guys. I hadn't stopped to think he might not be the one to answer the phone, but he picked up on the second ring.

"Hello."

"Hi, John. It's Therese."

The silence was so intense, it seemed like minutes, not seconds, passed before he spoke again. He sounded surprised. "Oh…hi. Is everything all right?"

"Yes, everything's fine." I rested my head against the wall. "I'm calling to ask your forgiveness, John. I'm so sorry I hurt you and…and…almost destroyed us."

"Well…" he seemed at a loss for words, "we all have our own way of dealing with hard stuff. I'm glad you took the time to think it through. I don't want you to have any regrets. Unfortunately, Huntington's will be part of my life, and my sisters'. Are you sure you can live with it?"

"Yes, I can. I want to spend the rest of my life with you, if you'll still have me. Huntington's isn't going to steal you away from me. We'll get through it…*if* it happens," I said with conviction.

"Of course I still want you," John said. "I love you, and I always will. Hey, why don't you fly to Pomona this Friday, and we'll celebrate us and my graduation together?"

He didn't have to ask twice.

6

As soon as I saw John at the airport, I dropped my backpack and ran into his arms, crying, "I'm so glad to see you. I never want to be separated from you again!"

All John's roommates were gone when we reached the house they were renting. I had been in the house the previous fall, and it had been a mess; it smelled, and the bathroom was disgusting. The OCD in me had made me clean it thoroughly, but I vowed I would never do that again. I didn't notice anything this time. Once we entered the house, we left a trail of clothes to John's bedroom. My passion ignited as he gently caressed me. Our kisses were hard; my hands were entwined in his hair to keep his lips on mine.

The next day, Lora, Dave, Marcia, and Big John arrived. Lora was the first to give me a hug. "Oh, I'm so glad you guys got back together. I knew you would!"

With tears in my eyes, I hugged her back. "I'm so glad I came to my senses, because I love your brother so much."

As Marcia and I embraced, I glanced over her shoulder and saw John talking with his father. "How did you guys get him to come?" I whispered.

Lora giggled. "We didn't give him a choice, did we, Moochie?"

Marcia nodded. "We told him we were picking him up on Saturday morning at nine, and he'd better be ready."

❧❧❧

Sunday evening, after a festive graduation and lots of food and alcohol, John and I were lying on his bed, tangled in each other's arms. My fingertips traced his lips. "My plane leaves in three hours. I wish I didn't have to go."

"Me, too," John said, hugging me tighter. We lay there a little longer, his hand brushing my hair from my face. "Remember how I've talked about traveling to Europe?"

"Of course."

"Well, last month I found out that one of the professors on campus was organizing a six-week trip for his architecture students. I asked him if I could go even though I was graduating, and he said that wasn't a problem. They leave July 1."

John jumped out of bed and grabbed his backpack. I sat cross-legged on the bed as he pulled out a spiral notebook. "I'm seriously thinking of going, Therese. It's exactly what I've been looking for." He handed me the open notebook. "Look, here's the itinerary and budget."

I stared at the page, trying to hide my disappointment. We'd just gotten back together, and now he was talking about leaving?

"We'll travel on the trains, stay in hostels, and eat with the locals. I'll get to see the most beautiful architecture in Europe! And the timing couldn't be better. It'll be only a slight detour before I start my career." He sat down and took my hands in his. "The challenge is whether I can make enough money in time. But I've got a plan that just might work, if I can paint four houses and schedule them one after the other. Anyway, I have to make a decision soon. What do you think, Therese?"

I had rarely seen John so animated. After our three-year long-distance relationship, not to mention the past several months, I wanted to be together. But he was looking at me with his big hazel eyes, so full of enthusiasm, and I remembered he'd made these plans when I wasn't in the picture. It would be selfish of me to say no. And with the new uncertainty in his life, perhaps he wanted to travel while he could, just in case he couldn't go later.

"John, if this is your dream, you should do it. The opportunity might not come again, and I agree, now is the best time."

"Really, Therese? You're not upset I'll be leaving?"

"Well, maybe a little, but I can see you really want to go. Besides, when you come back, it will be for good." I looked at him and smiled. "Well, it'd better be!"

Saying goodbye at the airport a few weeks later was hard, but as he walked away, I yelled, "Have a great time, and send lots of postcards!" The only good thing about Huntington's, I thought as I got into my car, is that it makes you appreciate the here-and-now and not dwell on the future. I decided my new motto would be "It's not about the destination; it's about the journey."

I worked a lot while John was gone, forty-five or fifty hours a week, not counting the work I took home at night and on weekends. But I didn't mind, because I enjoyed it. And I was saving for an event I had dreamed of since I'd been a little girl: my wedding.

❧❧❧

Once John returned, Lora and Dave offered their second bedroom to him. I was thrilled to have him so close, just thirty minutes away. No more driving eight hours on lonely Interstate 5 to see one another. No more long-distance phone calls.

John went to work for a temporary agency while he applied for career jobs. His first and only temp job was working in Weinstock's warehouse, unloading trucks. We couldn't believe the coincidence. Since the warehouse was my first stop each morning, to see what merchandise had arrived, we got to say "Good morning" to each other seven days a week.

In October, Dave found a flyer on a bulletin board in the Citrus Heights post office and passed it on to John. It was a job opening for an assistant architect for Placer County, in Auburn, the county's biggest city. Placer County stretched from the suburbs of Sacramento to Lake Tahoe and the Nevada border, but Auburn was only some twenty miles from Citrus Heights, where Dave and Lora lived. John applied for the job and was hired on the spot.

We set our wedding date for September 27, 1980, which allowed us a year to plan and save for our special day and honeymoon. We decided to have a simple wedding in my parents' church, Most Precious Blood Catholic Church in Concord, and I would wear my mother's wedding dress. Ever the pessimists, my parents still were not happy about the marriage. I said to them, "I am going to marry John, period. You can be part of planning our celebration or not. It's your choice."

Planning our wedding was validation of my commitment to John—and organizing every detail of the event really helped me stay calm, since the threat of HD was now a constant in my life. It also meant spending many weekends in the Bay Area, making all those arrangements with my mom.

One weekend, in the middle of addressing invitations, John threw down his pen. "I'll be glad when this is over. Then you won't be pulled in a hundred directions and I can have you all to myself. Come on," he cajoled, "let's take a break from this wedding stuff and go away for a weekend."

Over the next few weeks, he talked me into it. "I want to show you the Cahoon ranch in Carmel Valley, where my mother grew up. From what Dad says, the old ranch house is still standing."

∾∾∾∾

A hundred and twenty miles south of San Francisco on the Monterey Peninsula, Carmel, christened Carmel-by-the-Sea, is known for its white sand beaches, gorgeous scenery, and rich artistic history. Of course we took the famous 17-Mile Drive, which passes two renowned golf courses, impressive mansions, and attractions such as the famed Lone Cypress on its rocky promontory. The Lincoln Green Inn was a short walk to the beach. Built in 1925, it was elegantly decorated with French and English furnishings and lovely antiques. Flowers and ancient trees filled the grounds, and the smell of the sea was in the air. Once we unpacked, we walked to the beach, put out a blanket, opened a bottle of wine, and listened to the waves crash onto the shore.

About an hour later, the wind died down and the waves grew smaller. As we watched a fiery sun drop into the ocean, John took my hand and kissed it. "When we were young, Dad used to bring Cindy and me to Carmel to visit Aunt Louise and Uncle Jimmy. Louise is my mother's oldest sister," he reminded me. "Their ranch is not too far from the old Cahoon place, and we always stopped and looked at the old ranch house, which was abandoned even when I was a kid. I remember how Dad would get a faraway look in his eyes when we were there."

The next day, we drove the narrow, windy road through Carmel Valley, the rolling hills on either side covered in chaparral, grasses, and a few scattered oak trees. John slowed as we turned a corner and a dilapidated house with a "No Trespassing" sign in the yard came into view. "This is it!" he yelled as he turned onto a gravel driveway all but hidden under weeds.

John stretched as he walked around the car and wrapped his arms around my waist. I leaned into him, and we studied the structure together. The front porch was tilting to the right, and all the windows were boarded up.

Gazing at the rolling countryside, I said, "What a beautiful place to live. It must have been wonderful to grow up here."

"Yeah, I bet it was." He sighed. "I wanted to show you the house, but I really can't tell you much about it. I wish I knew more about my mother's family; Dad didn't talk about the Cahoon clan with us, and we never visited them, or they us. One day, I'm going to talk to Aunt Evelyn and Aunt Louise about their life on the ranch."

He jumped up on the porch and looked in the window; I leaned on the car and let the sun warm my face. As I looked at the ramshackle old house, I wondered once more about the mother John had never known.

"Can't see much. I'm going to check out the back."

Wading through the tall grass, I found John standing on a decrepit foundation covered with blackberry bushes. He thought it was what was left of a barn, because he'd seen pictures of his grandmother riding a horse.

When we got back in the car, I slid close to him and looked into his eyes. "Thanks for showing me the house. It gives me a little insight into your mom. I love you, and I know it's a hard subject for you to talk about." I kissed him, and our foreheads touched.

John took one last look at the house and revved the engine. As the car fishtailed on the loose gravel, rocks flew out behind us. "Let's get back to town and enjoy the wine-

and-cheese party at the B&B. We can watch the sun go down over the ocean again."

"Sounds good, but let's get there in one piece!"

The windows were open, and my hair was flying wildly. As I pulled it into a ponytail, I turned to John with a question. "Do you know how your parents met? I mean, she lived here and your dad lived in Martinez."

"Yes, Aunt Alice told me the story a few years ago. They met in the summer of 1946. Aunt Betty, my mother's second-oldest sister, lived next door to Alice in downtown Martinez, and Phyllis was living with her, helping with the kids. Dad visited his sister often, because he and her husband, Frank, had been in the army together and they were good friends." He hesitated. "I know a few more details about the Cahoon family, if you want to hear them, Therese. Aunt Evelyn shared this with my sisters during their visit last year."

Since knowing the truth wasn't going to change anything between us, I said, "Absolutely. It's part of our family history now." As I said those words, I could feel my heart rate rise.

"My grandfather committed suicide here in 1937, when he was fifty-three. He hung himself in the barn, and Phyllis found him hanging from the rafters. She was only fourteen."

My heart skipped a beat when he said *suicide*, and after this, we both grew quiet. When John glanced at me, I looked out the window, not wanting him to see the look on my face. "Your poor mother."

I had read that the most common psychiatric disorder associated with HD is depression, and that up to twenty-seven percent of Huntington's sufferers attempt suicide, although it's unclear how often it is to escape their physical symptoms. The real tragedy was that no one had understood why Charles Cahoon had acted the way he did, however his illness manifested, and no one knew what made him kill himself. The story of this family kept getting worse.

The tightness in my chest and feeling of dread was about to consume me, so I took some deep breaths, my all-purpose remedy. By now, I knew to change the subject. I reached for John and said, "I can't wait for our wedding! Where are we going on our honeymoon? You still haven't told me."

"That's because it's a surprise," John laughed.

7

Our wedding was beautiful, with a candlelight ceremony in the church followed by a reception at the Concord Grange Hall. At midnight, we were finally on our way to the Beresford Arms Hotel, in San Francisco's theater district, arriving so late we had to ring the bell to get our room key. We were so exhausted, we fell asleep in our clothes on top of the bed.

Our honeymoon destination was still a mystery to me, so during our two days in San Francisco, I searched through John's stuff whenever he wasn't looking. He must have been wise to me, because I didn't find any plane tickets or even an itinerary. When we got to the airport, I felt giddy. John stopped to look at departure times for Air Mexicali, then turned to me with a big smile. "Our flight to Guadalajara is on time. Viva la Mexico!"

I had never been to a foreign country and felt reassured when John began conversing with the flight attendant in Spanish. "Well, well, I'm impressed. I've listened to you and Lora banter back and forth in Spanish, but I never realized you were fluent." I'd known this man for four years, and there was still so much to learn about him. I looked around and said, "Hey, everyone, I have a Spanish-speaking husband. Woo-hoo!"

John pulled me close and we laughed when the attendant offered us each a glass of champagne. "Muchas gracias," John replied.

On the plane, John told me the story of his Grandmother and Grandfather Marin. On February 12, 1912, in search of a better life, Benita and Antonio had emigrated from Spain, first to the Hawaiian Islands to work for the Hawaii

Agricultural Company, which paid for their voyage. Their daughter Jessica was born there. After fulfilling their three-year contract, they booked passage to San Francisco. Antonio found work well south of the city, in the Santa Clara Valley, working in the fields and packing sheds. Their other children—Jack, Christina, Alice, and John—were born at home in San Leandro, in the East Bay. When John was around ten, the family moved to Martinez, first settling in Franklin Canyon and then in a house on Muir Road.

During World War II, they learned that the army barracks on an old airfield in Richmond was being demolished. Antonio and Jack bid twenty-five dollars on one of the buildings, and after they signed a liability waiver, it was theirs. They tore it down with crowbars, saved the wood, windows, doors, and nails, and hauled it all back to Martinez, where Jack helped his father build a house on their newly acquired five-acre property near the waterfront. When Big John came home after the war, he built a house next to theirs, though his son didn't live in it until he was six.

John kissed my forehead. "You know, I haven't spoken Spanish in a long time. It feels so natural, and it reminds me of them."

❧❧❧

John and I enjoyed the sights and culture of Guadalajara for a week. Then we flew to Mazatlan and stayed in a condo on the beach a few miles outside of town. Big John and Lucy had bought this timeshare in 1972 and used it for two weeks in the spring and two weeks in the fall. That first night, we ate dinner on a balcony overlooking the pool and the beach, a cool ocean breeze blowing through the condo. As we drank our sangria, we looked out at one of the most beautiful sunsets of my life.

The weather was gorgeous in Mazatlan that week. John and I didn't have a care in the world as we roamed the city's markets, lay by the pool, walked hand in hand on the beach, made love at all hours, ate whenever we were hungry. It was easy not to worry about Huntington's. I didn't make a single list.

One evening, we took a bus filled with locals carrying chickens, groceries, and crying children outside the city to watch a baseball game. As we found seats in an old stadium a far cry from San Francisco's Candlestick Park, the stands groaned and swayed under the weight of all the fans. I squealed, "I don't think these stands will hold all these people."

"Oh, Therese. These bleachers have probably held crowds for years," John reminded me. "It'll be fine. Just relax and enjoy yourself."

❦❦❦

Since John's job was in the Gold Rush town of Auburn, in the Sierra Nevada foothills, and my job was in downtown Sacramento, we looked for a place midway and found an apartment in Roseville, in the new Cirby Woods complex. It was less than a mile from the interstate that we drove in opposite directions. Roseville was growing from its railroad town beginnings into a major urban center. In 1980, the city was booming: Hewlett Packard had moved into offices here the year before and become a major employer; NEC Technologies, Inc., a Japanese computer company, was building a campus that would open in the next two years. New homes, restaurants, stores, gas stations, and strip malls were going up as well.

I was ecstatic that John and I were finally living under the same roof. Our split-level apartment had two bedrooms, one bathroom, and a cute kitchen with a bay window that my coleuses loved. Upstairs was a dining area and a sunken living room with a stone fireplace; a sliding-glass door opened onto a little balcony that overlooked a creek.

On my last day before returning to work, my mother and grandmother were helping us get settled. Mom was in the kitchen unpacking wedding gifts; since she felt everything needed to be washed first, the dishwasher had been running all day. My parents had accepted my happiness and never brought up any pessimistic or negative feelings about our future. I walked into the kitchen and gave my mother a hug. "You might want to take a break, Mom."

When John came home from work, he practically shouted, "Wow, the apartment looks great! I can't believe how much you got done." Mom and Grandma were sitting on the couch with their feet up on the coffee table, looking tired. John sat down between them, wrapped an arm around each, and said, "Let's go to dinner. I want to take you girls out to thank you for all your help."

Anyone looking at us would have seen a happy, well-matched couple starting what seemed a wonderful life together. Little would they know the challenge that lay quietly beneath our joy. Every day, I consciously reminded myself to live in the present moment. It was the small stuff I savored: waking up next to John, seeing him every night, eating dinner together, talking about our day, feeling his arms around me. Those moments were precious, and I selfishly saved them just for me.

8

*I*n the spring of 1981, John and Dave organized a men's softball league. They played every Tuesday evening at Rush Park in Citrus Heights, about seven miles from our apartment and just a few minutes from Lora and Dave's home. I loved watching John play, because he was so athletic and found such joy in the games, and they gave Lora and me time to make plans for the weekend. We were usually home by ten, just in time for our favorite TV show, *St. Elsewhere*. John would make popcorn, and we'd settle back on the old black leather couch that Marcia's boyfriend, Glenn, had given us.

Dave coached a women's softball team that Lora had played on for several years. When John and I watched her play, I was amazed at her strength. Only five-foot-one, she walloped the heck out of the ball, and she was the fastest runner on the team, even though her stride was half as long as mine. When one of Lora's teammates dropped out, the team asked me to join. Playing softball made me feel like a kid again. John said I was pretty good, but I think he was biased.

After every game, Lora brought out freshly baked treats: cinnamon rolls, brownies, cupcakes. Since she worked full-time like the rest of us, I wondered when she found the time to bake. But you witnessed kindness in everything Lora did. At one of our games, Chris, our best hitter, sprained her ankle, and Lora was the first one at her side. She got ice out of the cooler to keep the swelling down and then drove Chris to the nearest emergency room.

I'll never forget when Lora and I were visiting one of her neighbors. You could tell Rebecca was at her wits' end from her kids' constant fighting. Lora hugged her and said, "Go relax, Mom, I'll take care of the kids." She sat them down and talked with them in a calm, gentle manner, and we didn't hear a peep out of them the rest of the afternoon.

At such times, I couldn't help wondering if for some reason she had chosen not to have children, even before learning about the Huntington's. It seemed such a private matter, I couldn't bring myself to ask her, and John had no idea.

❧❧❧

We spent at least two weekends a month with Lora and Dave. John liked helping Dave around their house, and since both loved sports, they watched a lot of sports events on TV. Whenever Marcia and Glenn visited, the women would go shopping for the makings of a luscious Lora dinner. Sometimes even Lora needed a break, though, and we'd all go out to eat and to a movie.

The next time Marcia and Glenn drove in for the weekend, we went to a TGI Fridays for dinner. Waiting for a table at the bar, the women sat on the high bar stools and had drinks while the guys stood nearby, enjoying a beer. Marcia always had a cigarette with her drink, and now she lit one and took a drag. As she tilted her head back and blew out the smoke, her head made an unusual jerk. I didn't think much of it until awhile later, when we were seated at our table and were making a TGIF toast, and it happened again. I told myself it was probably nothing.

When the hostess had led us to our table, Dave poked John in the ribs. "Did you see the size of her boobs? Boy, would I love to feast on them!" he laughed. At the table, as the woman turned to leave, Dave said to her, "You look especially beautiful tonight." If I'd been sitting next to him,

I would have slugged him in the arm. Lora was playing with her napkin, trying to ignore Dave's flirting.

The menu was huge, and when the waitress came to take our orders, Lora said, "I don't know what I want. What's your most popular dish?"

The waitress chewed on her pen. "Well, the ravioli in red sauce is delicious."

Dave patted Lora on the head. "Oh, come on, Edith. Don't think too hard; you'll hurt your brain." He laughed, and this time Lora did slug him. I gave him a dirty look.

When John and I were getting ready for bed, I asked, "Why does Dave call Lora Edith? I know he's comparing her to Edith on that show *All in the Family*, but she's nothing like her. It's a stupid joke."

"Dave has always teased her."

"It's just not right. Lora laughs along with him, but I can tell it hurts her feelings."

A few weeks later, something similar happened, and I felt the need to talk to John again. "Dave's always the life of the party and everyone likes him, but he makes Lora the butt of his jokes, and they're often cruel. And haven't you noticed whenever we're in a restaurant, Dave flirts with the waitress until it becomes embarrassing? Yet Lora is constantly feeding his ego and does practically everything for him. I mean, for Christ's sake, he's a grown man."

John took a deep breath. I could tell the conversation upset him. "Yes, I've noticed."

"Lora always laughs, but for the life of me, I don't understand why she takes it. If it were me, I'd tell him to cut it out. Why doesn't she?"

He was quiet for a long time. "You may not like the answer, Therese."

"Well, maybe not, but please tell me."

"He's always been like that, a kidder. It's his macho way."

"You're right. I don't like the answer."

"You have to understand, Therese, the difference Dave made when he entered our lives. He was our savior."

"What does that mean?"

"The four of us were always stuck on the ranch, five miles from town, with little to do, especially during the summer. Dad wouldn't take us to the library, or to a friend's house, or to play in any sports or clubs, so we were bored out of our minds. When Lora met Dave, the summer before her sophomore year in high school—Dave was a year older—he became the center of her world. I was eight years old, and Dave showed genuine interest in me; he became the big brother I didn't have in my life, and father, for that matter. He owned a car, so we got to escape the ranch and do some fun stuff that didn't cost money, because we had none. Dave encouraged me to play in Little League and drove me to practices and games. He believed in me and was so positive, so different from Dad.

"He had a brother, Bill, who was my age, and we became good friends. I got to do things with them I'd never done before. And their parents treated Lora and me like part of their family."

"Lora never dated anyone else, then?"

John shook his head.

"So all of you are indebted to Dave, and Lora must feel she can never upset him. But I think his flirting makes her insecure—and I think he likes it that way. He controls her with his macho behavior. Poor Lora. She probably doesn't have much self-esteem."

John touched my cheek. "Yeah, none of us had much faith in ourselves except for Cindy. I never told you this, but Dave cheated on Lora early in their marriage. They worked it out, but the way he acts toward women surely doesn't help. But Lora has never argued with Dave, or questioned his decisions or behavior." What John said next really bothered me. "What he says goes, and she'd better not cross him. It's almost like she's living with our father."

❧ ❧ ❧

The next time Marcia came to visit, she stayed at our apartment that Friday night, because Lora and Dave were going to a wedding the next day. Over coffee that morning, I asked Marcia about Dave, but she dismissed my concerns. "Oh, he's just kidding her. He's always done that." And she repeated what John had said. "Our lives changed when Dave started going with Lora. In high school, Lora and I even double-dated, because I went steady with Dave's best friend. Oh, that reminds me of a story."

John put down his newspaper to listen.

"One day when we were in high school, I caught Lora wearing one of my new outfits. I'd just finished sewing it a few days before. Later that day, I found it wadded up in a heap on the bedroom floor. I stomped through the house until I found her, and we started throwing shoes, glasses, and books at each other. When we were done, the place looked like a war zone."

John couldn't stop laughing. "I remember that fight. I was nine, and I kept my distance until it was safe; I think I hid. Remember when Dad got home? He was so pissed. 'What the hell happened in here?' You guys made up some cockamamie story, and Dad believed it."

"She and I had lots of fights growing up. One time, Lora even threw a knife at me." Marcia laughed and shook her head. "I have to say we were pretty wild."

"Did it take long to forgive her about the dress?" I asked.

"Oh, no. Lora and I always shared a bedroom, and it was hard to hold a grudge in such close quarters. Besides, she's my sister."

Later, I asked John, "What makes you and your sisters so close?"

"Well, Dad was never there for us, so we depended on each other. We learned at a young age to forgive and forget, because we were all we had."

"Do you think Marcia would ever transfer to Sacramento to be closer to Lora and you?"

"I don't think so. She loves the city. It fits her personality, with its beauty and culture. When I was in high school, even though she worked there all week, she used to take me into the city on Saturdays. She'd get her nails and hair done while I walked around, and then we'd have lunch and go to a movie. She and her girlfriends had season tickets to the American Conservatory Theater, and when one of them couldn't make it to a play, I got to go."

The more I learned about the Marin siblings, the more I thought about my relationships with my own. My sisters and I weren't close and never had been. Unlike the Marin family, we'd had a mother at home, and since we lived in the suburbs, our neighborhood was full of kids, so we didn't play together much. Also, I realized, my parents had assigned labels to each of us at an early age: Ellen was the athletic one, Amy was the smart one, Jennifer was the spitfire, and I was the crybaby. Because of the stereotypes they had assigned to us, my father always teased us about our differences, and this kept us isolated from one another, perhaps destroying any camaraderie we might have had.

~•~•~•~

Jim, my boss at Weinstock's, had taken a position in Southern California with Broadway Stores, Inc. Management decided to restructure my department, and Brian, the men's-underwear buyer, became the new men's dress shirt buyer. Brian passed the underwear buying to me, along with the ties and men's jewelry. Now I usually went to the office on Saturdays, too, though I tried to get there early enough to come home by eleven and spend the rest of the day with John.

Assistant buyers were expected to visit Weinstock's other Sacramento stores once a month, to work with the department managers and make sure all the stock was on the floor. Those days, we worked at least twelve hours, but the really long days were when we drove to the Reno or Stockton store. At least we had to visit the Fresno store just once every three months, because then I had to spend two nights away from home. In the eight months we'd been married, I probably worked an average of sixty hours a week. Life was too short, and with the threat of Huntington's, every day with John was precious. That spring, I began searching for a new job.

Early that summer, a former professor of mine asked me to assist him in a market-research project he was conducting for the California State Fair. My job would be hiring, training, scheduling, and supervising twenty people who would conduct surveys during the seventeen days of the fair, which started in August. Of course I said yes, glad to leave Weinstock's behind while I continued searching for a permanent full-time job.

John turned twenty-seven in early September. Three weeks later, we celebrated our first anniversary in the traditional manner: eating the top portion of our wedding cake, which had sat in the freezer for a year. We each took a bite, spit it out, and laughed. After we threw the cake away, John ran down to his truck and carried up my anniversary gift. It was a classic standing Cheval dressing mirror, in a warm wood frame with an arched top and graceful curved legs. It even tilted. It fit perfectly into the corner of our bedroom. After we made love, I thanked God for keeping him and his sisters safe.

By October 1, the market-research project was winding down, and ten days later, Aratex Services (later Aramark Uniform Services) in Sacramento, which specialized in uniforms and career apparel, offered me a position as merchandise-control manager. Leading a department with twenty-four union employees, I'd manage a million-dollar budget, process and distribute orders to the sales team, and perform a monthly inventory. My new job started in two weeks. John had plenty of vacation time accrued, so we decided to visit Cindy—and Brad, her new husband—in British Columbia.

9

*C*indy and Brad, a middle school teacher, had married that September, but I'd been unable to attend because of the state fair project. I was so excited to see her again, to get to know her better, and to meet Brad.

Cindy had grown up in a very different world from her siblings. By 1952, when Cindy was born, Phyllis had had three daughters in four years and was physically and emotionally incapable of caring for a baby. Big John's oldest sister, Jessica, and her husband, Edward, lived on an adjacent ranch, and he paid them a hundred dollars a month to take care of Cindy. Their daughters, Ann and Marie, became Cindy's adopted big sisters. While Big John cracked the whip over Lora to manage the house and either ignored Marcia and, later, John or used them as verbal punching bags, Cindy was lovingly cared for by her aunt, uncle, and cousins, who took her to birthday parties, Blue Bird meetings, and other activities. Whenever John and I visited Big John and Lucy, I studied the school pictures on the hallway wall and noted the huge difference between Cindy's and those of her siblings. Cindy was always neatly dressed, with bows in her curly hair and a cheery smile. The others had messy hair, tight smiles, and a look of sadness, I thought, in their big hazel eyes.

When Cindy was nine or ten, Uncle Edward bought her a horse she named Candy. After school, John often spent the afternoon with his closest sister, and that summer, they rode Candy through the hills. The following year, her uncle bought Cindy a fast, spirited Arabian horse she called Apache. That meant John got to ride Candy by himself, and he followed his big sister wherever she went.

I don't know why, but when Cindy was in fourth grade, Big John moved her into his house. It was the happiest day of John's life, but Lora and Cindy had horrendous fights, almost coming to blows, because Lora couldn't boss Cindy around as she did Marcia and John.

More important, Cindy challenged her father from the day she moved in. She called him a bully and a know-it-all and told him she wasn't afraid of him. Cindy had seen the results of his verbal abuse and was determined not to take any. The confrontations upset Lora, because she felt it was her job to protect her dad. And all three of her siblings begged Cindy to keep her mouth shut, because when she instigated a fight with Big John, his wrath landed on all of them.

Three years later, in December 1965, Aunt Jessica, the matriarch of the family, died unexpectedly of a heart attack. It was a huge loss for Cindy and John.

After she graduated from high school, Cindy managed to stay with Lucy and Big John for six months, until Lucy began accusing her of stealing from them, and her father, of course, failed to stand up for her. She moved into a commune in Martinez down the street from the county building in which her father worked. By 1973, both Cindy and John were attending Diablo Valley College. John felt that living with friends in a common space reflected Cindy's open, sharing attitude. He admired his fearless sister, because she lived her life the way she wanted to.

While Cindy was in college, she worked for a dentist named Dr. Kramer, and once she got her Associate Arts degree, she took postgraduate courses in periodontal sciences and treatment and became a dental assistant. Cindy was a backpacker, skier, and nature lover, chafing against all the people and pollution she found in California. When she discovered that Dr. Kramer had a dentist friend in Vancouver, British Columbia, she contacted him, and he offered her a job. She packed up her Pinto and off she went, on the first of her many adventures.

❧ ❧ ❧

Cindy and Brad lived in White Rock, a town surrounded on three sides by Surrey and bordering Semiahmoo Bay. The second bedroom in their funky apartment was a converted porch, with single-paned windows that let the cold air creep in. As we unpacked, I said, "I'm glad I brought my flannel pajamas."

John looked up from his suitcase and said, "I'm not!"

I giggled as I put the last of my clothing in the dresser drawer and stood by the window. "Come and look at the view, John. It's beautiful!" His arms went around my waist, and I screeched as he pulled me backward onto the bed. I nuzzled against him as we listened to the rhythmic, soothing sound of the waves lapping the rocks.

The next morning, after Cindy and Brad had gone to work, John and I explored White Rock. It was a writer and artist's paradise that offered abundant inspiration. We strolled around the beautiful little town, read our books in a sweet café, took a long walk along the shore.

When we got back to the apartment, Cindy was creating some kind of tofu dish for dinner. "How was your day?"

"Wonderful. White Rock is so quaint! I love it," I said.

"I took the rest of the week off," Cindy said, "and I've got a lot of fun things planned. I thought we'd do some sightseeing on the bikes tomorrow. Brad and I each have a bike, and I borrowed one for you, John. We've got great trails here, Therese, and it's pretty flat."

I had noticed the last time I'd seen Cindy, at Christmas, how strong she looked. Dressed in her cycling clothes, she seemed even stronger now, her body a solid piece of muscle from her arms to her thighs. We biked in Stanley Park, a magnificent green oasis in the midst of Vancouver's heavily built urban landscape, and a national historic site. In addition to kilometers of trails, it had beautiful beaches, wildlife, great eats, and many natural, cultural, and historic landmarks.

After an hour, I needed a break. We sat on the shore of Lost Lagoon, a large bird sanctuary within the park. Cindy looked as if she had hardly broken a sweat. "What have you been doing to become so fit?" I asked her.

"Brad and I started running half-marathons last year, and we ran our first full marathon a few months ago," she said. "Running has become addicting to me, because when the adrenaline starts pumping through my veins, I feel like I'm on a high. We also cycle long distances with friends at least once a month. Two weekends ago, we biked three hundred miles over two days. With the mountains in this area, both sports are challenging. I love being outdoors, and Canada is so beautiful."

The next day, Cindy and I were off to Vancouver to shop. John wanted to bike on a more difficult trail he'd spotted, so he stayed in White Rock. We had lunch at Cindy's favorite vegetarian café; Cindy ordered, and when the food arrived, the aroma made my mouth water.

"I'd be tempted to become vegetarian, too, if I could make dishes like these," I said before stuffing my mouth full of noodles. "Though it would be hard to change John's diet, because he loves meat."

"Brad hasn't gone totally veggie, but he loves what I

make." Cindy motioned to the waiter. "Could we have another order of noodles, please?"

"When did you become a vegetarian?"

"Well, I'm not totally vegetarian. Sometimes I crave a steak or ribs. I changed my lifestyle when I moved to Canada. I eat fresh fruits and vegetables and limit my intake of refined sugar and enriched flour. I want my body to be healthy inside and out." She took a sip of herbal tea. "So how are you and John doing?"

I smiled. "We're great, and so happy to be living together." I paused, wondering if I should bring up the subject. "I don't know if you knew, but John and I broke up over Huntington's. I wasn't sure I could handle living with it hanging over our heads."

"Yes, Lora told me about the breakup. You know, I had just met Brad when we found out. I was upfront about it right away. After we'd been seeing each other for a while, he told me it didn't make any difference, because he loved me. I remember him saying, 'Nothing is certain in life.'"

I nodded at the familiar words.

As we talked about our lives, I was surprised at Cindy's openness, because her sisters certainly didn't share their feelings. By the end of our stay, I'd concluded that the four siblings had one important thing in common: All considered fun a priority. Over the past week, Cindy had described skiing at Canada's Mount Whistler, Lake Louise, and Banff; taking fishing trips to Alaska and vacations in Hawaii. A trip of some kind was always on the horizon, it seemed, and work was only the means to another adventure.

Their next destination was Australia. Brad had been accepted into an international teacher-exchange program: During the next school year, he would take the position of a teacher in Australia and live in his or her home, and the

Australian teacher would live in their apartment and teach Brad's class.

On our last morning, I found Cindy and John at the kitchen table eating cold pizza. "We were reminiscing about old times," Cindy said as she took another bite. "Join us."

I poured myself a cup of coffee and sat down. "Aunt Evelyn's family owned Freddie's Pizzeria in Lafayette. Lora worked there Friday, Saturday, and Sunday evenings, and if an order hadn't been picked up by closing time, she could take it home. We never got to eat out as kids and were forever hungry, so my sisters concocted a plan to get free pizza. Marcia would call late at night and order in Spanish so that no one would recognize her voice. 'Yo quiero un pizza de pepperoni and olive.' Once Lora got home, we'd wake John up, and the four of us would gorge on the pizza. The next morning, Lora would make coffee, and we'd eat the rest. To this day, I still love cold pizza and coffee."

I crinkled my noise. "Yes, I can see that."

When we left, John held his sister tight and said, "We have an extra bedroom. Come anytime and stay with us."

To his joy, Cindy replied, "We're thinking of driving to Sacramento for Christmas and taking a few days to ski at Lake Tahoe. Brad has never been there. I'll let you know in a few weeks."

he best thing about my new job was that I didn't have to work ridiculous hours—that and the fact that I made more money than I had at Weinstock's. Before I knew it, it was Christmas. Cindy and Brad drove down from Canada, and John took a day off and skied with them at the Squaw Valley Ski Resort, in Olympic Valley, where the 1960 Winter Olympics had been held.

It was so nice to see the Marin siblings together again, their bond secure and their happiness contagious. My OCD had calmed considerably since John and I had married, and I felt it had a lot to do with the Marins' spontaneity and positive attitude.

Once buds started appearing on the trees and daffodils poked through the soil, Lora and John were dubbed our "weekend fun directors," charged with setting up one or two get-away-from-it-all excursions a month. We went camping in the Sierra, boating on Folsom Lake, biking along the American River or lazily rafting down it. Sometimes we just barbequed at Lora and Dave's; other times, "the girls" went shopping while "the guys" worked on a project.

At this point in our lives, we saw Lora and Dave on most weekends and Marcia a couple times a month. The Marin siblings had always drawn strength from one another, and with HD lurking, their need to be together must have been even greater.

My sister Amy had followed my footsteps into California State University, Sacramento, and would soon graduate with a degree in English. Unfortunately, she had retained the worst personality traits of our parents, their criticism and negativity. And her OCD was much more serious than mine.

That was apparent in her eating habits. She wouldn't touch anything but food she considered pure and healthy (when obsessive, a condition known as orthorexia nervosa). She wouldn't eat any kind of fish, no matter where it was caught, for fear of digesting mercury.

My parents had no sympathy for her eating habits, but on her graduation day, they searched hard for a restaurant with something on the menu that would please her. After we tried three places, we wound up in a pizza parlor, where Amy ordered a small salad. Lunch was tense, to say the least. As John and I drove off, he said, "The Crutchers need to chill and have a little fun."

Amy got a job with a mortgage company in downtown Sacramento, lived alone in a small apartment, and was, in my view, miserable. And she'd begun showing signs of anorexia, becoming incredibly thin and unhealthy-looking. I hated seeing her like that, so we invited her on our annual Memorial Day weekend camping trip to Silver Lake, off Carson Pass, south of Lake Tahoe. She was such a drag, complaining and pouting and not engaging with anyone, we didn't invite her to do anything with us again.

❧❧❧❧

One Saturday in June, the plan was for "the girls" to go shopping while "the boys" installed a hot tub in Lora and Dave's backyard. When Marcia and Glenn drove up, Lora and I grabbed our purses and jumped into Marcia's Datsun 280Z. Sitting in the back, I found a box of tapes and started to look through them. "Are these self-help tapes?" I asked.

"Yes. They're from est, for Erhard Seminars Training. Werner Erhard's ideas focus on personal responsibility, accountability, possibility, and transformation. All the big companies are sending their professionals to his five-day training classes, or buying the tapes."

Lora turned around from the passenger seat and took a couple from me. "How long have you had these, Moochie?"

"Pacific Bell bought them for me last month. It's nice to listen to them while I'm driving to see a client. You can borrow them if you like."

I admired Marcia's determination and tenacity, knowing how she had moved up the career ladder at Pac Bell without a college degree. These tapes were no doubt another strategy to improve her expertise and expand her personal skills, but the timing was interesting.

At Macy's, Marcia and I shopped for clothes while Lora disappeared into the housewares department. When we met her there an hour later, her face lit up as she showed us a Cuisinart food processor. "Look at this, you guys. Having this could save me so much time and energy." She looked at the price tag. "Ouch!"

"Maybe it could be a business expense," I said. "Do you and Anna ever think of starting that catering business you've been talking about forever?" Anna was an old friend from Martinez; in the late thirties, her mother had gone to Alhambra High with Big John.

"Oh, we're still in the planning stage."

I looked at Marcia. "I think your sister must be in heaven, thinking about cooking all day instead of working for the accountants."

At lunch, Marcia said, "You know, Lora, having your own catering business has been your dream since you were in high school. You and Anna would make a great team. You should do it."

I nodded vigorously. I didn't know if Marcia was thinking

what I was, but I couldn't help adding, "Yes, Lora, you should go after your dream!"

None of us could resist ordering a piece of chocolate pie with our coffee. As I dug into mine, I noticed a twitch in Marcia's shoulder; it was very slight, but it happened several times. Had Lora noticed it, too? I considered asking her if the opportunity arose, but I was pretty sure I knew how she would react. None of the Marins ever wanted to talk about Huntington's.

When we got back to Lora's, the sliding-glass door was open, and we could hear the three men grunting and groaning as they moved the hot tub into place. Suddenly, Dave screamed, "Goddamn it! Lift it up! You're smashing my fingers!" He ran into the kitchen and ran cold water over his hand. The water ran red in the sink.

Lora was immediately next to Dave and grabbing his hand. "Let me look at it. You smashed it pretty good, but you'll be fine," she told him soothingly. "I'll get some hydrogen peroxide and bandages."

While she was patching him up, Marcia and I started dinner. "Lora seems to enjoy being needed by her husband, and she's so comfortable dealing with blood and gore," I said. "You can tell she likes taking care of people."

Marcia nodded. "Yeah, Lora has always been an empathetic person. I'll bet you didn't know she was a Candy Striper. She was in a work program at the veterans' hospital in Martinez her senior year. I think she would have made a great nurse, but Dad discouraged her, because he thought she'd get too involved with her patients."

Just then, Lora came into the kitchen. "Moochie, why don't you get out the wine glasses and pour us some wine? I cook much better when I've got some alcohol in me." She looked at me and chuckled. "I'm kidding."

❧❧❧

Later that summer, John and I were in Mazatlan again, relaxing at the Marin condo, only this time with Lora, Dave, Marcia, Glenn, Cindy, and Brad. The weather was beautiful, and the condo's pool reflected the clear blue sky. I was sitting at the pool's edge, dangling my feet in the water and watching a catamaran with a royal blue and white sail heading toward shore. Once it hit the sand, the passengers jumped off and new folks climbed aboard. The rest of the family was lying on lounges, soaking up the sun. When we felt adventurous, we walked down to the beach and played in the warm Pacific.

That evening, we stood outside the condo and flagged down two pneumonia carts, junky old golf carts driven by young and old toothless men. I loved downtown Mazatlan, with its markets lined with bright-colored blankets, traditional embroidered Mexican blouses and dresses, ponchos, jewelry, T-shirts, hats, piñatas. And the produce! There was always an array of chilies, cactus paddles, aromatic herbs and spices, as well as scrumptious Oaxacan cheeses. It was fun weaving in and out of the aisles and bartering with the vendors. Since many cruise ships docked in Mazatlan for a day, the town was always festive and swarming with people.

We shopped for a couple of hours and headed to the infamous Señor Frog's, a popular restaurant on the main drag overlooking the ocean. A blast of cold air blew our hair back when we walked in. We all sighed, "Ahh." In the bar, an assortment of fish and sea creatures, large and small, stared down at the customers. A colorfully dressed waiter took our drink orders, and soon a fish-bowl-size margarita appeared before each of us. Lora held her monstrous glass high and said, "This is the perfect time to tell you our good news. Anna and I are doing it—we're starting our catering business next month! I'm going to work full-time until Anna lines up enough jobs to keep me busy in the kitchen. I'm so excited!"

We all clapped and cheered. "Congratulations, sis. I'm proud of you!" John applauded.

"That's wonderful, Lora," I said. "If you need any servers, John and I can help. You only need to pay us with your delicious food."

Dave held up his glass. "Here's to Lora and Anna's catering business. May it be a success!"

❧❧❧

I was the first one up the next morning and began making coffee. The others fell out of bed not long after and gathered at the kitchen table. We all looked like a bunch of hung-over drunks, which we were. Our heads drooped as we wrapped our hands around hot mugs of black coffee spiked with amaretto and Kahlúa.

By noon, the Marins were ready for their next adventure: parasailing. As Lora and I stood in the ocean up to our knees, I shaded my eyes and watched Dave flying high beneath a huge yellow, red, and blue canopy. "You're crazy if you think I'm going up in that thing, Lora."

Dave glided down into the water like a feather falling from the sky, hardly making a splash. John was next, and as he stood in the surf behind a jet boat, we watched two men tighten his harness. When they stepped aside, the boat's engine suddenly roared, and John flew into the air like a tossed puppet.

"Oh, my God, he's going to die!" At that moment, it

appeared my prediction might come true, because the jet boat stopped dead in the water, and John fell straight into the ocean with a huge splash. As soon as his head bobbed up, he waved and yelled, "Don't worry. I'm fine! They just ran out of gas."

My heart was still pounding as Lora and I sat down on our beach towels. "You Marins are fearless. You'll try anything."

She nodded and said, "It's my turn next. I can't wait."

Life was good for the Marin siblings; all were healthy, with no visible signs of Huntington's—I didn't even notice a twitch in Marcia. On the plane ride home, I stopped reading my novel and looked out the window. How I admired the special relationship these siblings had. They never fought or argued; compromise was easy for them. All four possessed enormous hearts, were the most forgiving, nonjudgmental people I'd ever met. And they all loved me, with all my faults and insecurities. If only I had a magic lamp and a genie who would grant me one wish. My wish wouldn't be for a million dollars, a big beautiful house, or a new car. It would be for time to freeze just where it was. That way, none of these people I loved would ever have to face Huntington's.

11

*J*ohn and I had been married for almost two years, and when we began talking about buying a house, the usual insecurities popped up in my brain. What if John gets sick? Could I make the mortgage payments on my salary? Could I maintain the house by myself? I pushed those thoughts away and replaced them with more reasonable questions: You've always wanted your own home, haven't you? You don't want to pay rent for the rest of your life, do you?

We agreed it was the right time to make this investment in our future. We both had good jobs, and buying a home was in the normal progression for couples building a life together. Of course, most happily married couples never doubt they have a future.

One day, John, who by then had come to know Placer County well, came home full of excitement. "I found a house for us, Therese! It's in Loomis, a fixer-upper, but it has real potential. I can't wait for you to see it."

Since he had studied architecture and worked in construction during summer breaks from college, I trusted his ability to see past what was there and visualize what it could become. Loomis, a rural area nestled in the foothills of the Sierra Nevada, was about thirty minutes east of Sacramento along the Interstate 80 corridor. It was said to be a friendly, old-fashioned community.

The night before we went to look at the house, I lay in John's arms, delighting in his enthusiasm as he described the place once more. "The house sits on an acre, with a well, a septic system, and a pool! It has three bedrooms and two bathrooms, and the original garage has been converted into a family room, but there's enough land for us to build a three-car garage." John's voice faded as I dreamed of verdant pastureland, cows grazing lazily outside the kitchen window.

I left work early to meet John and our realtor, Brenda. I couldn't get past the magnitude of the decision, and the terrible questions nagging at me. The old anxiety pushed hard against any optimism I could muster. To calm my fears, I did what I always did: develop a plan. Since I managed our finances, I would be as thrifty as possible and save as much as I could.

John and Brenda greeted me at the car. The house was incredibly shabby—paint peeling, windows broken, a roof that needed replacing—but there was a nice farm feeling to the place. John grabbed my hand as we walked to the front door and knocked. "Remember, Therese, keep an open mind. It's a fixer-upper. We'll remodel, paint, and build a garage. We'll make it our own."

I squeezed his hand and nodded.

A woman shouted, "Come on in. It's open." As soon as we opened the door, the smell of frying fish assailed us. Brenda gasped and glared at the woman standing at the stove. Her kids were at the kitchen table, throwing food at one another. The woman raised a spatula in the air and said, "Sorry about the smell. My boy caught fish today and wanted it for dinner."

Ignoring the obnoxious odor as well as we could, we began to look around. I tried to act casual, but the place was a sight to see: smoke-stained ceilings and drapes, dirty carpets, holes in the walls and doors. An enormous ski-resort fireplace sat in the middle of the front room, full of trash. In the bedrooms, we noticed hundreds of tiny holes in the walls; pellets from a BB gun littered the floors.

John was not blind to the shock on my face. He quickly

guided me into the second bathroom, in which a lonely toilet sat. "How about we wallpaper this bathroom, and I'll put a standup shower in here?"

"Yes, then the guestroom would have its own bathroom," I said, trying to envision the transformation. "It could be really cute."

Brenda had been quietly following us and trying to get a sense of how I felt. "It's a great little starter home, and the price is terrific!" She gently touched my arm. "Come on, Therese. Let's go look at the backyard and pool."

Out back, the grass was green and lush; blackberry bushes hid the fences marking the property line. There were no homes behind the house, just open fields, where cows really were lazily chewing their cud, and it was so quiet. A peaceful feeling blanketed me as I looked out at the open space. A dilapidated shack sat at the far end of the property, a tall cottonwood tree hanging over it. "What's in the little shed?" I asked.

"It's the pump house. Brenda said it's a hand-dug forty-foot well, and it generates five gallons per minute. That's a good flow," John explained.

I walked over to the pool and stopped short. "Oh, my God. This is the most disgusting thing I've ever seen. I can't even see the bottom. Yuck!" I just stared at the filthy pool, shaking my head. A frog grazed my leg as it hopped into the water. "Yikes!"

John was immediately at my side. "What's the matter?"

I stepped back from the pool and began to laugh. "A frog just jumped in. You know what this is? It's a cement pond!"

"It can be fixed," Brenda assured us. "There are companies that specialize in cleaning pools. We'll write in the contract that the seller must clean the pool and have the equipment in working order before the deal closes."

Looking like a little boy who'd just been handed a new toy, John wrapped his arms around me. "I knew you'd see the potential. And isn't the pool great? We can have barbeques and pool parties. Everyone will want to come to our house!"

❧❧❧

We became official homeowners on September 3, 1982, three days before John's twenty-eighth birthday, at the bargain price of fifty-eight thousand dollars. The first night in our new house, we sat on the floor eating Chinese food out of the boxes. We cracked a bottle of champagne, lay on the mattress, and made love by candlelight.

Now that we owned a home, one that needed a lot of work, the nature of our weekends changed. John considered remodeling our house "fun." I was happy just working side by side and watching our house take shape.

When I'd told my parents about the house, they had offered to help, so we invited them for a weekend before the month was over. My handy father had worked on many projects around our house while I was growing up. That morning, I was standing in the living room wearing goggles and gloves and holding a ten-pound sledgehammer, ready to help John knock out the concrete slab where the fireplace had been. We heard a gentle knock, and the front door opened.

Mom and Dad stopped in their tracks and their jaws dropped as they looked around our godforsaken house. Mom's smile turned into a frown. "Oh, my God!"

Since negativity had filled my childhood, this reaction was hardly a surprise, although in this case, I could hardly blame them. I grabbed the bags they'd brought and gave them each a hug. "Remember, Mom? I told you and Dad it was a fixer-upper. It's only temporary. Thanks for picking up a few things. It's saved me a trip."

John shook Dad's hand and hugged Mom. "Thanks, Rita."

Mom took a deep breath. "Oh, you're welcome, sugar. I guess I was taken aback for a minute."

"That's all right, Mom. You should have seen the look on my face when I first saw it. Come on, let me give you the grand tour and tell you our ideas." As we left the room, my dad was putting on his work gloves.

Once we explored the house and property, Mom retreated to her comfort zone, the kitchen. "I'll start the casserole in a little while, because it'll take an hour to bake." She opened the oven door, closed it, and murmured, "Maybe I'll clean the oven first."

⚜ ⚜ ⚜

Our first project was building the three-car garage, so that John had a place to store material and I could have a washer and dryer. Over the next few weeks, he spent hours drawing designs, calculating costs, pulling permits, and getting the plans for our new garage approved by the county. The morning he planned to pour the concrete-slab foundation, he was as excited as a kid on Christmas.

Dave got there around eight, and I took him outside where John was happily pouring bags of sand and water into the concrete mixer he'd rented. When I turned to go back in, he grabbed my arm. "Hey, Therese, can you call Lora? She's not feeling well. I don't think she can go shopping with you today."

"Sure, I'll call her right away."

The phone rang for a long time.

"Hi, Lora. It's Therese." I pressed the phone hard against

my ear, and grew concerned when all I heard was crying. "I'll be right over."

When Lora opened the door, she looked awful; her skin was a light shade of gray, and her eyes were red and puffy. I took her arm and led her to the couch.

"Lora. What's wrong? I've never seen you like this."

She wrung her hands and fidgeted. "I had a miscarriage on Wednesday, and yesterday my doctor did a D&C. I was only a couple of months along." She tried to smile, but her lips were quivering. "I've been pregnant five times since Dave and I've been married, but I can't get past the first trimester."

"Oh, Lora, I didn't know. I'm so sorry." Tears welled up in my eyes, but I shook them off. I needed to be strong for my friend. "What can I do?"

Her head hung so low, I dropped and tilted mine, but she wouldn't look at me. "Nothing, Therese. There's nothing anyone can do." Her body sagged, and tears began rolling down her cheeks. "I had gynecological problems when I was a teenager. I think that's why I can't carry a child to term."

I grabbed a napkin off the kitchen table and handed it to her.

She wiped her eyes and said, "My doctor wants me to have a hysterectomy, because of the scar tissue in my uterus. He's convinced I will never be able to have a baby. But I'm not ready to give up yet."

I desperately wanted to be as good a friend as she had been to me, but when I hugged her, she stiffened and pushed me away.

"Thanks, Therese, but I'll be fine. I need to forget about it and move on." She straightened and then stood up. "Don't worry about me. It'll only take me a few minutes to get ready."

"Are you sure you feel up to shopping today? Maybe you should rest. Don't you and Anna have a big party tomorrow night?"

"Yes, but I want to get out. I need to get a few things, and it will take my mind off this."

"Okay." I was stunned she could switch gears so readily when I was still grieving for her loss.

She headed to the bedroom and I followed her. Before she could close the door, I asked, "Have you gotten a second opinion, Lora? It might be worth talking to another doctor."

She swiftly turned around to face me. "I don't want to talk about it anymore, Therese."

❧❧❧❧

Later that evening as John and I watched TV, I twisted toward him and put my feet in his lap. He started to massage them, and I melted into the couch. "Oh, that feels good! Don't stop."

John squeezed my toes and said, "Chinese toehold."

After a while, I swung my legs around in front of me and turned off the TV. "Did you know Lora's had several miscarriages?"

"No, I didn't." John's brow furrowed. "I wonder why they never told me?"

"She said she'd had some sort of female problems when she was young. Her doctor wants her to have a hysterectomy, so it must be serious, because she's only thirty-four— pretty young to have that procedure done. I'm really worried about her physical and emotional state, John."

"Hmm. I never knew she had these problems, but being the boy in the family, I guess I wouldn't have heard about those kinds of things." He paused, and I could tell he wanted to say more. "You know, Therese, I worry about my sister for a lot of reasons."

"What do you mean?"

"I haven't shared much about Lora's early life, because it's not a pretty story. Promise me you won't talk with her about any of this. Okay?"

"Of course."

"Aunt Jessica and Aunt Evelyn helped Phyllis when Lora and Marcia were toddlers, but after Cindy was born, Dad demanded a lot from Lora. Aunt Jessica watched over Lora and Marcia as well as she could, but she was raising her own children, caring for Cindy, and helping Uncle Edward on the ranch. At a very young age, Lora was supposed to run the household and have dinner on the table when Dad walked in the door. Lora worked so hard to please him, and Dad never appreciated all she did for him.

"Our well-being never entered Dad's mind, so when Phyllis came home from Napa State Hospital for a visit, Lora had to take care of her, too. When it was time to leave, Phyllis screamed and cried and had to be carried to the car. It was the doctors who stopped the home visits." He paused. "But every now and then, Dad brought her home anyway. I remember standing at the front door watching this scary, strange-acting woman. I ran off and hid in the barn. Grandma came and got me and took me to her house.

"Dad was such a tyrant," he continued, "and since we were alone so much without adult supervision, Lora was the same with Marcia and me. Sometimes her wrath could be painful. She picked me up by my ears and slugged me so hard, it left bruises. She told such scary stories, I was afraid to be alone. One time, I dropped a carton of eggs on the floor, and Lora held it over my head for two years.

Whenever she couldn't get me to do something, she'd threaten, 'I'm going to tell Dad about those eggs you broke.'

"Anger just spewed out of Lora then. She took it out on everyone, because she was the boss. Marcia and Lora fought constantly, and once Cindy moved home, the fights got worse. One time, Lora threw a butcher knife across the room at Marcia, and it stuck in the wall. I was a little kid scared shitless of my big sister. After school, I usually followed Cindy to Aunt Jessica's house just to stay away from Lora for as long as I could."

Hearing what Lora had endured so early in life was painful—and a little baffling, because the Lora John described was the complete opposite of the Lora I knew and loved. I understood her conduct as that of a child growing up without a mother, devoid of fatherly love or much support, a girl mad as hell at the world. You would never know she bore such scars. These Marin women kept their secrets close, hiding the wounds of their childhood, never giving a hint of what they had endured and overcome. No wonder they wanted to avoid facing any more pain.

12

When the weather turned cold and rainy, John and I started working on indoor projects. Our bedroom and bathroom were first. We painted, lay down new carpeting and installed new closet doors, replaced the bathroom vanity and repaired the shower. In the family room, we tore out the old carpet and put in new, exchanged the large single-paned window for a double-paned bay window, replaced the sliding-glass door. We installed a wood-burning stove just when we needed it. As for the new garage, the walls and roof were up, and the washer and dryer were in.

John was so hot to get things done, I had to remind him we needed breaks from our remodeling fun to have regular fun. So once a month, we had a play date with Lora and Dave, and Marcia and Glenn joined us whenever they could drive in from the Bay Area. One fall evening, we arrived at the Citrus Heights Marie Callender's a few minutes late, and Dave waved us over to their table. After the flurry of hellos, I sat down next to Lora and hugged her. "Hey, how was your week?"

"Oh, pretty good. Anna has some big parties lined up for us."

When I turned to Marcia, she didn't look up, just picked up her wine glass and took a big sip. My brow furrowed as I scanned the table looking for a clue to what was wrong, but I couldn't read a thing on anyone's face.

John flagged down the waitress and ordered us drinks. He leaned back in his chair and said with a loud sigh, "I'm so glad it's Friday!"

Dave flirted with the waitress, as usual, and I pursed my

lips. After a few minutes of chatting, I still had the feeling something was amiss. Marcia wasn't a big talker, but tonight she hadn't said a thing other than hello. Also, Glenn wasn't there, and Marcia hadn't said why.

All of a sudden, Marcia blurted out, "I don't know if you heard, but Pacific Bell is splitting into two companies, Pac Bell and AT&T. I was informed yesterday morning that my job in the San Francisco office is being eliminated."

The rest of us stared at her and said, "What?"

"It was a shock to me, too, but the good news is I've been offered another position. The bad news is it's in New Jersey. They told me if I don't take it, I am out of a job."

Lora put her hand on Marcia's. "Why didn't you call me, Moochie?"

Marcia reached in her purse and pulled out a pack of cigarettes. "You have enough on your plate." She took a cigarette out of the box and lit it, and when she took a drag, her hand jerked. She quickly moved it under the table.

No one else seemed to have noticed. Trying to lighten the mood, John raised his glass. "Congratulations, Marcia. You're starting a new chapter of your life, one that includes driving in snow! But we will miss you."

We all raised our glasses. "Here, here!"

"So now I guess you and Glenn will have a long-distance relationship, like John and I did," I said. "It's really not that bad; I mean, you'll miss him, but you will plan time together. And you know that saying about absence...."

When our food arrived, Marcia tried to smash her cigarette in the ashtray, and her hand jerked again. It took her a couple of tries to put the cigarette out. Trying to ignore what I'd seen, I went on talking about love and long-distance relationships until John gently bumped my leg under the table.

Marcia shifted in her chair and took another sip of wine. "Glenn and I broke up last night. We haven't been getting along that well anyway. He has a lot of baggage from his first marriage that he still needs to work through." She put her napkin on the table and stood up. "I'm going to the ladies room."

Lora was immediately out of her chair.

My hand instantly went over my mouth and slowly slid to my heart. "Oh, no. Boy, do I feel like a jerk."

John reached over and took my hand. "It's okay, Therese. You didn't know."

When Marcia and Lora returned to the table, I said, "I'm so sorry about Glenn, Marcia." She shrugged her shoulders and grabbed her wine glass. The silence was killing me, so I changed the subject. "What do you know about your new position?"

"Well, from what I've been told, it's similar to my job here. Another marketing rep who's also been with the company a long time is moving to New Jersey, too, so at least I'll know one person there."

"Will you need any help packing?"

To my surprise, she said, "Yes, you guys can help me pack in two weeks. My new job starts November 1. I'm flying to New Jersey next week to meet my new boss and find an apartment."

❧❧❧

The following weekend, John and I were working inside, because it was pouring rain again. John had been in the attic all morning, adding insulation, and was in the shower washing off the prickly fiberglass that had stuck to his clothing and hair. I spread a blanket on the concrete floor where the fireplace had been and threw down some fat pillows. When John came out of the bedroom in clean clothes, he asked, "What's going on?"

"We're having a picnic inside today!"

He stretched out on his side and leaned on his elbow. "I'm sure going to miss Marcia," he sighed. "It will be so weird without her. At least she's only a phone call away. She'll visit during the holidays, and maybe next year we can visit her."

I opened a bag of potato chips and handed it to him. "It'll be strange not seeing her," I agreed. "She's been a big part of our lives ever since I've known you; I feel like I'm losing a sister. How do you think she'll handle moving so far away from you and Lora?"

John put his sandwich down. "Marcia will do fine at her job, but not knowing many people will be tough. She's pretty shy. And being away from Lora will be really hard for both of them."

A week later, we were on the road at six-thirty to get to Walnut Creek around eight, which would give us eight hours to pack before the moving van arrived. When we got there, Lora and Dave met us at the door. The mood in the apartment was glum, so John turned on the radio. He clapped his hands and rubbed them together. "Okay, let's get cracking! What do you want us to do, Marcia?"

"You and Therese can finish packing up the kitchen. Boxes and paper are in the living room." Wrapping her dishware and glasses in newspaper, I noticed that Lora and Marcia were never far apart. I watched them whisper to each other as they worked; sometimes they'd laugh, and sometimes they'd wipe tears from their eyes.

Around noon, someone ran to Burger King and brought back burgers and fries. Since the legs had already been removed from the kitchen table, we sat on the floor, Marcia's leg touching Lora's. They dipped their French fries into the same bowl of ketchup and tasted each other's milkshakes.

"How are you feeling about all this, Marcia?" I asked. "This is a big move for you, being a California girl and all."

Everybody stopped chewing and stared at me. I'd touched a nerve by using the word *feel*, wondering about a truth Marcia could not share. Waving me off with her hand, she walked into the kitchen. "I'm fine. Don't worry about me."

What other reply would I expect from a Marin? They so rarely shared what they felt. It must be so lonely with those emotions stuck inside, I thought. They all react the same way, as if they'd been programmed.

By three o'clock, some thirty boxes lay scattered throughout the apartment. Marcia and Lora carried suitcases and a few boxes to Marcia's car. She was driving the roughly three thousand miles to New Jersey alone, even though Lora had wanted to go with her and fly back. Marcia and her sister had never been far apart, and they depended so much on each other. I had a bad feeling about the move, but what could I do? I pasted a smile on my face and tried to convince myself that John knew better than I: They'd probably talk on the phone every night, and everything would be all right.

Once the moving van was loaded, we all stood around in the empty apartment. I held back tears as I hugged Marcia. "Be careful driving, and please call Lora or John every night so we know you're fine, okay?" She nodded, crossing her arms and staring at the carpet.

When John hugged her, he kept his arm around her shoulders. Lora stood on her other side, and the three moved close together. It was such a private moment, I pretended to look for something in my purse. After a few minutes, Dave pushed them apart. "Hey, it's my turn!" John wrapped his arm around my waist, and we went out to wait by our car.

After a few minutes, Dave came out. As we waited for Lora, John said, "Hey, do you and Lora want to grab a bite to eat? I'm starved."

❧❧❧

We met in Martinez at the Golden West Pancake House, a place these Alhambra High graduates used to hang out after Friday night football games. At the table, Dave looked around and said, "Oh, man, I haven't been in here since my senior year."

John laughed. "When I was going to Diablo Valley College, my friends Josh and Rick and I would meet here on Saturday mornings around two a.m. After partying all night, we needed coffee and food before we went home to crash. Boy, those were crazy times."

As they talked and laughed, I could tell Lora was very upset, though when she noticed me looking at her sympathetically, she hastened to say, "I'm fine. I really need to get back to work. Anna and I have a big catering job to prepare for next weekend."

Lora excused herself when we finished eating, and after about ten minutes, John nudged me. "Can you go and check on Lora? She's been gone awhile."

A couple of little girls came running out of the restroom, and I scooted out of their way and waited for Lora to come out. "Are you okay?"

"Yes, of course. Did Dave send you?"

"No, John asked me to see how you were."

"Well, he didn't need to do that. I'm just fine."

Once we were on the road, I told John, "When Lora came out of the restroom, her eyes were watery, and she kept clearing her throat. She seemed put out that you'd sent me to check on her. Is something going on that I should know about?"

"I'm sorry I put you in a bad position, Therese. I think she's bulimic again. Marcia does, too. Over the past few months, I've noticed that every time we eat together, she immediately goes into the bathroom when she's done. I think she throws up."

"What did you say? Bulimic? Again? You've never told me she had an eating disorder." I glared at him. "What the hell! Why has no one ever mentioned this? I'm part of this family, too, though sometimes you'd never know it."

John was quiet for a moment, then he turned his head toward me and said, "Yes, unfortunately, Lora has some bad habits. Dave thinks if he ignores them, they'll go away. Marcia and Lora both struggled with their weight growing up—you know, always on some sort of diet."

"Bulimia is a far cry from a diet, John!" I felt a headache coming on and massaged my forehead. My mind was reeling, thinking of all the meals we'd eaten together. "Why didn't you tell me? She's important to me, too!" I looked out the window. "God, there are so many secrets in your family!"

"I didn't tell you because I wasn't sure! You should know by now, we don't talk about things. We're just there for each other. I had my suspicions, and tonight you confirmed them." He sighed. "It's not something you just blurt out, especially about your sister. For Christ's sake, she's thirty-five years old!"

John was so upset, his hands were gripping the steering wheel, and his knuckles were white. After a few minutes, he tried to put his arm around my shoulder, but I moved away. "Oh, come on, Therese. What would you have done if you'd known about it?"

"I don't know. But it hurts being left out." The tears I'd kept back all day ran down my face. "Shit, if we knew one of my sisters was bulimic, the rest of us would have had an intervention. But I guess nobody wants my suggestions."

John didn't say anything, just turned the radio on.

When we got closer to home, he let out a deep breath. "I'm sorry. Old habits are hard to break. The reason I said *again* is because Lora struggled with bulimia when they were first married. She got real skinny and didn't look like herself." He turned the radio off. "Now that Marcia's gone, we can't compare notes anymore. I guess I'll just have to talk to Dave and you. Next time, I'll tell you when I suspect something."

Let's see if you do, I thought. I'll believe it when it happens.

❧❧

About six months later, just after softball season began, Dave called the house early on the morning of our first game. "John, can you coach the girls' team today?"

"Sure, but what's going on? Should we pick up Lora and take her to the game with us?"

John's side of the conversation drifted into the bedroom as I made the bed. Hearing Lora's name over and over, I came out of the room and stood in front of him as he hung up, my hands on my hips. John's hands went up in the air like a shield. "All I know, Therese, is that she's having some sort of kidney problems and is in Sutter Memorial Hospital. We'll go see her after the game."

"Has she had kidney problems before? You know, people aren't admitted into the hospital unless it's serious. Is this something you haven't told me about, like the bulimia?"

"No, Therese. This time I really don't know anything about it."

After the game, the whole team went to see Lora. When there were just four of us in the room, John stepped close to the bed. "What's going on with your kidneys, Lora? I didn't know you had a problem."

Lora looked up at her brother innocently. "Oh, I must have mentioned it to you. You probably forgot."

"No, you never told me anything about it."

"Don't you remember when I contracted hepatitis B, when I worked in that dental office years ago? How could you have forgotten that? Don't worry, I'll be fine. I promise not to miss another game."

Frustrated, John grabbed Dave's arm and pulled him into the hall, hoping to get the real story from him.

I had been standing quietly at the back of the room. Lora looked terrible. Her skin and eyes had a yellow tint, and she was bloated. She'd chewed her fingernails down to the quick. I scooted into the chair next to the bed and leaned in close to her. "Lora, we just want you to get well. There will be lots of softball games. Your health is the most important thing."

John stomped out of the hospital and all the way to the car. When I caught up to him, I tugged on his shirt. "Hey, hey, calm down. What did Dave say?"

"Nothing! He stuck to the same story as Lora. They're both hiding something. The diagnosis of hepatitis is bullshit!"

Lora was discharged two days later, and when I called the house to see how she was doing, Dave answered the phone. "She's sleeping right now. I'll tell her you called. Why don't you give her a couple of days to call back?"

"Humph, I think he doesn't want me talking to her, or she doesn't want to talk to me," I told John. "I agree, they're hiding something."

❧❧❧❧

Throughout the summer, John and I continued working on the house, with many friends and our families helping. It was becoming a warm and inviting place, and as we completed each project, we were filled with a sense of accomplishment and pride. The garage was finished; we'd replaced the gravel driveway with concrete; John had built a deck from the house to the garage so that I didn't have to tromp through mud and dirt; and now he was designing a breakfast nook for the kitchen. When friends or family members visited, they were amazed at the transformation.

We had just remodeled the second bathroom and John was almost finished tiling the floor. It was Saturday around noon, and John had been on his knees all morning.

"Hey, why don't you take a break for lunch, honey?"

"Sounds good." He grabbed a soda and sat at the kitchen table. He seemed lost in his thoughts, but eventually, he came back to earth. "Last weekend, when Dave and I were repairing the fences, he told me something that's been bothering me ever since."

I was fishing lunchmeat and cheese out of the refrigerator and waited for him to continue.

"He thinks Lora has a drinking problem."

"What?" I stood up so abruptly, I hit my head. "Ouch!" I closed the refrigerator door with my foot and carried the sandwich fixings to the table, sitting down with a thud. "You've got to be kidding! That's the most ridiculous thing I've ever heard."

"Well, he's her husband, and I think he knows what he's talking about."

He grabbed the package of bread so hard, I thought the

bread was ruined. He took out two slices, smoothed them out, and started making a sandwich.

"You know, I've thought a lot about it since he told me. Remember when I lived with them before we got married?"

"Yes."

"Well, I got up in the middle of the night a couple of times and caught Lora drinking. The first time it happened, I went into the kitchen for a glass of water and Lora was standing at the refrigerator, drinking wine out of the bottle. When she saw me, she made an excuse that she couldn't sleep and thought a little wine might help. We never talked about it again."

"You never mentioned it to me."

"At the time, I didn't think it was a big deal, and I forgot about it. Now I've remembered another time, when she was sitting on the couch drinking vodka straight out of the bottle. She didn't notice me, and I went back to bed pondering what I'd seen. I wasn't sure what to do or even if it meant anything, so I talked to Dave. He blew me off. He said she must've had a bad day." John drummed his fingers on the table and stared out the window. "I didn't know what else to do, so I dropped it. Maybe I shouldn't have."

"Hmm. It's been four years since you lived with them. Have you noticed anything else that would make you think she's an alcoholic? I haven't."

John scratched his bristly whiskers. Suddenly, his eyes widened. "You know something? When we were kids, Lora used to steal booze out of Dad's liquor cabinet and replace it with water. The three of us thought it was funny, but maybe that was the beginning." He stopped and gave me a quick glance. "This is crazy! What am I saying? That my sister has been an alcoholic her whole life?"

"I don't know, maybe. What did Dave want you to do?"

"He didn't say. I think he just needed someone to talk to. How about we invite them over for dinner this Friday? Maybe you can pull her aside and get her to talk."

"What makes you think she'll talk to me? I'm not Marcia. She rarely tells me anything." I shook my head. "I'll do my best, but if she doesn't want to talk, we'll have to come up with something else."

We planned our strategy, but Lora called the night before and said they couldn't come. We tried the next weekend and got the same response. It was hard not to think that something was up. One evening after work, we stopped by their house, and John peeked in the garage. Lora's car was there, so we knocked on the front door. We could hear the dogs barking, and they were never in the house unless someone was home. But Lora never answered the door.

13

*P*lacer County proved to be an excellent place for John to work, since it was growing rapidly and offered many opportunities for a young professional. Just after our third anniversary, a position became available in the county planning department, and John got the job. He would assist the Placer County Board of Supervisors and the county's planning commission in preparing for growth, enforce the county's zoning ordinance, and review and make recommendations on land development.

Both John and I worked with young married couples that were starting families. This opened a long conversation as to whether or not we should have children. I was having a hard time getting past the risk involved, agonizing over bringing a child into the world when quite possibly condemning him or her to the life of uncertainty we led.

When I decided to marry John, I had consciously accepted the fears I would have to live with. To keep my OCD in check, I tried to control the important aspects of my life, such as our finances and my career, to focus on the present and stay optimistic about the future. For the most part, I'd been successful. But now, my concern for Lora, and not knowing whether her bulimia and drinking had been caused by a stressful childhood or the depressive—or other— symptoms of HD, was opening the door to my demons.

John would turn thirty next year, entering the age range— thirty to forty-five—during which, we'd been told, Huntington's symptoms most often present themselves. During our many discussions, John decided he did want to have kids. He understood my apprehension, of course, and when he suggested we investigate adoption, we contacted an agency, Sierra Forever Families, in Sacramento. We attended a workshop, listened carefully, and took home all the paperwork.

As the months went on and we talked and talked until we couldn't bear another word on the subject, John told me he could live with whatever I decided. I should have been grateful for that, and I was; but it put before me another life-changing crossroad, created another huge decision that had to be made alone.

In 1968, the year after Woody Guthrie died, his second wife, Marjorie Guthrie, had created the Committee to Combat Huntington's Disease (now the Huntington's Disease Society of America). When I'd been so torn up over whether to stay with John, I'd made a donation and asked for information. Marjorie had responded with an inspiring personal letter, and I'd been receiving the group's quarterly newsletters ever since. Once John and I married, we contributed as much as we could afford, but John never once looked at a newsletter. I usually carried them to work and read every word at lunch.

The December 1983 newsletter had been in my briefcase for a week, and when I finally looked at it, I couldn't believe what I saw. The headline story read, "In a surprise break-through, a genetic marker was discovered which localized the Huntington's gene to an area close to the tip of the short arm of chromosome four. This discovery would pave the way for a pre-symptomatic test for the disease using DNA-linkage analysis. It is expected to become available in the next couple of years."

I couldn't wait to show John the article and tell his sisters about it. Driving home that day, I thought, Oh, my gosh, this is great news! Now at-risk individuals won't have to live with the unknown and can have some control over their lives. Knowing was key, as far as I was concerned, because only then could a plan be devised.

John read the article, but he didn't share my feelings. "I guess it's good news if you want to know, but I don't. It would be great to find out I don't have the mutated gene, but what if I tested positive?" He looked at me sadly. "I'm afraid it would destroy us, Therese."

"But John, this could help me decide if I want to have a baby! If you don't have the mutated gene, the child couldn't inherit it from you." I hesitated. "You wouldn't ever consider being tested?"

"No. I'd rather live my life with the hope I don't have the mutated gene than find out I do. If we decide to have a child, we will have to live with the risk."

When I called Lora, I got the same reaction. Marcia dittoed that, and Cindy just asked for a copy of the newsletter. I resigned myself to the fact that John didn't want to know his status right now. Maybe he'd change his mind in a couple of years, when the test became available.

~~~~

A couple of days before Christmas, my mom, grandma, two sisters, and I ventured into the Sun Valley Mall in Pleasant Hill, about twenty minutes from my parents' house. We drove two cars in case Grandma got tired. When she did, Amy and Jen weren't done shopping yet, so I offered to take her home. I talked on and on about John, my job, the latest projects at the house. When Grandma interjected, "When are you and John going to have a baby?" the timing took me by surprise.

I stuttered and stammered and finally said we didn't know if we ever would, because of the threat of Huntington's. Not having children had never been an option in my faithful

Catholic family. I stopped at a stoplight and looked at my grandmother. She said, "Sometimes you have to take a leap of faith, Therese. Nothing is certain. And besides, I believe John is going to be just fine."

I was equally surprised when my mother felt the same way, at least about the leap of faith. It wasn't long before all this support melted my apprehension, and I could honestly replace it with hope. Hope that John didn't carry the mutated gene, so that our child wouldn't be at risk. Hope that, with the research being conducted, if my child did inherit HD, a cure or therapy would be found by the time he or she developed any symptoms. Four years ago, I had taken one big chance; now I was ready to take another.

Over the next few months, John and I didn't use contraceptives. I figured what was meant to be, would be. I thought a lot about Lora; she was such a dear friend, and I couldn't bear the thought of hurting her. Though I never doubted she would have been a loving mother, she was already thirty-five, bulimic, possibly alcoholic, at risk for HD, and she lived with a man who had never grown up. I wasn't sure she was strong enough to handle another child.

When I got pregnant, I told Mom and Grandma the good news and considered the best way to tell Lora. But John beat me to it, shouting over the telephone, "We're expecting a baby in October! Can you believe it, Lora? I'm going to be a dad, and you're going to be an aunt! Can you guys come over for dinner on Saturday to celebrate?"

Jennifer, Amy, and Jen's boyfriend, Matt, were already there when Dave and Lora showed up with a bottle of wine. When Lora reached out to hug me, she had tears in her eyes. I wanted to believe they were tears of happiness for us. We had a wonderful evening. John and I both noticed that Lora didn't touch the wine.

❧❧❧

My doctor was one of five female physicians at A Woman's Place, in Roseville. The waiting room had comfortable padded chairs, and photographs of serene landscapes were displayed on the textured-wallpaper. Emily Hamilton, M.D., was also pregnant with her first child, which was even due around the same time as mine. John accompanied me to my first prenatal appointment. When Dr. Hamilton asked if we'd like to hear the baby's heartbeat, John's face lit up, and it was hard to contain our excitement. At that moment, it all became very real.

After that appointment, John became a man with a mission. "We've got seven months to get the nursery painted, carpeted, and wallpapered, finish the kitchen nook, and build a pantry so that you have more storage."

"I just have one request. Please build a fence around the pool," I said.

John laughed. "Therese, the kid isn't even born yet." But he put the task close to the top of the list.

Though Dave was over often to help with our projects, we didn't see Lora much, because her business was booming. The first weekend that she wasn't catering a party, we had them over for dinner. I wanted to do something just for her, to have her sit at our table and relax. Lora, of course, brought the most delicious homemade hors d'oeuvre, bacon-wrapped chestnuts soaked in teriyaki sauce. And being the kind person she was, she never made me feel uncomfortable about being pregnant.

❧❧❧

Lora and Anna had been catering for two years, and we thought their business was doing well until we ran into Anna's husband, Steve, at the store one afternoon.

"They had more business than they could handle, so they hired a woman to help six months ago and paid her in cash," he told us. "Turns out she was on welfare and didn't report her earnings. The welfare department just found out and reported them to the state. Now they owe back taxes, and on top of that, someone, probably the welfare gal, turned them into the state licensing board for preparing food in a residential kitchen, not a commercial kitchen." We couldn't believe we hadn't had a clue about any of this. "And to top it off, the health department shut them down last week and revoked their license."

Dave had been changing jobs a lot, two times in the past year, and we'd known he wasn't making as much money but assumed—because, once again, no one told us anything—that Lora's earnings were making up at least some of the loss. When John and I asked how we could help, they told us they were filing for bankruptcy. The stress was apparent; Lora had deep lines in her forehead, heavy black half-moons under her eyes. We felt their boat was sinking, and ours didn't have long enough paddles to reach them and keep them from drowning.

❧❧❧

John turned thirty on September 6, 1984. It was hard to believe he would be a father soon, and I'd be a mother. My boss at Aratex was giving me a six-month maternity leave, and I was deliriously happy. Mom had been busy digging my old baby garments, bonnets, and toys out of her cedar chest. She'd already presented me with a yellow crocheted sweater and bonnet made by Grandma that I'd worn home from the hospital in 1955. She had crocheted a yellow baby blanket to go with them.

My due date was October 8, my twenty-ninth birthday,

and as I reflected on my pregnancy, I saw how fortunate I'd been: no morning sickness or swollen ankles, and I'd put on just twenty-five pounds so far. John and I never talked about the risk we had taken in conceiving this child, but every now and then, I had a restless night.

By early October, I felt like a beached whale. The eighth fell on a Sunday, so I had a few more days to get organized before we greeted our child.

The Monday before, John made me breakfast. "Remember what the doctor said. Don't overdo it, and take a nap when you feel tired. I'll set up the changing table and bring in the dresser tonight after I put the new knobs on." He rubbed my belly. "Wow, he's really moving a lot today."

"Yes, he is." My hand went over his. "I can't wait to put the clothes in the dresser. I'm still amazed at how tiny they are."

The next morning, the telephone rang at seven a.m. John was in the shower, and I reached for the phone. "Therese. It's Dave." He sounded angry, which was unusual for him.

I rubbed my eyes. "What's the matter?"

"I want you and John to know I'm admitting Lora to the drug-rehab center at Roseville Community Hospital. She doesn't want to go, but I'm insisting. She needs help."

"You're doing what?" I said, motioning to John as he came out of the bathroom in his robe. I handed him the phone, trying to grasp what Dave had told me.

"Hey, Dave." I watched John's shoulders slump slowly, as if he were being deflated. When he hung up, he said, only half in disbelief, "Lora's going into rehab, because she is an alcoholic."

As I struggled to get out of bed, I said, "This is unbelievable and crazy! I've never seen Lora drunk or, for that matter, even drink excessively." John helped me to the living room and made me sit down. I hid my face in my hands. "Why doesn't she trust us? We could have helped."

"I don't know, Therese," he said, pacing the room. "Goddamn it! I shouldn't have pussyfooted around with her. She's such a good liar! When Dave told me his suspicions, I should have confronted her. Hell, I should have done it years ago." He ran his hands through his hair in anguish. "I'll drive to Roseville at lunchtime and see how things are going."

The thirty-day drug-recovery program allowed the patient to live at the facility, then called Starting Point Drug and Rehabilitation Center, while undergoing treatment. During that time, the patient attended both group and individual sessions, with an option to join twelve-step meetings aimed at helping recovered patients maintain their sobriety.

When John got home from work, I asked immediately, "How did it go?"

He fell onto the couch next to me. "Well, she was mad as hell when I got there. And she had the shakes real bad. Dave and I talked with the counselor to understand how the program works. After he explained things, I asked for some statistics on the program, like how many people finish it and stay sober? He said about eighty percent finish the thirty-day program. Once they're out, it's a different story. I was happy to hear they follow their patients for a year. But the return rate is about forty percent, which I don't consider good. He emphasized to both of us, 'Once the patients are discharged, they're on their own.' They have to stick with the program and religiously attend AA meetings and stay connected with their sponsor. 'Only a few can do this alone,' he said. 'They need support and positive reinforcement.'

"After that, Dave filled out all the paperwork, and then he had a private meeting with the counselor. Before I left, he asked if I would call Dad. The counselor stressed to both of us that for Lora to be successful in the program, we need participation from family members."

After dinner, John called his father. It was a difficult conversation, to say the least. John repeated more than once, "Lora is an alcoholic, and she needs our support. The counselor suggested as many family members as possible be involved…. Come on, Dad, Lora has never asked you for much. For that matter, none of us have. You need to do this for her."

I could hear Big John yelling from across the room. "That's the stupidest thing I've ever heard. Lora's not an alcoholic. What is Dave thinking, putting her in there? You know Lucy's not well. I have to stay here, because she can't get up by herself."

John was fuming, pacing up and down and stretching the phone cord to its limit. "Well, Dad, I guess you've chosen Lucy over your kids once again. Can't teach an old dog new tricks, huh?" He took a deep breath. "You know I lived with Lora for a year after college, and I can tell you, she does have a problem. If you decide to come, her first session is tomorrow morning at nine. Get here at eight, and we can talk more about it. You can stay the night if you like."

But once more, the father of this lovely woman let her down. It didn't surprise me. Why would we expect him to support his daughter now, when he had ignored, neglected, and used her as she was growing up?

After four days of the program, it became clear to the counselors that Lora was unwilling to address her drinking problem. "In the sessions I've attended, she refuses to admit she even has a problem," John told me. "Everyone else does, but until she recognizes it, she can't begin to recover. And Dave isn't really helping. He thinks it should be an easy fix, like a broken leg. I keep telling him it doesn't work that way."

Another issue weighed heavily on my mind, but I didn't dare talk about it. Because an early and prominent symptom of HD is depression, a person with Huntington's can turn to alcohol as a way to self-medicate. With all her other problems, Lora must have been terrified of having Huntington's, because it wasn't an abstract disease to her. The memories of watching her mother's struggle must have remained vivid in her mind.

After John had attended four of Lora's sessions, he came home with upsetting news. "Dave told the group that Lora's hospital stay last year wasn't about hepatitis B," I started nodding, "but the beginning of cirrhosis of the liver."

I gasped and my eyes starting filling with tears. "What did she say about me coming to her sessions? You told her I want to help, right?"

"Yes, I asked her, Therese." He looked away. "She doesn't want you there. She doesn't even want me there, but I'm not going anywhere. She is so angry. I don't think it would be good for either of you."

I was so frightened for my friend. She was heading down a road of self-destruction—unfortunately, one she'd been on for years, though she'd hidden it well—and we were powerless to stop her. "Well, I will be there for her when she gets out," I said as I took John's hand. "But for now, I will support you, honey."

❧❧❧

Keith Anthony Marin was born on October 6, 1984, in the same hospital Lora was in, one week into her rehab. At first, I was a bit disconcerted that she was in the same facility. But after looking into Keith's angelic face, I felt he'd been destined to arrive at this time and place, to create balance in all our lives. The miracle I held in my arms renewed my hope and faith that Lora would prevail in her struggle. I prayed that once Lora looked at Keith, she could also draw strength from him.

"Knock, knock, can I come in?" asked Lora, peeking into the room.

"Of course!" I reached out to hug her, but she backed away, staying just beyond arm's reach.

"Congratulations! John told me the wonderful news this morning. I'm so happy for you guys."

"Thanks, Lora. I'm still kind of in shock." A woman had followed Lora into the room and was standing off to one side. "Who is this with you?"

"This is my new friend, Margie. I can't go outside the ward without her. Guess they think I'll escape or something," Lora joked.

I smiled and said hello, then turned back to Lora. "Do you want to see your nephew? We can go to the nursery together." Lora kept her distance as we walked down the hall, Margie trailing behind her. At the nursery window, I pointed him out. "That one's Keith. Isn't he cute?"

"He's darling, Therese. I can't believe I'm an aunt now." Lora turned her head away.

Wanting to change the subject, I could only think to ask, "So, how is rehab going?"

"It's going okay. I'll be fine."

I put my arm around her, and she stiffened. Playfully shaking her, I said in what I hoped was a light tone of voice, "You won't believe it, but there's a baby bigger than Keith in here. Let's see, where is that bruiser? Keith weighs nine pounds, one ounce, and this guy weighs at least eleven pounds."

Other new mothers were crowding around the window with their families, and there was a lot of oohing and ahhing. Margie touched Lora's arm. "It's time to go back to the unit," she reminded her gently. "Your session starts in thirty minutes."

Back in my room, John had been patiently waiting for me. As I climbed into the bed, the phone rang, and he answered it. "Hi, Marcia.... Yes, Keith and Therese are fine. Thanks for the beautiful flowers.... Well, we wish you were here to see him. He's so cute. And big! It's hard to believe my little Therese gave birth to a whale."

Then he turned away and began talking in a low voice. It wasn't hard to figure out what they were discussing. It made me sad, but just then, a nurse walked in with Keith and placed in my arms this little person I'd been waiting for my whole life. When John hung up the phone, we each held one of Keith's tiny hands. Staring into his bright eyes, I think we both saw hope.

14

*B*aby Keith and I were discharged five days after he was born. Walking through the front door with a newborn in my arms, a realization hit me: Our lives would never be the same. This child given to us to love, nurture, and protect was now our first priority.

Lora had ten days left in the program, and I felt I was deserting her. My emotions were fragmented: one minute, joyous our child was here and healthy; the next, distressed and upset that my friend was fighting a foe I wasn't sure she could conquer.

John was under a lot of pressure as he continued to attend Lora's sessions while working full-time and adjusting to a newborn. I listened when he wanted to talk, but I didn't push, because I knew how hard it was on him to see his alcoholic, bulimic sister in lockdown. I was overjoyed to note how his mood lightened whenever he looked at our little bundle of joy.

Mom arrived for a week the day after I got home, and I'd never been so happy to see her. Our days were focused on Keith's needs, which were utterly basic: eating, sleeping, being bathed, changed, and soothed. With my mother giving me the confidence I needed, I began to relax and enjoy motherhood. I found such contentment in nursing and cuddling this tiny person who depended on me.

And it felt good to talk to an objective person, someone who validated my roller-coaster emotions. My fear that Lora had Huntington's was escalating, and when I shared my concern with my mom, she became teary-eyed. But she agreed that discussing it with Lora or John would serve no purpose.

One day, John came home looking downtrodden. "Did something happen at Lora's session?" I asked. Being a true Marin, he responded with a shrug. Mom took Keith into the nursery to give us some privacy.

"Come on, honey, what's wrong?" I persisted. "I'm not any different than I was before I had our baby. I want to help if I can."

John sat at the kitchen table massaging his forehead. "I'm so worried about her. I'm not a counselor, but I can see she's not making any progress. She still puts on a front, as if everything's all right, but I know the true Lora."

In bed that night, we held each other. "I love you, John." I felt him relax and was amazed at how quickly he fell asleep. Everyone finds a way to deal with stress, and sleep was John's.

I listened to his rhythmic breathing and stared at the ceiling for so long, I finally wandered into my baby's room and sat in the rocking chair. When Keith fussed, I picked him up. "Don't cry, little man. It's okay." I cradled my newborn in my arms and nursed him; once he drifted off to sleep, I put him in his crib and gently patted his back. Then I moved to the window, pulled up the shade, and stared into the darkness.

Since Lora had gone into rehab, my demons had started appearing at night. With my hormones fluctuating and the lack of sleep, my resistance had been faltering ever since Keith's birth. Now I took a deep breath, but my throat constricted and my chest tightened. How I wished I could not worry about HD until something happened, if it ever happened. Hoping to push my terror away, I crossed my arms and squeezed my body as tightly as I could. My eyes went to my sleeping angel, and I prayed. "Dear God, protect this innocent child, who deserves nothing less than all the joy in the world. I pray I have not condemned him to a life with Huntington's. Please help me be strong."

Struggling to hold back tears, I stood at the crib and made a solemn promise to Keith. "Since I brought you into this world, my darling child, I will always be there for you, no matter what."

My head started to hurt and I was shivering, so I went back to bed. Two hours later, I went into the bathroom and passed a blood clot the size of a child's block.

John knocked on the bathroom door. "Are you all right, Therese?"

I walked out of the bathroom shakily and lay on the bed. Mom heard us talking and came into the bedroom. "What's the matter?"

"Therese isn't well, and she passed a blood clot. I'm taking her temperature."

Mom was frowning as she took the thermometer from John and shook it hard, just as she'd done so many times when I was a kid. "Let's give her some ibuprofen, and I think you should call her doctor." She sat on the bed next to me and put her hand on my forehead. "You're burning up, sugar. Your temperature is a hundred and two."

When John got off the phone, he stood in the doorway. "The doctor told me to take her to the emergency room, where she'll have an order waiting to admit her." He took Mom aside as I got dressed, but I could hear them. "She thinks Therese has an infection and should be treated in the hospital. Can you stay with Keith until we figure things out?"

"Of course."

All the way to the hospital, wrapped in a blanket, my body was shaking and I couldn't make it stop. Between sobs, I murmured, "Oh, God, what's happening?" I pulled the blanket tighter and whimpered, "I just want to be home with my baby." I slid closer to John. "Is that too much to ask?"

"It'll be okay, Therese, don't worry." My head jerked backward as he stepped on the gas.

Even though I knew something was wrong, my baby was all I could think about. Suddenly, I had a terrible thought. "Oh, no, Keith will be hungry when he wakes up, and I won't be there! I never thought something like this would happen."

When Dr. Hamilton arrived at the hospital at five a.m., I was hooked up to an IV with the first of many bags of antibiotics. My fever was a hundred and three, and I'd passed two more clots. "Therese, you probably have a staph infection in your uterus. That's the reason for the clotting. This happens sometimes when you have a C-section. We need to stop the infection so that it doesn't cause scar tissue, which could potentially make it difficult for you to conceive again."

Hearing that, I burst into tears. John brought me close and kissed my head as my cry turned into a howl, like the sound of someone losing her mind. John called Mom, and she brought our starving, wailing child to the hospital. The nurses moved a bassinet into the room for Keith and a bed chair for John, who watched the nurses change the antibiotic bags and carry Keith to me when he was hungry. When I looked particularly worried, he tried to lighten my spirits by saying, "Well, at least all I have to do is go downstairs for Lora's session."

Five days later, I was discharged once again, the recipient of nine bags of antibiotics. I weighed just a hundred and ten pounds, while my child had developed a double chin and was wearing clothes for a six-to-nine-month-old baby.

❧❧❧❧

Once Lora returned home, her stint in rehab seemed like a bad dream, at least to me. Anna was happy the chef was back and they could bid on catering jobs again. She had taken care of some of their problems by renting an industrial kitchen in which to prepare food, paying the fine to reinstate their business license, and setting up a payment plan with the state for back taxes on their errant employee. But I couldn't help wondering if the pressure of running a business was too much for Lora.

I invited her to the house several times, but she always had an excuse. "Do you think Lora is mad at me for having a baby?" I asked John.

"What? That's crazy. Lora isn't like that."

"Then why has she shut me out of her life ever since Keith was born? Maybe I'm being too sensitive about it. I mean, I think it's really painful for her to see us with a baby."

"I don't think that's it, Therese. You know Lora has a lot on her plate these days, with the business, attending AA meetings, staying in touch with her sponsor. Dave said they have a lot of parties booked during the holidays; in fact, he asked if I could bartend at some of them."

"Well, I'm glad you can help. And maybe that'll give you a chance to see how she's doing," I said.

"I doubt it. She hides things so well. I'd forgotten how secretive she can be."

That year, both sides of the family invited us to Thanksgiving dinner. "Why don't you ask your family to come to my parents' house?" I suggested to John. "Lora deserves some down time from cooking—for God's sake, that's what she does for a living now. Everyone likes to get away from their job once in a while."

Once again, the answer was no. "Dave's dead set against

it," John told me, "and I know why. He wants the leftovers. And of course Lora agrees with him." A deep sigh escaped him. "Sometimes I just want to shake the guy and tell him to be more considerate of my sister."

"He's so selfish!" I said. "Doesn't he have any compassion? She doesn't need any more pressure. Besides, he's not the one who'll be slaving over the stove."

At least it would be a small crowd this year, since Marcia was in New Jersey and Cindy and Brad were skiing in British Columbia. As I swaddled my precious little guy in a blanket and put a warm hat on his head, I felt thrilled to be showing him off to the Marin family. Keith was such a happy baby, and he'd begun reaching out to the world, grasping our fingers and focusing on moving objects. I was so happy when Lora hugged us both and smiled as she gave him a kiss. She did look tired, though.

The table was beautiful, set with Lora's Noritake china, crystal wine and water glasses, cloth napkins, and a holiday-flower centerpiece. Dave carried the golden-brown turkey out from the kitchen. Lora set down her moist oyster stuffing and the gravy boat, followed by mashed potatoes, homemade cranberry sauce, and whipped yams with marshmallows. I added the savory rolls, fresh butter, and a bowl of black olives. It looked as if we were going to feed half the state.

Just as Dave was sharpening the knife to carve the turkey, Lora excused herself, saying she had a headache. When we'd begun eating and she hadn't returned, I went to check on her and on Keith, but she didn't come out until we had all finished dinner. She looked more exhausted than before, and I could smell alcohol on her breath. As we began clearing the table, she wouldn't look at anyone; I could feel the tension growing as Dave pursed his lips and turned on a football game.

After that, even more of my conversations with John revolved around Lora. Her precarious situation, and knowing that alcoholism can be a manifestation of Huntington's, had triggered my OCD, and feeling helpless increased my anxiety. Being at risk for HD was such a terrible thing to live with, always wondering when you dropped something or stumbled if it was clumsiness or the beginning of the end. That kind of terror could drive a person to drink. If I were her, I thought, I might be drinking, too.

❧❧❧

Marcia called most Saturday mornings, catching John before he got involved in a project, and when he was done, she and I talked for a few minutes. She seemed to enjoy her job, but I could hear loneliness in her voice.

Four days before Christmas, she flew in from New Jersey. Still on maternity leave, I'd had so much fun decorating the house. John picked her up from the airport, and as soon as she walked in the door, she dropped her bags, threw her arms in the air, and said, "I'm so glad to be back in California."

John couldn't wait to show Keith to his sister, and as soon as Marcia sat down, John put the baby on her lap and tickled his cheek to make him smile. "Keith, this is your Auntie Marcia." She held him so awkwardly, it was clear that she had never been around babies. I gave her a bottle to feed him, and he fell asleep in her arms as he took his last gulp. As John watched her feed his son, I could see how happy he was to be with Marcia again.

"Do you want something to eat?" I asked. "It's so cold out. I made minestrone soup this morning."

"That sounds great, Therese," Marcia replied. "This cold is nothing compared to New Jersey, though. I had to buy a wool coat, gloves, and boots. Pants aren't my thing, as you know, but I broke down and bought a couple pair, because my legs were freezing."

"Bet you're getting pretty good at driving in the snow," John said.

"Well, I bought snow tires, and they do help." She laughed. "I'm sure people hate to be behind me, because I drive so slowly, especially when it's icy."

After John showed Marcia the house and all the projects we were working on, I put the soup, sourdough bread, and butter on the table. As we ate, I noticed a slight spasm in Marcia's shoulder. My concern over Lora had lowered my resistance, and the demons took this opportunity to pounce, slowly crawling up my back into my psyche as her twitching continued. I shrugged my shoulders up and down to combat the stress mounting in my body.

"Oh, how I've missed this! There's nothing like San Francisco bread," Marcia said. "You can't find real sourdough anywhere in New Jersey." As she buttered a slice, the knife slipped out of her hand and onto the floor. "Darn it."

"Don't worry. I'll get another one." I looked at John to see if he'd noticed anything, but he was busy eating. I handed Marcia another knife and prayed I was overreacting.

pple blossoms appeared on the little apple tree in the front yard, and the newborn calves in the pasture were staying close to their mothers. It should have made me smile, but this year, spring triggered an emotion I'd never expected: separation anxiety. My six-month maternity leave was almost over.

Phyllis had shown signs of Huntington's in her late twenties. Lora and Marcia were struggling, and my gut feeling was that both were showing symptoms. As my anxiousness over leaving Keith, as well as everything else, mounted, my remedy was to keep him close to me all day long. I did my chores with him on my chest in the baby carrier, and when he napped, I stayed in his room. The only time he left my sight was when he was in his crib for the night, although I'd wake up around one or two each morning and wander into his room. The idea of staying home was constantly on my mind, but I knew that was not an option.

Now that I had a child, my need to be prepared had intensified, and having good health insurance and two incomes was crucial. I'd cherished my time off, but I knew returning to work was the only way I could feel in control again.

On my first day back at work, John and I left Keith with Shana, a young mother with two little boys. She and her husband lived in Penryn, a small town about three miles from Loomis. Handing over my baby to her was probably the hardest thing I'd ever done. I cried all the way to work.

My first week back was exhausting, and I was so glad when Friday night came. When the phone rang on Saturday morning, John answered it, and the next thing I knew, he was running out the door, yelling that he'd call me when he got to Lora's house. The wheels on his truck were screeching as he drove away.

When I finally heard from him, I heard panic in his voice. He'd found Lora passed out on the floor of her living room, drunk, and Dave was nowhere around.

With the help of her former counselor, Lora was admitted to Starting Point again. Dave hesitantly reentered the picture, and over the next week, he and John worked with the counselors and attended Lora's therapy sessions. We were all hopeful that this time, she would become healthy and strong.

❧❧❧

The following Friday evening, I planned to visit my friend on the way home from work, so John picked Keith up from the sitter. As I walked into the hospital, I thought about what I would say to her. I'd never known anyone who'd gone through a rehab program for alcoholism, although of course Lora was still the same sister-in-law whom I loved and cherished. When I got to the Starting Point center, the door was locked and I had to press a buzzer to get in—the place truly was locked down. I jumped when a voice came over the intercom and asked for my name and who I was visiting, and jumped again when the door opened with a grinding-metal sound.

After signing in, I went to a big reception area painted an industrial gray. It had lots of windows, couches, tables, and plants, even a thirty-cup coffeemaker and a plate of cookies, but it still had an institutional feeling. Over the next fifteen minutes, more people arrived, and patients began coming in through a door at the far end of the room. As the volume of noise rose, I couldn't sit still any longer and started pacing.

Finally, a man with an official tag pinned to his shirt entered the room from another door and came over to me. "I'm Scott, Lora's counselor," he said, shaking my hand. "I'm sorry to tell you this, but she won't come out. She's just not ready to see you. Next time, I suggest you call me before you come. Here's my card."

I walked out to my car with anger rumbling inside me. On the drive home, though, a feeling of helplessness overwhelmed me. By the time I reached our house, I was grieving for the friend I felt was lost to me.

Over the next couple of weeks, I settled into work, still missing my baby all day long. Then Scott called one evening and requested a meeting with Dave and John. The night before the appointment, John called Marcia, and I heard bits of the conversation, which ended with John saying, "Her counselor wants to talk to Dave and me tomorrow, and I don't think it'll be good news. I'll let you know what happens."

The next evening, John didn't say much until he'd finished eating the stew I'd made in a crockpot that day. "Lora's counselor feels Starting Point can't give her what she needs to be successful. She's stubborn and defiant and still won't admit she has a drinking problem. She hasn't hit rock bottom, and until she does, he says, she can't move forward." He took another bite of cornbread and wiped his mouth with his napkin. "Anyway, he proposed that she be placed in a women's rehab center in Minnesota for three months. Studies show that removing patients from the environment that's creating the stress can be beneficial."

He went over to his briefcase, took out a brochure from The Wayside House, and slid it across the table.

"Well, it looks nice. If this is where she needs to go to get well, she should go."

A couple evenings later, the doorbell rang, and there stood a tired-looking Dave. John pulled him in and guided him to the kitchen table, where he sat down heavily and then quite dramatically dropped his head into his hands. He had more bad news. His insurance wouldn't pay for a third rehab for Lora, and they couldn't afford it.

John said, "You and Lora have to swallow your pride and ask Dad for the money. He won't make it easy, but she's got to go. I'm afraid of what will happen if she doesn't."

"That's a good idea," Dave said. "Asking your dad for the money might be the answer." He relaxed back into his chair. "You know, Lora and I have never asked him for a thing since we've been married. I'm going to call him first thing tomorrow."

As we got ready for bed, I asked, "Do you think your dad will give them the money? From the stories you've told me, he's pretty stingy."

"I think it's worth a shot. To tell you the truth, I'm more worried about Lucy than my dad. She's never liked my sisters. No matter how hard they tried to have a relationship with her, and they really tried, she treated them like shit. I'm pretty sure she makes the final decision in their house."

Adding a baby to your life brings a whole new meaning to the word *busy*. But now, instead of spending every spare minute on our house, we set aside Sundays for enjoying our little boy together. Since both my boys woke up at the crack of dawn, they had some father-and-son time, and I got to sleep in.

That Sunday, I was leaning against the kitchen counter, watching my husband give his son his undivided attention. The scene tugged at my heart, knowing that John's father had never spent any time like that with him. When the phone rang, John casually leaned against the wall as he answered it. The minute he heard his father's voice, his body language changed and he became stiff as a board. Big John's voice was booming so loudly, John held the phone away from his ear; I was about six feet away, and even I could hear him. "Did you know she asked me for five thousand dollars to go to some place in Minnesota? I'll be damned if I give her any of my hard-earned money."

By this time, I could tell John was about to explode, so I moved over to him and started rubbing his back. Enunciating every word, he said, "Dad, let me be clear. She could die if she doesn't go."

He changed the phone to his other ear and listened for a few minutes.

"Really? Come on! You owe it to her." Then he looked over at Keith and lowered his voice. "Okay, Dad. If you want to see her, you'd better come soon."

After he hung up, John took Keith into his arms. Keith squealed and flapped his arms like a bird, which brought John back into our happy world. But anger soon returned to his face, and he started pacing, bouncing the baby up and down.

"Come on, John. Sit down." I guided him to the couch and sat next to him, giving him a minute to calm down. "Didn't he give Lora the money?"

"Yes, but not really." He hugged Keith as if to shelter him from the harsh words. "He gave her a loan. Lucy wrote up a contract stating they must repay the money in five years and insisted they sign it." He ran his hand through his hair. "Oh, well, at least she has the money, and that's all that really matters."

"Yes, now she can go and get well."

John looked at me and said, "I don't know why I'm so upset. His reaction is nothing new. Not one of us ever asked him for a dime when we were growing up, because if we did, we'd get an earful. Half the time, Marcia and Lora had to spend their own money on groceries, and the worst part is, Dad expected it.

"One time when I was about eight, my shoes had holes in the bottoms, and I had outgrown my pants. Dad responded the same way he always did when we needed basic things. 'How do you expect me to pay for it? I have to pay property taxes, Grandma has to go see a doctor, Napa State Hospital wants money, and my car needs work.' I put cardboard in my shoes and wore them the rest of the school year. It was even harder on my sisters, because clothes were so important to them. I have to say, we all became very resourceful at a young age."

᳿᳚᳚

The day Lora was discharged, Keith and I went to the hospital to say goodbye. John had gone ahead of us to spend more time with her. Since I hadn't seen Lora in a month, I knocked apprehensively and peeked into the room.

John motioned us to come in, and Lora said, "Hi, Therese" but didn't make eye contact with me. Instead, she went over to Keith and tickled him. "How's my little nephew today? Still as cute as ever! Saint Patrick's Day is tomorrow, and John and I were remembering the Saint Paddy's Day parade in San Francisco. Alhambra High School used to participate, and since I was the head majorette, I led the marching band."

Yeah, yeah, I thought; talk about the good old days to distract yourselves from the present and the hot water you're in. John took his son in his arms and added, "I loved going to that parade and watching the floats and clowns and especially the horses. I was seven the first time we went, and it was special, because we did it as a family."

When the reminiscing ended, I asked, "Can I help you with anything, Lora? I can swing by the house if you need something."

"No, no, thanks. Dave is bringing my stuff. I wish I could go home, but there's not enough time. Anyway, don't worry about me. We'll get through this."

She turned and began packing her bag. I waited, staring at her back. Finally, I said, "Bye," grabbed Keith from John, and slammed the door on my way out.

When John found us in the waiting room, Keith was crying, and so was I. "It's okay, Therese. Don't cry."

"She dismissed me," I whimpered. "She didn't even say goodbye. I don't know what to do anymore. All I want to do is be a supportive friend."

"I know," John said.

16

*O*ver the next month, I settled into working full-time again but struggled with not seeing my baby nine hours each day. Keith was growing and changing so quickly, and it weighed on my heart that I wasn't there to witness everything. One evening when I picked him up, Shana told me, "Keith started crawling today." I gritted my teeth and smiled; it wasn't her fault I hadn't been able to see it. Most nights, I cried all the way home, reminding myself that this was the price I had to pay to feel secure.

John sensed my need to be close to my infant. My dear, sweet man quietly did most of the chores, never complaining or making me feel guilty. By April, we had worked into a good routine and my fears had subsided a bit, because Lora was not around and we didn't talk about her, although I thought about her every night.

Returning to work and earning a paycheck again helped me regain my confidence and squash my doubts. And I was sleeping better, probably because I was exhausted. In any event, the demons weren't waking me up, and our son kept me focused on the present. John and I watched Keith in amazement. In only eight months, he'd grown from a helpless nine-pound newborn into a smart, lightning-fast eighteen-pound little guy. He was like a sponge, absorbing everything he saw, heard, and touched. Curiosity was his middle name and crawling was his game. I'd never seen a child move so fast on all fours.

Lora seemed happy enough in Minnesota; at least she sounded upbeat in her letters, which arrived about every two weeks. In one letter, she wrote, "I got a job, a requirement of the program, and walk to it each day. The counselors are great, and the women in the program are, too." Her closing words were always on the order of "Don't worry about me. I'm doing fine."

Every couple of weeks, John met Dave for lunch. John, of course, wanted to know how his sister was really doing, though I doubted Dave would know. John also was curious about the contract Lucy and Big John had made them sign, and one afternoon, Dave brought it with him. I almost wished he hadn't, because John came home in a terrible mood. "I can't believe they're charging them interest! Ten percent, no less. That's ridiculous."

～❧～❧～❧

Lora's return date was fast approaching, and John smiled when he spoke about it. "You know, Lora can be strong and very determined. I think these three months away is just what she needed to get her act together."

But in early June, just a week before she was due to come home, Dave dropped a bomb, telling John at lunch that he didn't want Lora back and that he'd bring her car and clothing to our place on the weekend. I was so angry when I heard this, I called him a bastard and a coward and swore Keith and I wouldn't be there when he arrived. Yes, I threw a temper tantrum, and it felt good to let it all out.

John and I agreed that the least we could do to help Lora in her quest for sobriety, in beginning a new life, was to offer her our home. I still considered her my friend, no matter what she thought. Before John left for the airport, he said, "Hope I see my old sis, not the defiant one who left three months ago."

It felt so good to hug Lora again, and to see her take Keith from my arms and kiss him. Both John and I noticed immediately that she appeared to use her anger as motivation. Even her posture reflected her determination. We kept close tabs on her anyway, without being obvious, just to make sure she stayed focused.

Without Lora, Anna had had to close their catering business, of course. Within a few weeks, Lora had found a full-time sales job with the Ramada Inn in Sacramento. By then, she was attending AA meetings five nights a week and working hard on her six-month sobriety pin. One evening, she asked to use the phone in our bedroom to call Anna and came out teary-eyed. It was brave of her to call her; it had to have been a difficult thing to do.

With all three of us working, the weekdays were full, and most nights, we didn't see Lora until late, after her AA meeting. John could tell that the weekends were tough for his sister, so we always planned some kind of outing. Having a small child changes what you do for fun, but she seemed to enjoy getting out, even if it was to the Sacramento Zoo or for a picnic in the park.

Every night, I silently prayed she would stay strong and healthy. She was working so hard and deserved to be happy. We felt blessed that we could share Keith with Lora, but there were times when sorrow was written all over her face. Dave had been her true love. When I noticed that sadness, I'd ask her to take care of Keith so that, I said, I could get something done.

Because she wasn't making much money at the Ramada Inn, Lora got another job, as a sales rep for the Russ Toy Company (Hasbro). The job came with a company car, which was great, because her car was on its last legs. Eventually, she started spending a lot of time away from the house; we didn't know where, and she was evasive when we asked. John turned thirty-one in early September, and when

Dave showed up at his party unannounced, Lora informed us that she had invited him and didn't think we'd mind. We didn't mind, but we were worried.

And one Saturday morning in early October, Lora made an announcement. "Dave and I are getting back together. We're selling the house, paying off our debts, and renting a place in Roseville to start fresh."

John's jaw tightened. "It's not healthy for you to go back to that environment. Dave hasn't changed, Lora. He'll push your buttons again and trigger your insecurities and doubts."

"No, he won't," Lora insisted. "I've changed; I'm a lot stronger now. Besides, he's my husband, and he loves me."

Two weeks later, she moved out.

❧❧❧

With the busy lives we led, it wasn't hard to shove Huntington's to the back of my mind. At the same time, I consciously had to stop my forward momentum and take time to be thankful for the life John and I had. Hassles at work or the refrigerator giving out or Keith cranky with an ear infection—these were small, petty distractions I didn't let upset me. John was healthy, not showing a sign of HD, and our child had brought a joy to our lives I'd never experienced before. My heart was bursting with the love I felt for my two favorite boys.

That Christmas, Cindy and Brad stayed in Canada, but Marcia flew in for the holidays. She looked a little thinner, and she was wearing shoes without heels, which was uncharacteristic of her. Both she and Lora were barely five-foot-one, and both had always worn really high heels.

On Christmas, Lora, Dave, and Marcia drove to Martinez to visit Big John and Lucy, and the three of us followed in our car. John and I would spend the afternoon with them and then head to Concord and my parents, who tolerated a toddler a bit more. You'd think we were moving out of our house, with the stroller, fold-up crib, suitcases, bags of baby food, and all the gifts crammed in the car. Traveling light was a thing of the past.

After we'd exchanged presents and Keith was running around with fistfuls of torn wrapping paper, John announced, "I wanted you all to know, I'm now the Placer County facilities manager. I get to play boss and get the management benefits." John beamed with pride and at the positive response from his sisters, Dave, and even Lucy, though his dad just had to make a negative comment. We all ignored him as John explained, "I'll be in charge of planning, constructing, managing, and operating Placer County's buildings, properties, infrastructure, and assets. Parks and custodial services will be under me also. I'll manage about fifty employees."

The day after Christmas, Keith came down with a cold, and we decided it was best to head home. We stopped at Big John's house, but Keith was sleeping, so I stayed in the car with him. When John returned to the car, he told me that Marcia had just taken a spill in the backyard; her knee was so swollen, they were thinking of taking her to the emergency room. As we drove off, I added that information to the incidents I'd witnessed: the twitches in her hands and shoulders, loss of balance, all the things she'd dropped or knocked over. Once again, panic began rising in my chest.

When Dave, Lora, and Marcia came to our house on New Year's Eve morning, John helped Marcia hobble into the kitchen. The bagels I'd made that morning were still warm as I put them on the table with cream cheese, jam, and lunchmeats. As Marcia reached for her soda, her hand jerked, and she knocked over the glass.

Later that day, John was leaning against the kitchen counter eating another bagel. "I love these things, Therese." On his last bite, he turned to go out to the garage.

Before he got away, I said, "Did you notice anything different about Marcia since we saw her last year?"

He turned around. "No."

"Well, I sure hope I'm seeing things, because I've noticed little twitches in her body. Didn't you see her hand jerk as she knocked over the glass? And she fell at your dad's house. It's not normal, John."

As I spoke, John had been inching toward the sliding-glass door. "I didn't see any of that." He opened the door and slipped out.

❧❧❧

A few weeks into the new year, a blizzard hammered the New York-New Jersey area with so much snow and ice, we saw pictures on the television news. Big John called a couple of days later, and since we only heard from him when he was pissed off about something, John immediately looked apprehensive. I bent my ear to hear some of their conversation, and when the word *hospital* was repeated several times, my heart rate soared. I watched John scribble a hospital name and phone number on the pad next to the phone.

Marcia had been in a serious car accident that morning and had totaled her car. John dialed the hospital as fast as he could and asked for Marcia's room, but no one picked up the phone. He called again, and someone at the nursing station told him that Marcia was in the radiology department having a CAT scan.

It took an hour for John to track down the doctor who

was treating her. When the doctor placed him on hold for a moment, John whispered, "She has a concussion, and he wants to keep her in the hospital for a couple of days for observation. If the CAT scan comes back normal, she might be discharged on Thursday."

I couldn't help wondering how soon she would be able to fly, because I had a strong sense there was more to the story than we knew.

The alarm clock said one-thirty as I turned over for the tenth time. I grabbed my book off the nightstand, went into Keith's room, sat in the rocking chair, opened the shade, and read my book under the glow of the full moon pouring through the window. The smell of baby powder had its usual effect on me, and I was soothed for a time. About an hour later, I climbed back into bed, and just as I was nodding off, the demons whispered in my ear. "You know the truth, Therese. You can't deny it."

That Saturday, Big John picked Marcia up at San Francisco International Airport. Lucy, of course, wasn't too keen on having Marcia stay with them, so I'm sure she made it uncomfortable for her. Early the next morning, John got a call from his dad, barking out orders—to fly to New Jersey, pack up Marcia's belongings, and ship them to California. Confused, John couldn't take it in until he talked with Marcia, and unfortunately, she confirmed that she wasn't going back to work. When their father came back on the line, John made it clear that since Big John was retired, he was the logical one to go to New Jersey.

But once he hung up, John walked to his drawing table like a zombie. He turned on the light and stared down at his work, but I knew he wasn't seeing a thing. I draped my arms over his shoulders and nestled my cheek into his neck. "Honey? I hate to say this, but you know...there's a real possibility Marcia has Huntington's."

John crossed his arms and glared at me. "Why do you say that, Therese? You don't know."

"Well, hon, I've been suspicious for a couple of years. Even before she moved to New Jersey, I saw twitches in her hands and shoulders. The last time she was here, she fell and hurt herself. And she was wearing flat shoes—Marcia has never worn flat shoes!"

He bolted out of his chair and stomped to the kitchen. "Anybody can fall, Therese. You're wrong! I don't want to talk about it anymore."

I followed him, pleading, "Honey, I'm not saying it to be mean. We have to be prepared. And I need to talk to you about it, because if I don't, I swear I'll go crazy."

He started pacing like a lion in a cage. After a few minutes, he came over to me and placed his hand on mine. "I'm sorry I snapped at you, but this is my worst nightmare. The possibility of another sister having...it," he paused, "well, it's overwhelming. It's just not fair!"

I raised my eyebrows in disbelief. He does suspect Lora has Huntington's, I thought. He just wouldn't say it.

❧❧❧

We were both restless that week, awaiting news about Marcia. John was very quiet. He'd perk up a little when he was with Keith, but eventually, the worried look returned. It seemed to help when he met Lora for dinner one night.

One evening, I gave Keith a bath, lathered him in baby lotion, and dressed him in his soft pajamas. We settled into the rocking chair, and I dropped my head onto his and breathed in his sweet, pure smell as he quickly fell asleep in my arms. As I focused on the rhythmic, rocking motion, my body calmed and my mind cleared. How I wished I could capture this peace, keep it in a bag, and pull from it whenever I needed strength.

When the phone rang, I jumped, just as I had with every phone call that week. Feeling a bit dizzy, I took some deep breaths before joining John in the bedroom. "Was that Marcia?"

"Yes." He folded his arms across his chest. "Dad made an appointment for her with a neurologist at the UC San Francisco Medical Center in two weeks. They'll conduct a battery of tests and collect our family history. We'll have to wait until the tests are complete to know anything."

I wanted to shout, "What the hell is the battery of tests for? What do they suspect, for God's sake? Huntington's?" I couldn't say any of this aloud, so I curled up next to John and let him guide the conversation as he wrapped his arms around me.

"You know, with all that's going on with Marcia, it's made me think about a lot of things. Marcia didn't get the credit she deserved when we were growing up, because Lora was so aggressive and bossy. But she did a lot around the house; she looked after me, and she wasn't mean."

"Yes, it always sounded as if Lora did everything."

John nodded. "You probably didn't know she was a majorette in high school, like Lora. She was a good student and wanted to attend college full-time, but Dad didn't support women going to college. Of the four of us, Marcia was the most industrious and organized. She saved money from her birthday and Christmas to buy material and make her own clothes. She was so proud of her work.

"I wish she'd never left California!" he burst out. "You know, I asked her about the accident. She doesn't remember much, only that when she left the apartment for work that morning, it was snowing and the road was icy. The next thing she knew, she was waking up in ER with a bad headache."

"Well, I guess the truth will be told once she sees the neurologist. I sure hope the doctor examining her knows something about Huntington's disease."

"Dad said the neurology department at UCSF is one of the best in the country. They'll assess her through physical and cognitive exams first. If they can't determine whether she has it or not, they may ask us for blood samples."

It—the tiny word for Huntington's that could bring me to my knees. I wished it were an animate object that I could chop into a million pieces, burn to a crisp, and allow the wind to blow far, far away.

"I'm beat," I said, "and you must be, too. Let's go to bed." We turned out the light, and I lay my head on his chest. "How do you think Marcia is handling all this? I have always had such a hard time reading her. She's like Lora in that way."

"Therese, we weren't allowed to show any feelings or emotions when we were growing up. Dad couldn't tolerate or deal with them. He was the only one permitted to express them, and unfortunately, he did it hatefully. When I think back to all the stomach aches I had as a kid—wow, they were sure proof of my stifled emotions." He caressed my arm. "I guess you have to accept us the way we are."

Our kiss was long, and I held onto him as if I'd never let go. "You know I always will."

About two a.m., I woke up in a cold sweat. Slipping into the bathroom, I splashed water on my face and changed my pajama top, because it was soaking wet. The demons had stolen into my dreams tonight.

Marcia and I were walking on an unfamiliar path in an

eerie, shadowy forest. Crows squawked above us, and we ducked as bats swooped close to our heads. My heart was pounding and my mouth was dry. When we came to a fork in the road, I wasn't sure which way to go. All of a sudden, darkness descended on us. My anxiety grew until I began to panic. I looked at Marcia, who shrugged. "Don't look so worried, Therese. Everything is going to be all right."

Suddenly, we heard a rustling of leaves behind us—someone or something was coming up fast. I grabbed her hand, took the road on the right, and yelled, "Run! Follow me!" I let go of her hand and ran as fast as I could, but after a couple of minutes, I slowed down and looked back to see where Marcia was. My heart jumped into my throat. "Oh, God!" I cried. She had fallen to the ground.

When I ran back to her, twigs were breaking on my right and on my left. I looked in both directions, but the forest was so dense, I couldn't see anything. I yanked Marcia up and screamed, "Come on! We have to move!" Again, I bolted ahead of her, yelling with all my might, "Help, help! Somebody help us!" I heard a loud commotion behind me, and I stopped in my tracks, sweat trickling down my face. When I turned around, my hands went over my mouth as I whispered, "Oh, my God. It got her." I fell to my knees and wept.

17

On March 1, 1986, Big John drove his daughter to the UCSF Medical Center. I'd been worrying about the Marin siblings for eight years, though it felt more like fifty, and many times I'd just wanted to flee. This was one of them. I dreamed of escaping with John and Keith into a world that had no illness, no genetic disease, where we could live happily ever after. But that was a fairy tale. The reality was—and I had no doubt—that Marcia had HD. My fear was almost consuming me, but, of course, it was nothing compared to what Marcia must have been feeling.

The neurologists at the medical center had a rating system, which they used clinically and in research, to evaluate a patient's motor, cognitive, behavioral, and functional abilities on a scale from zero to four, four being the most severe dysfunction. Marcia would be evaluated in fifteen areas, among them gait, tandem walking, rigidity in arms, tongue protrusion, and ocular pursuit.

John called that evening to find out how it went, but she didn't say much, only that the doctors would call with the results in three weeks. He tried to be upbeat, but you could tell it was a hard conversation. Even Big John was at a loss for words. Once again, I wished with all my heart that I could simply stop time, so that no more cells in Marcia and Lora's brains would die and they wouldn't have to experience any more pain or sorrow. And that way, HD could never find my love.

❧❧❧

John and I kept as busy as we could, and Keith certainly helped with that. Filling our home with tantrums, cries, and laughter, he constantly reminded us that life would go on even after Marcia received her diagnosis.

One evening at dinner, John started sharing stories about Marcia and Lora. Whenever he began a story I had already heard, I listened gratefully and laughed all over again. I'd realized long before that whenever the Marin siblings faced a stressful situation, they turned their thoughts to happier times.

"In high school, Lora and Marcia did everything together. They even double-dated, because Marcia went steady with Dave's best friend, Art. They had shared a bedroom their whole life, so they were always whispering secrets to each other and teasing me about not knowing their innermost thoughts."

Nodding and smiling, I listened intently.

He stopped to eat a few more bites of steak and salad. "Marcia was a good student. She worked hard and never complained, and she always brought home awards. Her first job, at sixteen, was at Mode O'Day, a dress shop in Sun Valley Mall." Lost in his thoughts, he continued, "San Francisco fit her personality, and I think she felt it was where she belonged."

I said, "Marcia always looked fabulous, never had a hair out of place. I never told you this, because it's a girl kind of thing, but I always envied both Lora and Marcia, because they had the most beautiful, creamy complexions, and their faces glowed when they smiled."

"Do you remember the trip Marcia and I took to Canada to visit Cindy right before I left for Cal Poly? It was quite a trip." He chuckled.

"I do, but what happened on that trip that's so funny?"

"Before we left, Marcia and I had agreed that, since it was a two-day drive, we'd camp one night. She pulled up at

Dad's house in her '68 Mustang, and when I got in the car, she was wearing high-heeled sandals, a silk blouse, and fancy jeans. I said to her, 'I thought we were roughing it? You look like you're going out on the town.' Of course she ignored me.

"We drove all day and camped in the redwoods up north that night. I set up the tent and made dinner as it got dark. The temperature dropped dramatically, and by the time we were done eating, it was freezing. We climbed into our sleeping bags and read our books by flashlight. The next morning, she made a mad dash into the campground bathroom with her electric-curler set."

I laughed. "That sounds like the Marcia I know."

"The look on Marcia's face when we got to Cindy's place was priceless. It was a rustic log cabin, with no electricity, no running water, a wood stove to cook on. The place was totally Cindy, a simple, uncomplicated, nonmaterialistic lifestyle. But I have to give Marcia credit, because she never complained once."

The morning Marcia was to learn her test results, I raised the shade in our bedroom and the sun poured in, brightening my mood for a moment. Neither John nor I mentioned her as we got ready for work, and by the time I got to my office, my stomach was churning. I had such a hard time getting anything accomplished, I grabbed a cup of coffee and went outside for a break. I leaned against the building and prayed.

That evening, the room seemed to grow cold when Marcia called and I watched John's reaction. My big, strong man crumpled in front of me, slowly wilting and then bending in two like a broken twig. I grabbed the phone and said, "Hi." All of a sudden, Marcia started talking in a flat tone of voice.

"You know, the last few months at work have been hard. Many of my co-workers said I slurred my words and thought I was drunk." She paused for so long, I wasn't sure she was going to continue. After a minute, she blurted out, "I had to stop wearing high heels, because I was losing my balance. My memory was getting so bad, I started writing myself notes. Joyce, my supervisor, called me into her office and asked me what was wrong. I didn't have an answer for her, because I didn't know what was happening."

"I'm so sorry," I said, bowing my head.

Over the next few days, as the news began to sink in, the demons were my constant companions. At work, I had to close my door sometimes and talk myself down from the mountain I wanted to jump off.

John had been so quiet since that evening. I knew he wanted me to just let him be. But I needed to talk to someone, so one night before he got home, I called my mom. I'd tried hard not to cry, because John didn't like tears, but at the moment, I felt it was warranted.

"Oh, God, John is thirty-two years old, and I have a two-year-old child, a full-time job, a mortgage, and a car payment. And now two of the four Marin siblings have Huntington's, I know it!"

❧❧❧

When Cindy heard the news, she came straight to Martinez, snatched Marcia from their dad's house, and headed to ours. When I hugged Marcia, her eyes didn't seem to focus, and her body was making an involuntary dancelike movement, reminding me of what I'd read so long ago: The word *chorea*, from the Greek word for *dance*, was once part of the name of this disease.

When Marcia needed to use the bathroom, John helped her there and closed the door. Cindy told us she thought Marcia was in shock. She was encouraging her to get out of their father's house as soon as possible, because it was such a negative environment. She asked how Lora was doing, and John just shook his head. "I really can't tell you. You know how she is."

When Marcia reappeared, John stressed to his sisters that they could stay with us as long as they liked. Cindy had brought us a bottle of wine, and now I lifted it from the counter and read, "British Columbia Winery Pinot Noir. Sounds good. Do you want a glass of wine, Marcia?"

"No, the doctor said to avoid alcohol, since my balance is already affected. Do you have a diet soda?"

"Yes." I took Keith's hand and we walked into the kitchen, where I retrieved a soda from the refrigerator. "Here, honey," I said, pointing to Marcia. "Go give this to Aunt Marcia."

Keith ran off squealing and stopped when he hit her knees. As he handed her the soda, Cindy said, "Ahh, how sweet is that?"

John opened the can for his sister and sat down next to her. As I watched from the recliner, she seemed to go in and out of a trance. All of a sudden, Keith caught her attention, and she laughed as he crashed his cars on the living room floor. Slowly, life returned to her eyes and her body relaxed a bit. She reached for her soda on the coffee table, but her leg jerked and the can went flying.

"Sorry. I didn't mean to do that."

"Of course not," I said, grabbing the roll of paper towels in the kitchen. While I was cleaning up, I patted her leg. "It's no big deal. John, can you get another can of soda, please?"

At dinner, Cindy shared some news with us. "Brad and I are getting a divorce." I choked and reached for my glass of water, then quickly excused myself to take Keith into his bedroom. He didn't need changing, but I had to get away for a minute and compose myself.

"No more bad news is allowed in our life," I told John after we'd gone to bed. "My sister Ellen is getting a divorce, too, and Lora and Marcia…. Can we run away," I asked, "live on love, and leave all this behind?" He thought I was kidding.

When I woke up, Marcia, Cindy, and John were at the kitchen table. Marcia was giggling, and I was elated to see such a smile on her face.

"What's so funny?"

"Oh, we're talking about Lora and the trouble she caused," Cindy said. "Remember the night the Mercury blew up, and the time she thought a convict was going to kill us all? Lora always exaggerated."

I wondered if John and Cindy were laughing about the past, a common Marin coping mechanism, to defuse their own fears. In addition to Marcia, how could they help being terribly afraid for themselves?

John couldn't stop laughing. "Oh, yeah. She was coming home from Freddie's Pizzeria late one night when the Mercury burst into flames, as Lora put it. Dad should never have bought it, but when you're a teenager, you don't complain when you're given a car, even if it's a piece of shit. Thank goodness, Uncle Jimmy was following her home."

Marcia spilled her coffee, and John just kept talking as I cleaned it up and got her another cup.

"Uncle Jimmy left the car in Lafayette and drove Lora home. The next day, Dad took the truck and hauled what was left of the car back home. He was so pissed, even though it was his own fault."

"And what's the story about the convict trying to kill you?" I asked.

Cindy stirred milk into her coffee and started laughing

again. "Well, it was two in the morning, and Lora was coming home from a date with Dave. A roadblock had been set up on Morello Road, and the sheriff was stopping and checking all the cars before letting them through, because someone had escaped from the Contra Costa County jail.

"When they got home, Lora woke everybody up. Since we had no neighbors and were all alone, she was sure the guy would come to our house and murder us."

"Lora could always be counted on to tell a gruesome story with a lot of detail," John added. "I was only nine and very gullible. We were afraid to stay in the house, so we made Dave drive us over to Uncle Jack and Aunt Faye's house until Dad got home."

On their last night before returning to Martinez, Cindy shared a little bit about Brad and the breakup. "I want a home of my own. Brad says he doesn't want to be tied down with a house. He doesn't want to lose his freedom to travel when school is out, and he won't be able to do that with a mortgage, he says. He doesn't like to do things with our friends anymore, and now he wants to go off and take stupid pictures with his two-thousand-dollar camera without me. I want a partner to share my life with, not just somebody to live with. So he can be alone, because I'm leaving and moving into a gorgeous Victorian house in Vancouver with three good friends. They're like family, and I'll ski, hike in the wilderness, climb mountains, and party with them. They'll help me forget about Brad, and I'll move on with my life."

The only good thing in hearing all this was that the breakup hadn't been because of Huntington's disease. Cindy deserved to live as rich a life as possible, since it could end far too early. If she did have the mutated gene, at least she'd have filled her life with wonderful experiences.

18

*M*arcia heeded Cindy's advice, and once her belongings arrived, she moved into an apartment in Pleasant Hill. It was a nice town in the East Bay, where Marcia had lived before leaving for New Jersey, so I wasn't surprised by her choice. When I spoke to her on the phone, though, I sensed her loneliness. Many of her Pac Bell colleagues had moved to jobs in other cities. It took about two hours to drive to Roseville, where Lora lived, and Loomis wasn't any closer. Much to my disappointment, I learned that Big John hadn't visited at all since he'd moved her in, although he lived only ten miles away. Once again, he let one of his children down when she truly needed his support. Lucy, I felt, never thinking of anyone but herself, added to the disconnect between father and daughter.

But a few of Marcia's high school friends still lived in the area, and she reconnected with them. And Concord, where my parents lived, was just twelve miles or so from Marcia's place. We visited my parents every couple of months, and they always invited Marcia to dinner on those Saturday nights. Even better, they were happy to babysit while we took Marcia to a movie or drove into her favorite city, San Francisco, for a few hours.

We were doubly grateful to my mother when she started spending one day a week with Marcia, going grocery shopping or visiting the mall or doing errands with her.

❧❧❧

We met Lora and Dave just a couple of times each month, but it was easy to see they were back to their old selves.

Dave teased Lora incessantly and made her the butt of his jokes; she always laughed and waited on him like a servant. We both felt Lora was heading down a slippery slope, and we didn't know how to help her. John talked with Marcia on the phone frequently, which seemed to ease some of his anxiety. His phone conversations with Cindy, always longer than those with Marcia, also helped.

I often invited Lora to go shopping with me, but got the same reply each time. "Sorry, I can't go today. I've got work to catch up on."

When Lora invited us to a Father's Day dinner with Big John, Marcia, and Lucy, it irked me that she wanted to please her father when he didn't seem to give a rat's ass about her. I didn't like spending time with either the man or his wife, but I did it for John, because, as he'd told me, sometimes he just wanted to see his only parent. And I was so happy when Lora called. It had been so long since we'd had a good conversation. But she started saying goodbye once she'd told me the time and what to bring. "You know how much Dave loves your fudge pie."

I couldn't help interjecting softly, "I'm not trying to be nosy, Lora, but we're wondering if you're still attending AA meetings? When you lived with us, you said they were really important."

After a long pause, Lora responded sharply, "Yes, I'm going, Therese. See you Sunday."

I wished I could believe her.

When we arrived, Marcia, Lucy, and Big John were already there, sitting on the patio under a wide umbrella. Big John and Lucy barely acknowledged Keith, sitting and smoking their cigarettes while Dave grilled the steaks and Lora served appetizers. When Lora offered the plate to Lucy, she greedily grabbed several and put them on her plate, saying as she did so, "Well, you've been home almost a year, Lora. When are you going to start paying me back?"

Lora started backing away and practically ran to the sliding-glass door, but not before Dave took the opportunity to rag on his wife. "Lora, before you go inside, why don't you smile and show everyone your new capped teeth?" She froze as he laughed and added, "Just as soon as we pay off those beauties, Lucy."

Lora grinned half-heartedly and charged into the kitchen. I passed Keith to John and followed her. "Lora, just ignore her. You know she has no social skills. How can I help?"

She didn't look at me. "Will you take out the plates and silverware, please? Everything is just about ready."

When I stepped back outside, I was sure I looked like a rabid dog, foaming at the mouth and baring my teeth at Dave. I wanted to shout, "That's what happens to bulimic people with years of practice. You're the problem, asshole!" Meanwhile, Dave had the nerve to walk around with a beer in his hand, offering wine and beer to the rest of us.

I could feel the blood pulsing in my carotid artery. "What the hell, Dave? Why in God's name are we drinking alcohol in front of Lora? You know that's not a good idea."

"She's okay with it. Just because she can't drink doesn't mean we can't." I wanted to get up and leave right then, but John gave me a look, so I took some deep breaths and tried to calm down.

Lucy never moved from her chair, so when we finished eating, I started picking up and helping Lora in the kitchen. I was glad when Keith got fussy and we could say our goodbyes. Once we were in the car, I started in. "Same old Dave, sucking the life out of Lora. Geez, Louise, there was alcohol everywhere! He's so hurtful and inconsiderate, and for the life of me, I don't know why she takes it. She was so strong and confident when she came back last year. What happened?"

John moved a hand off the steering wheel and squeezed my thigh. "Therese, Lora is allowing it to happen. She could stop the verbal abuse anytime if she wanted to, but she won't, because she's desperately trying to hold onto Dave. And maybe he believes that after three rehabs, she's fixed now and has the willpower to say no."

In July, Dave and Lora came to our house for the afternoon, because it was going to be a scorcher. We weren't serving any wine or beer, only lemonade and soda. I couldn't help feeling our efforts were in vain, however, since Lora probably had a bottle in the big purse she always carried. It wasn't hard to see that she was drinking again, and heavily. The last time we'd played softball, she had perspired profusely, much more than the weather and exercise warranted. When I mentioned it to John, he sighed. "It's how her body gets rid of the alcohol."

My hope of offering a relaxing day to my friend vanished the minute I saw her. Lora was only thirty-nine years old, but she looked sixty. Her once-creamy complexion was dull, her forehead had deep creases in it, and her eyes drooped. She hadn't looked this bad since her last stint in Roseville Community Hospital.

I quickly asked Lora to keep me company in the kitchen, and she sat at the table as I made the salad. It wasn't long before she told me through tears that she had had another miscarriage. I wondered how much more she could take, physically and mentally, and that's when I had a horrible thought: Her time is running out.

❧❧❧❧

I never forgot that John was now in the high-risk age range and would be for another eight to thirteen years. Over the past few years, I had realized that this uncertainty, which I had taken on willingly, had opened my heart to love much more deeply, and acknowledging that my world could change in a heartbeat made my life with John so much richer. Life was just too precious to waste a minute arguing over any small stuff.

I had learned to overlook shortcomings and compromise without anger. And the Marin siblings had taught me about forgiveness and unconditional love, traits not common in my family. I forgave Dave time and again and never for a moment stopped loving Lora, even when she hurt my feelings.

Letting go of the anger I felt when I couldn't control a situation calmed my OCD to a manageable level, and lessening my anxiety allowed me to relax and find joy in the simple things. Perceiving the future as a blank canvas helped, as did not dwelling on it. Keith remained the best method of staying present, and I drew strength from being physically near John, ever the optimist. Staying focused was key to this constant battle.

John and I had continued making yearly donations to the Huntington's Disease Society of America. Around Thanksgiving, I read in the newsletter that a pre-symptomatic test for HD was not only commercially available now but that testing was being done at more than twenty sites around the country, including the UCSF Medical Center. The test was based on something called the DNA-linkage-analysis technique, or indirect testing: It involved tracing the inheritance of markers linked to the HD gene, rather than the gene itself. That meant collecting DNA samples from at least one affected family member and multiple unaffected family members. The test was considered ninety-five percent accurate at best. As more markers closer to the HD gene were identified, the test became more accurate.

Three years earlier, when we'd learned a test would soon be available, neither John nor his sisters had wanted to learn their gene status. Since then, of course, we'd had Keith, and I wondered if John had changed his mind. This time, when I showed him the newsletter, he wasn't quick to reply, so I waited patiently. Much to my surprise, he agreed to have the test done.

Once he said the words, I was a woman on a mission. My first task was to contact the testing center at UCSF Med Center to request information on how to start the process. I called John's sisters to tell them his decision and ask them to provide blood samples; all three agreed. John's Aunt Betty had died in 1980, and his Uncle Ben was seriously ill. Aunt Evelyn and Aunt Louise, the only two siblings to have escaped HD, were also part of the puzzle. Both agreed to participate and to get a sample of their brother's blood sent to the lab as well.

My plan seemed to be going well until we got a phone call a few days later. Lora was hysterical, Dave told us, thinking that giving blood for John's test would reveal her gene status, too. I tried to reassure her that only John's gene status would be revealed.

Now all I needed was to have John's blood drawn and sent off to the lab. That Saturday morning, John said very little as we ate breakfast and Keith sat in his high chair stuffing Cheerios into his mouth. As I cleaned his hands and face and packed his bag, I kept an eye on my husband.

John remained quiet on our way to the lab. All of a sudden, he pulled over and stopped the truck abruptly, then sat staring out at the hood. Finally, he looked over at me and said, "Therese, I love you and I want to do this for you, but I can't." He leaned forward and rested his head on the steering wheel. "I just can't do this. I have to live my life with hope—hope that I'm free of this terrible disease. If I go through with this and my result is positive.... I'm sorry. I hope you understand."

He was right, and I leaned across Keith, in his car seat between us, and begged his forgiveness. "It was selfish on my part. I got caught up in the excitement of taking the test. I feel awful for causing more stress and pain to your family." Wiping away tears, I promised, "I will never ask you to be tested again."

19

With the help of her father, and I have to give him credit here, Marcia bought a new car, which she drove to Roseville two weekends a month to stay with Dave and Lora in their four-bedroom rental house. With the diagnosis of HD, Marcia was collecting disability benefits. Working was no longer an option, because her gait was so unsteady and she couldn't remember things.

The general population hadn't a clue about this rare disease, and sometimes made cruel assumptions about people suffering from HD—that they were alcoholics or on drugs. It seemed so cruel to see her so alone. We were very glad when, after a year, she decided to move closer to her siblings. John found her an apartment in north Natomas, a new community just outside downtown Sacramento, about forty-five minutes from us. Cindy flew in to help with the move and get Marcia settled. Their cousin Marie, Aunt Jessica and Uncle Edward's daughter, lived just a few miles away. Back in the seventies, Marie had also lived in Walnut Creek; she was part of the group of women who'd gone to the theater in San Francisco on a regular basis. Once Marcia was in her new apartment, Marie included her in activities with her friends, and Marcia began staying with Dave and Lora most weekends.

John and I connected with the three of them as often as we could, but our lives were changing as well. We had decided to have another child, and I was three months pregnant. It was an easier decision for me this time, because we agreed on the importance of Keith's not being an only child. He had no cousins on John's side of the family, and none on my side who lived in California. If John carried the mutated HD gene, both children would be at risk, and having each other for support would be crucial.

John had been the facilities manager for Placer County for two years now, and talk around the county was that he was being groomed to become the board of supervisors' administrative officer. I'd worked at Aratex Services for almost seven years and had recently been promoted. As regional merchandise-control manager, I had to travel to Aratex plants in Fresno and Redding, California, and Medford, Oregon, to coordinate group buys with the merchandise-control manager at each plant to lower the cost of materials. On top of my new, stressful job and worrying about John, I was trying to be a good mother and thoughtful wife. At times, I felt I was on the edge of losing it, and sometimes I did.

One night, as I drove home from the babysitter's, Keith was jabbering nonstop in the back seat, and it was driving me crazy. I'd hit my limit and stomped on the brake, turning around and yelling, "Keith! Mommy needs some quiet time. Stop talking!" His eyes grew big, and tears streamed down his face. As soon as we got home, I ran inside with him, sat on the floor, held him close, and rocked him. All I could manage to say between sobs was "I'm sorry."

❧❧❧

On Saturday, September 6, 1987, John turned thirty-three, and we invited friends and family to celebrate. As usual, I silently rejoiced. I was also feeling fortunate that, as with my first pregnancy, I'd not had any morning sickness, although I felt a lot more tired this time.

John's smile was especially wide and constant, because

Cindy had come for his birthday and for the Marin family picnic, which would be in Martinez the next day. It was a hot Indian-summer day, and in the late afternoon, after most of our guests had left, we went into the backyard with John's sisters and Dave. John walked behind Marcia on the grass and caught her just as she lost her balance. He sat in a lawn chair next to her and braced his chair against hers.

Lora and Cindy were sitting on the pool steps and splashing their feet in the water. "Remember how we used to go to Aunt Jessica and Uncle Edward's ranch and swim in the reservoir?" Lora said. She scooped up some water and threw it on Marcia. "How many rafts do you think we built through the years, Moochie?"

As the water hit Marcia's legs, she laughed and said, "I don't know. All I remember is how they usually fell apart once we drifted out to the deep end. Then we'd swim back to shore and build another one. They were real Tom Sawyer rafts." As she crossed her legs, her chair tilted, but John was there to stabilize it.

"And remember why we needed to cool off in the first place?" Cindy asked. "Huh, huh?" She shook her finger at Lora. "Because somebody made us pick and can fruit all summer long. My God, it was hot, working at the stove for hours on end. I couldn't wait to jump in the water. You were such a tyrant, Lora. You threatened us with bodily injury if we didn't help."

Dave dove into the pool and swam up to the steps. "And I remember you made some money selling fruit for quite a few years," he said, pointing to John. "I'll never forget that old brick fruit stand you built on Highway 4."

"You're right. I sold fruit there every spring and fall from age eight. It was so boring sitting there for so many hours. Grandma felt sorry for me and would come and keep me company. When I was twelve, I got to go to Disneyland with your family using the money I made. Dad told me—I mean, yelled at me, 'If you want to go, you'll have to pay for it yourself!' I didn't have enough money, but your folks took me anyway."

John looked over to check on Marcia. "The stand came down when I was fourteen, because Lora got me a job at the dentist's office, cleaning after hours. By fifteen, I'd saved four hundred dollars. I bought a Suzuki motorcycle and escaped the ranch on my own."

❧❧❧

Witnessing this sinister disease steal things she loved from Marcia's life was heartbreaking. It made me think of the European Jews under the Nazis, stripped of their freedom, every possession and joy taken from them, locked up in concentration camps, isolated from the world, most of them never returning. Huntington's was shrinking her world ever smaller. She couldn't take up a hobby because of her lack of coordination. Reading was a problem. After John found burn holes in her carpet and couch, she even quit smoking.

This woman who had taken such pride in her appearance now had to wear tennis shoes with Velcro straps, since handling buckles and shoelaces was impossible. Her stylish jeans and slacks had been replaced with elastic-waist pants, because she couldn't manipulate buttons or zippers. Her head and body were constantly moving, so sitting in a chair at the beauty parlor for an hour was difficult. Her hair was often unruly and her skin unclean. She didn't even try to put on makeup anymore.

But Marcia lifted my spirits by never complaining. When I took her shopping and offered a suggestion, such as buying a wide-collared shirt that went over her head, she always nodded and let me help her try it on. When I evaluated her apartment, she graciously listened to my ideas for helping her stay safe. We removed all the small rugs, for instance, and John installed a handle in her shower and put a shower chair in the tub. Through all the huge adjustments in her life, I witnessed remarkable strength on her part and drew inspiration from this gentle, brave woman.

That November, as we sat around Dave and Lora's dinner table, Marcia announced, "I'm going to fly with Marie and a few of her travel-agent friends to Hong Kong next month. Marie will have to work some of the time, but I can hang around with her friends. Hong Kong is a cosmopolitan center; it has ultramodern skyscrapers, and the streets are immaculate. We'll take tours and sightsee, and Marie's set us up to take a sunset cruise on a Chinese junk. And boy, am I looking forward to the shopping."

When she returned from her two-week adventure and showed us the photographs someone else must have taken, she wore a big smile. Being the sweetheart she was, she'd brought back silk robes and jade bracelets for Lora, Cindy, and me.

20

Our beautiful baby girl, Vanessa Ann Marin, was born at Roseville Community Hospital on January 25, 1988. Weighing in at nine pounds, she was a keeper, like her brother. Dr. Hamilton told me that when she'd handed our little butterball to my husband and he was coddling her, he started teetering, and the nurses quickly slid a chair up behind him—it happens all the time with new dads, she said. We were deliriously happy and felt our family was complete.

At times, I felt guilty about my bliss—our two wonderful children and the love John and I shared—while Lora was unable to have kids, struggling against alcohol and bulimia, and probably had HD, and Marcia was desperately trying to hold onto her independence.

By 1988, John had worked for Placer County for nine years and was starting a new job: He had been appointed administrative officer to the county board of supervisors, a top management position with a hefty bump in salary. Serving at the will of the elected board, he would be chief of staff, formulating consistent policy positions, reviewing development proposals, and interacting with community groups and constituents. Now his office was in the Placer County Administrative Center. A geodesic structure nicknamed "the Domes," it had been designed by R. Buckminster Fuller, a renowned inventor, engineer, mathematician, and visionary considered one of the great thinkers of his time.

Shortly after Vanessa's birth, John and I began discussing whether I could take a couple of years off. The travel my job required would be even more stressful on our family life. I dreaded leaving my infant with someone else, having missed out on so much with Keith. After carefully evaluating our finances, we decided we could swing it for a few years. My boss at Aratex had been good to me, and he'd just given me another long maternity leave. I felt bad about quitting, so I immediately set up a meeting with him and resigned.

My energy returned quickly after Vanessa's birth, and once that meeting was over, I began to relax and enjoy being with my children. Like Keith, Vanessa was a happy baby. Having the whole day with them was heaven; I could even sneak in a nap when they slept. It took about six weeks for Keith to take an interest in his sister. How I hoped they would develop a close, lifelong bond like John had with his sisters.

With all my attention on my children, my demons raised their ugly heads only when I was with Lora or Marcia; as soon as I was home with the kids and John, they retreated. But much to my dismay, three months after I'd resigned from my job, the old anxiety crept into my brain and never left. John was making good money, and we had a substantial amount saved, but the threat of HD continually lurked, and I was unable to manage my fears.

I became obsessed with how little life insurance we had on John. As a county manager, he was covered for fifty thousand dollars under a Placer County group life-insurance policy, but without my bringing in a paycheck, that wouldn't last more than a couple of years. I applied for additional coverage under the group plan, but it was denied. Six independent insurance companies also denied John coverage. Deciding whether or not to provide life insurance to someone whose mother had died of Huntington's disease, it appeared, was a quick and easy "No."

I almost laughed when I told John what one insurance agent had said to me. "Mrs. Marin, just have your husband tested. If he's negative, we'll be glad to write a life-insurance policy on him." I threw my hands in the air and said, "Can you believe that? He thinks it's so simple. I wouldn't be applying if we knew!" For weeks, John heard me rant and rave about genetic discrimination. Coincidentally, the next newsletter from the Huntington's Disease Society had an article on that topic, noting that its legal department was beginning to focus on this new kind of discrimination faced by HD families.

Finally, I applied for mortgage-disability insurance, which gave me some peace of mind. If John became disabled, the policy would take care of our monthly mortgage payment until he returned to work. Of course, if he were disabled because of Huntington's, that would never happen. When John asked what he could do to calm my fears, I told him, "Never age."

He hugged me and said, "Therese, try to live in the day and enjoy our children. All will be fine."

I thought I knew this man inside and out, yet sometimes I could not understand how he could remain so optimistic and calm. After all, he was the one at risk.

Over the next month, I searched for possible solutions to help me feel more protected. Then an idea hit. Since I'd be out of the workforce for a few years, continuing to build my resume was important. The best way to do that, I thought, was to add to my education. With John's support, I began researching master's-degree programs that would be a good fit.

Like my mother, I had an empathetic heart, was sensitive to others' feelings and needs (sometimes to my detriment, because I wasn't a tough boss). My aspiration now was to help people who were in need of healthcare services to stay independent. The fact that two of my sisters-in-law would probably need such services at some point greatly influenced me. Since I had a degree in business administration and had worked on a managerial level, the master's program in healthcare administration through California State University, Long Beach, was just what I was looking for. Better yet, I could take classes on the CSU campus in Sacramento, my alma mater.

That summer, I applied to the university and was accepted into the program. When I got the letter, I took Keith's hands and whirled him around the family room, both of us giggling, while Vanessa kicked her feet and hands in her swing. I was almost giddy with excitement. It looked as if I could complete the coursework in two years, after which came a required six-month internship. If all went well, I could graduate in 1991 and, with firsthand knowledge of the business side of the healthcare system, find a job at one of the three hospitals in the Sacramento area.

Anybody watching me that day would have thought I'd won a million dollars. What I'd gained was so much more: a weapon to annihilate my fears and shore up my defenses.

In early September, we celebrated John's thirty-fourth birthday. The next day, after Keith and I picked apples off our little tree and made a pie for dessert that evening, the kids and I made a trip to the college bookstore. Being on campus again invigorated me and fueled my confidence. Keith pushed Vanessa in her stroller while I strolled down memory lane. I showed Keith Jenkins Hall, my dorm building, and told him, "This is where Mommy lived when she went to college."

The bookstore looked about the same, and it was easy to find a copy of *The Law of Hospital and Health Care Administration*, the eight-hundred-page textbook for my first class. I had to remind myself that business law had been one of my favorite undergraduate courses. When I saw the price—almost eighty dollars—I told myself it was an investment in my future.

A few nights later, the three-hour-a-week class began, and I was thrilled to be back in the classroom. It was refreshing to interact with adults after being with children all day. Now my days focused on two things: my children and completing my homework while they napped or played. I found joy in studying again, in learning new things and working toward an important goal.

❧❧❧

On the first Saturday in October, I jumped out of bed to find Vanessa already in her playpen with a bottle and Keith in front of the TV with a bowl of Cheerios and fruit. John came up behind me and said, "Shhh. They're both occupied for the moment." I giggled as he picked me up and carried me into the bedroom. We fell on the bed, passionately kissing as I wrapped myself around him. "I'm sorry it has to be a quickie," he said, "but you know they don't have a very long attention span."

Afterward, he asked casually, "So what do you want for your birthday, Therese? It's coming soon."

A few days after that, John presented me with a gift-wrapped little box tied with a bow. It held a membership card to the Courthouse Athletic Club, a gym in Auburn that John had belonged to for years. I shrieked. "Oh, yeah! Thank you, thank you! This is exactly what I wanted." I raised my arms like Sylvester Stallone as Rocky and danced around the kitchen.

The following Saturday, John had another surprise for me.

"I asked Dave and Lora to watch Vanessa for a couple of hours while we go to the gym together. They've offered to watch the kids so many times, I decided to take them up on it. Keith can come with us and play with the other kids in the childcare area."

I hadn't been in workout clothes in a long time and felt kind of frumpy, like you do after having a baby or two, while John looked lean and mean. But we were doing something we'd never done together. We dropped Vanessa off with all her stuff and happily went on our way. Three hours later, when we knocked on the door, no one answered, and I heard Vanessa crying. John opened the door and yelled, "Hello! Lora? Dave? Where are you?"

I ran into the kitchen to find a distraught Vanessa in her stroller. I picked her up and said angrily, "Where are they? I can't believe they left her alone like this!"

Keith looked up at his dad and asked, "Where's Uncle Dave and Aunt Lora, Daddy?"

Just then, Dave ran through the front door, breathless. "I've only been gone a few minutes. Is she okay?"

John said, "Yes, she's fine. What's going on? Where's Lora?"

Dave said, panting, "We had a big fight, and she ran out of the house and drove away. I cut through the bushes to try and catch her on Cirby Way, but she ignored me and sped off. She shouldn't be driving."

When it came to my children, I was like a mother bear with her cubs. I grabbed the diaper bag and glared at Dave as I stomped past him. "That's it. I should have known you two are not responsible enough to take care of our daughter."

Marcia stopped by our house a week later, before going to Lora and Dave's for the weekend. Mom was there, to help with the kids while I went to the library and John got some chores done around the house. As I drove off, she was sitting in the front yard with Vanessa on her lap as Keith kicked a soccer ball around. Marcia had pulled up a chair next to her.

Mom was in the kitchen when I got home, getting ready to serve one of her chicken-broccoli casseroles, homemade applesauce, and garlic bread. While she was occupied, John told me quietly that Marcia had confided her fears about Dave and Lora's relationship. She felt a lot of tension when she was there, she'd said. They had huge bills from her two stints in Starting Point, and she thought Lora's depression had worsened and that she was drinking again.

By then, Lora had been working for the Russ Toy Company for more than two years (and Vanessa and Keith had been the recipients of many samples: Transformers, My Little Ponies, Sesame Street dolls). She was often on the road in her company car, and I never stopped worrying about her driving. If she didn't kill herself, she might kill others.

A couple of weeks passed without incident. One night, John said, "I talked with Dave, and he won't say whether or not Lora's drinking again. But all the symptoms are there. He has his head in the sand, as far as I'm concerned."

"This is so frustrating!" I cried. "I feel like we're waiting for a time bomb to go off, with no way to stop it."

21

*B*efore I knew it, the first semester of my master's program was winding down and I'd soon be taking final exams. Keith, now four, and I decorated the Christmas tree as eleven-month-old Vanessa watched us hang the ornaments. When we were done, I put a wooden gate around the tree, and the two of them stood outside it like statues, captivated by the twinkling lights and all the presents wrapped in Mickey Mouse Christmas paper and shiny bows. Watching them brought back Christmases of my own childhood, good memories with my sisters and parents, celebrating with our aunts, uncles, and cousins when we lived in Kansas. And John was so happy, since Cindy would be coming for the holidays and the four siblings would be together again.

A few days before Christmas, Dave called, and there went my festive mood. His news didn't really surprise me. "I'm leaving Lora for good and filing for divorce. I can't live with her any longer."

Since John had had so many unsuccessful conversations with him, we decided I should go try to reason with him. Even though I was angry with Dave at times, I always forgave him, and I certainly wanted to help. He didn't know or care where Lora was, he said. "I cannot live with an alcoholic anymore. For God's sake, my parents were alcoholics."

On the way home, I wondered how either of them could be sane after the roller-coaster they'd been living on for the past four years.

Once the holiday decorations were packed away, I started looking forward to my next semester. Because I was in a small program, some classes were offered just once a year. In addition to taking Decision Making and Control for Health Administration, I'd had to sign up for Financial Management for Healthcare Providers, since it wouldn't be offered again until the following year. If I didn't take the class now, it would push my graduation date back, and I wanted and needed to return to work as soon as I could.

Both classes required a lot of work, so I studied and did homework whenever I could: in the morning before the kids woke up, when they napped, after they went to bed. On nice days, we went to a park in Rocklin, about ten minutes away, where Keith could burn off energy for a couple of hours. Even though Vanessa was walking by now, she was happy in a swing so long as it was moving; with one hand, I kept her swinging, and with the other, I held my book. On the nights John didn't have a meeting to attend, I had dinner on the table when he got home and retreated to the bedroom to study after we ate.

Being so busy kept me from worrying about Lora and Marcia, although I still fed myself a spoonful or two of guilt. Ever since Keith had been born, Lora's addiction had consumed her life and bled into ours. We had done everything we could to support and help her, but now it was up to her. That's what I kept telling myself anyway.

Dave moved out in mid-January. He'd paid the rent through February, so Lora had time to find a smaller place and pack; in March, we moved her into a one-bedroom apartment in Roseville. She avoided any discussion about her situation that day, so we made small talk, and the children couldn't even make her smile. Whenever we took a break—and with the kids, there were many—she slipped away. It was obvious each time that she'd been drinking.

When we left, John hugged her and said forcefully, "If you need anything at all, call us, anytime."

Lora jutted out her chin and said with a forced smile, "I'll be fine. This is just temporary; with time, Dave and I will work it out. Don't worry."

My first instinct was to shake her and yell at the top of my lungs, "What's wrong with you? You need to get your act together, because this time, he is not coming back!"

After that, John and Marcia devised a plan to keep close tabs on her. John would call her on Mondays; I called on Wednesdays; Marcia called on Friday nights; Cindy called on the weekends. Every week, we tried to coax her to our house for dinner, but she usually had some lame excuse or backed out the night before. On weekends, I arranged for a sitter on Saturday or Sunday, whichever day Lora agreed to, and we'd take her to a movie or out to dinner; then John and Marcia would compare notes. Because I had so much schoolwork, I stayed home to study sometimes while the babysitter watched the kids.

One May evening, I came home elated to be done with my last final. John informed me that a couple of human-resources people from Russ Toys had shown up at Lora's apartment, taken her company car and computer, and fired her. I stared at him in disbelief. "How much more can she take? If this isn't rock bottom, I don't know what is!"

He nodded, looking pained. "I don't know what's going to happen to her next."

Loving, supportive sister that she was, Marcia loaned her car to Lora while she looked for work. I was secretly relieved, because Marcia's reactions had become so slow, I felt she shouldn't drive anymore. The last time she'd come to our house, our neighbor had been driving behind her. He told us later, "She was weaving all over the road. I thought she was going to go right off into the irrigation ditch." Yet telling Marcia she could no longer drive was too hard to think about then.

Lora landed another job, and all was quiet for a while. Her old car had been sitting in our garage for the past year; when John got it running, Marcia got her car back. That summer, I had to take an additional class again. It wasn't easy to concentrate on the particulars of Marketing in the Healthcare Industry.

22

*M*onday, July 7 was a scorcher. The air-conditioning wall unit was on high, but it didn't help all that much. I lathered the kids with sunscreen, put hats on their heads, found the wading pool in the garage, and had Keith drag it into the front yard and turn on the hose. I moved my chair close to the fence, where there was a little shade, and read while the kids played in the water.

I had awakened that morning with a headache, unusual for me. When the phone rang, a sharp pain shot across my temple as I ran inside and grabbed it, watching the kids through the window. It was Marcia and she sounded upset, something rare for this Marin sibling. She hadn't been able to reach Lora for two days.

I ran outside and brought Vanessa in, telling Keith to stay in the pool. My hands shook as I called their father. "Hi, honey. Sorry to bother you at work. Marcia just called, and she hasn't talked to Lora for two days, and we're worried. If she hasn't heard from her by the time you get home, I think we'd better go to her apartment."

After dinner, we packed up the kids, drove to Roseville, and knocked on Lora's door; then we went to the manager and inquired if she'd seen Lora in the past few days. When we asked to see the apartment, she reluctantly let us in, but there was no sign of Lora. We started calling her friends and coworkers, with no success.

That was the first of many sleepless nights. John was up more than he was in bed. He talked to Marcia twice a day. He even broke down and called Dave to see if he knew anything. The kids and I went to her apartment on both of the next two days; the manager got pretty tired of my asking if she'd seen my sister-in-law. The three of us tried to stay positive, but it was hard. I kept mentally revisiting the last time we'd seen Lora, trying to recall any clue that might help. On Thursday evening, I was glad to go to class and think about something else. In bed that night, of course, my mind drifted back to her. It seemed as if she'd been missing a lifetime.

Finally, on Friday morning, Marcia phoned to say she'd heard from Lora, and she was leaving to pick her up at a rehab facility in Modesto at noon. She sounded rushed; it was already ten-thirty, and she had an eighty- or ninety-mile drive ahead of her—which would take hours, the way she drove these days. I quickly called John and shared the news. It felt as if a ton of bricks had been lifted off my shoulders. But I wondered about the details of Lora's disappearance, and whether she'd tell us the truth.

When John got home, he had a smile on his face, the first one I'd seen in days. When the phone rang, we both lunged for it, knowing it was Marcia. John listened intently and then said, "But Modesto? How did she get there?" I paced in a circle, trying to pick up pieces of the conversation.

John hung up with a stunned look on his face. Rubbing the back of his neck, he told me, "Last Saturday, when she was walking home from the liquor store—you know, the one down the block from her place—the police stopped and arrested her. They kept her in jail for twenty-four hours and then transferred her to a facility in Modesto; it's called New Hope Recovery. I don't know why she had to go so far away, but Marcia spoke with the woman who discharged her today, and she said when a person is arrested for being drunk in public, that's where the court sends them for five days, to dry out."

My heart hurt when I heard these words, and I was too

shocked to speak. I wanted desperately to believe in the name of the facility. Instead, I suddenly realized, as clearly as if she'd whispered it in my ear, Lora is going to die, she wants to die, and nothing can stop her. But couldn't she see it was killing her brother and sisters and me?

❧❧❧

The next evening, I scheduled a babysitter so that John and I could visit Lora without distractions. We knocked on her door, waited, knocked again. Her car was in the parking lot, so we knew she was home. After a couple more minutes, John shouted, "We know you're in there, Lora! We're not leaving until you open the door!" Her neighbor on the right opened his door and said, "I'm going to call the cops if you keep on with that yelling and pounding."

Probably because she didn't want to face the police again, Lora opened the door an inch and peeked through the crack. That was wide enough to see that the whites of her eyes were as yellow as the sun; her face was swollen, and her eyes were ringed with heavy, dark circles.

She hesitated, and then the door opened slowly. She had turned around to hide her face, but she couldn't hide her body. I'd never seen anything like it. Her ankles were three times normal size; they reminded me of elephants' legs.

As soon as we got in, John began firing off questions. "Why didn't you let us know where you were? We were so worried about you! It was like you'd dropped off the planet, Lora."

She said, "I'm sure Marcia gave you all the details. I really don't want to talk about it." Then she said the words I'd come to despise. "I'm okay. Don't worry about me."

When I took a step toward her, she backed away. I felt

like we were dancing around an elephant in the room, literally. "But Lora, why didn't you call and tell us where you were? We were so worried about you. I was afraid you were dead."

When she continued to offer no response or explanation, John got out a pen and wrote BROTHER in bold letters on his business card, then put it on the refrigerator door with a magnet. When we left, he slammed the door so hard, the building shook.

Remarkably, her new employer, Larsen's Paper Company, didn't fire her, probably because she'd made up a good story; Lora had become very good at that. Driving was still my biggest worry with her, and I hoped and prayed she was smart enough not to drive when she was really drunk. She had to make a living, and coming to stay with us was out of the question. I couldn't have someone I didn't trust in the house. That thought certainly fed my guilt—what was I saying? That this woman I cherished was such a wreck, I didn't want her around my kids?

John and I talked with Lora a couple times a week. Marcia talked with her every day, and she allowed Marcia to see her most weekends. She still wouldn't come visit us, not even with Marcia. I couldn't shake the feeling we were waiting for the other shoe to drop.

❧❧❧

I was looking forward to the fall semester until I found out that the only class I could take was Human Resources in the Healthcare Industry, at a Kaiser Permanente in Sacramento. Dr. Denise Carpenter had been its director of human resources for eighteen years, and the night class would be held in her office. My youngest sister, Jennifer, had studied human resources in college and was now working in HR at Raley's corporate office, in Sacramento. It sounded dull as dry toast to me.

Four days after John's thirty-fifth birthday, the phone rang about nine p.m. My heart skipped a beat, as it had been doing whenever the phone rang. It was someone from Mercy Hospital in Sacramento, asking in a cool, unemotional voice for John Marin, the brother of Lora Marin. John was just coming out of the bathroom, and my face must have been white as I handed him the phone. "It's Mercy Hospital, asking for Lora's brother."

He took the receiver, and it was a terrible thing to watch this strong, loving man wilt like a flower. In a strange monotone, he said, "Thank you. Goodbye."

I hadn't realized that while John was on the phone, I'd been slowly backing away from him. Now he was walking toward me like a robot, and I became even more frightened. My hands went over my ears to shut out the words he was going to say. As my back hit the wall, his arms went around me like a shield. "Lora fell and hit her head. She has a cerebral hemorrhage, and she's in a coma. She doesn't have much time left."

My legs lost all strength, and John held me tight. I felt as if I were in a dream, a very bad dream, heading for a dark place. He shook me gently. "I've got to call the family, Therese. Are you all right?"

I shook my head to banish the demons. "Yes, yes, I'll be okay." I felt so shaky when John released me, I didn't move.

He telephoned his father, Marcia, and Dave, telling them to get to Mercy Hospital as fast as they could. He grabbed his coat and ran out, saying he would call me when he knew more. Once I heard the car start, I slid down the wall, curled into a ball, and wept. This generous, beautiful woman I'd loved for so long was slipping away, and no one could do a thing about it. Her life had been too much to endure alone; and despite the love of her siblings, she had been alone in an essential way for most of her life, abandoned by the two men who were supposed to nurture and take care of her.

Time stood still while I waited for John's call. I thought of my husband and how strong he was, how much I wished I could be stronger for him. The phone rang around midnight, and I grabbed it, holding my breath.

"She's gone."

My hand covered my mouth, pressing hard to suppress the scream that was growing inside me. The scream came out in a long whimper and the phone slid out of my hand, somehow finding its way back to the cradle. Sinking to the floor, I let the endless tears begin to flow.

Loralee died at 11:49 p.m. on September 10, 1989. She was forty-one years old.

Around one a.m., I fell asleep on the couch and dreamed that Lora was outside, in the field across from the house. I yelled and waved to her and ran in her direction, but I couldn't reach her. No matter how fast I ran, she slipped further and further away.

John arrived home around three and woke me. I wrapped my arms around him, my only weapons against his grief. It was too distressing to look into his sorrow-filled eyes, so I buried my face in his chest. I wondered if he ever got tired of being so strong. Like the wonderful man he is, he tried to comfort me. "Therese, she was only meant to be on this earth for forty-one years. I know now this life was too hard for her. She didn't have the strength to keep going."

His body sagged from its heavy burden of heartache as he walked into the bedroom. I followed in a kind of trance, watching him lie down and instantly fall into a deep sleep.

I stood at the foot of the bed staring at him, grateful that he could always find an escape from pain or fear in that way.

How I wished such sleep could find me as well, but my eyes felt as if toothpicks were holding them open. I started pacing around the house, wandering from room to room. I took comfort from my children, stroking their cheeks and kissing them, thanking God for all I had, though sorrow was choking off my breath.

I continued pacing until six-thirty, when I couldn't wait any longer to call my parents. When my father, who was always up early, answered, I squeaked out a few words. Then Mom got on the line, and I heard her gasp and say, "Oh, no." After that, she let me talk and talk, which I did until the kids woke up.

The children made me smile as I dressed and fed them. Keith helped me carry his matchbox cars and trucks into the front room; Vanessa followed, and they started playing. As I walked past Keith to the kitchen, he grabbed my hand. "What's wrong, Mommy?"

Kneeling beside him, I kissed his angelic face and wondered how we were going to tell him his wonderful Aunt Lora was dead. "Oh, Mommy's a little sad today."

A few minutes later, John walked out of the bedroom, dressed in his business clothes. In the kitchen, he took my hand and said, "Let's sit down for a minute." I searched his eyes. "I know this is painful, Therese, but I have to tell you what happened last night. It was amazing."

"Amazing? How could anything amazing be part of this tragedy?"

"I know, but what we witnessed was incredible. I've never seen anything like it. Once Marcia, Dave, and Dad got there and we were all standing around the bed, the lines on Lora's face disappeared. Her skin was glowing, and she looked young again. She transformed right before our eyes—all of us noticed how she changed in a matter of minutes."

He shook his head, as if he still couldn't comprehend what he'd seen.

"She died right after that. I think she was waiting for us to get there." He sat back in his chair. "Maybe this was her last gift to us: letting us see her at peace."

23

*O*ver the next few days, Dave reentered the Marin world, playing the bereaved husband and making the funeral arrangements with the help of Big John. Except for John, Marcia, Cindy, and me, the family didn't know the two had separated, let alone that Dave was filing for divorce. Naturally, Dave didn't reveal to anyone that he had washed his hands of Lora. Nor did anyone else—the Marin siblings excelled at keeping such secrets. No doubt all agreed with John, who said, "It's not worth talking about. It won't help Lora."

And then there was me, an anomaly in the world of the Marin family. My emotions, which the Marins detested, were flying out of control. When Dave left Lora, I had hoped never to see him again, and I was so angry with him for playing this game, I was unable to hide it.

When Cindy flew in from Canada, the kids and I picked her up at the airport. The funeral would be that Sunday, and we planned to leave for Martinez on Saturday and stay over. That morning, we drove to Marcia's apartment to get Cindy and Marcia, then settled in for the two-hour drive. Keith sat next to his Aunt Cindy and chatted up a storm as Marcia and I stared blankly out our windows. I thought I might explode if I didn't tell the siblings how I felt, so before we reached their father's house, I turned to face the back seat.

"I will never forgive Dave for watching Lora kill herself while he took no responsibility for her downhill spiral." No one spoke, and I think it was the first time I was glad they didn't say anything.

When we got there, Big John threw the door open, his eyes bulging and his face bright red. Vanessa immediately backed away and hid behind my legs. "Why did you let your sister die?" he shouted at John. "What the hell happened?"

I picked Vanessa up and gently pushed her head into my shoulder, so that she didn't have to see this angry man. As Big John and his remaining children moved into the living room, I heard Lucy say, "John, it's not his fault Lora died. Leave him alone. What's wrong with you?"

Later that day, Cindy went to Connolly & Taylor, the funeral home in Martinez, to check on things. "I couldn't believe it when I saw her," she told us. "They had slicked her hair back from her face, and her makeup was awful. I teased her hair and put pink blush and lipstick on her. Now she looks like Lora."

To me, it was as if she were saying, "Let's make Lora up so she doesn't look dead." This was such a bad joke that I started laughing, while everyone stared at me.

That evening, relatives and friends came to the viewing at the funeral home, and I was repulsed, everyone gawking at the body. Even Lucy came, but she proceeded to make a scene by fainting. This forced Big John to choose yet again between his wife and Lora, and his wife won, as usual. Heaven forbid she might allow her husband a little time with his dead daughter. Lora had waited her entire life to get some response from him: love, affection, support—something. But it never came, and there would be no more second chances.

The kids were restless, so I took them into the lobby and waited for it to be over. After a while, though, John came out with Cindy and asked me to walk with him to the casket. Cindy held Vanessa and took Keith's hand. As I walked back inside, it was as if I were moving through slowly drying concrete. I'm sure John had a sense of the words screaming in my head. Please, don't make me look at my dear, sweet Lora. Let's just run far away from this place with our children.

Once we were at the casket, my eyes were drawn to her face, but I quickly turned away. I banished the image from my mind and replaced it with one of the kind, generous, glowing Lora I loved. That is the picture tattooed on my heart.

The funeral service, the next afternoon, was at Oakmont Memorial Park & Mortuary in Lafayette, about twenty-five minutes from Martinez. Randy and Kelly, neighbors who had known John since he was fourteen, offered to watch our children. Lucy didn't go to the service, thank goodness, claiming she was too upset. At the chapel, the five of us sat in the front pew as people arrived and a low mumbling filled the room. Many of our friends had known and loved Lora, and it warmed my heart to see they'd driven all this way to say goodbye. Finally, a clergyman stood at the podium and the room became quiet. I watched his mouth move, but his words didn't register. Whatever he said was a bunch of crap anyway. He hadn't known Lora.

A soft rain began to fall as we stood at the gravesite. John's eyes were glistening as he took my hand. "This is perfect. Lora loved the rain." Her casket would rest atop her mother's. Tears streamed down my cheeks, and I was helpless to stop them.

Back at Big John's house, John's aunts, uncles, and cousins kept saying, "What happened? I can't believe it. It was so sudden!" All I could muster when they asked me was "She fell and hit her head. She fell and hit her head." They would wait for me to continue, but I couldn't. Even if I could have, where would I start?

Aunt Christina approached John and cried on his shoulder. "Only last month at the family picnic, she looked and acted fine. Oh, John, I'm going to miss Lora so much."

After an hour of this, I felt like running out the door. And watching Dave circle the room, receiving undeserved sympathy from everyone, filled me with rage—good thing he never spoke to me or even made eye contact. I didn't want my anger spilling onto the others, so I took my children into the bedroom where their toys were, opened a window, and breathed deep. My wish for my husband, Marcia, and Cindy was to find comfort in knowing how all these people had loved their sister, that she would be remembered. I had no doubt Lora would live in the hearts and minds of her family forever.

❧☙❧☙

A week after the funeral, our minds began to unfreeze, and we started wondering how Lora had been injured and how she got to Mercy Hospital. When John said he was going to ask Dave, I had to laugh.

After many phone calls to the hospital, John tracked down the doctor who had cared for her in the intensive-care unit, and he filled in a few pieces of the puzzle. Lora had come in by ambulance, unconscious, with a large hematoma on the side of her head. We hadn't known that she'd been on Coumadin, a blood-thinning medication, because cirrhosis of the liver was causing her kidneys to shut down. Whatever had happened to her had resulted in head trauma that caused bleeding in her brain.

The next evening, we received an unexpected phone call from another person who asked for John Marin, brother of Lora. I almost dropped the phone when he said those names in his cigarette-raspy voice. His name was Joe, and he had been Lora's AA sponsor for the past few years. She had been with him on the day she collapsed.

Joe told us that when he and Lora had met for coffee that day, she didn't look well, and he asked if something had happened. She said she'd locked herself out of her apartment the day before. She knew she could get in through the sliding-glass door, which she left slightly open so the dogs could run in and out, but the gate to her little yard was also locked. She'd climbed over the fence, fallen, and hit her head. It had been pounding ever since, she told him, and she felt nauseous and dizzy. Then her eyes rolled back in her head and she passed out.

Joe called 911 and followed the ambulance to the hospital. John had been Lora's emergency contact, but as her sponsor, Joe felt confidentiality kept him from telling anyone but the doctors what had happened, so he'd given John's number to someone at the hospital. Then he'd read her obituary in the *Sacramento Bee*.

John walked to the window in the family room and stared out as he told me Joe's story. Afterward, he was silent for a long time. Then he said, "I'm so glad he called. Now we know what happened to her."

"Oh, I am, too." I bowed my head and thanked the Lord this man had been with her. Otherwise, Lora might have died alone.

A couple of weeks passed, and we never heard from Dave. John thought it was just too painful for him to see us, but I believed otherwise. John didn't say it, but on some level, I think he missed him. They just had too much history to be ignored.

I realized that Dave wasn't to blame for Huntington's or for Lora's inability to bear a child, but he was responsible for using her to feed his macho ego. And I resented him for not standing by Lora, as I had made the decision to stand by John, no matter what. Forgiving him this time was not going to be easy.

Each time John mentioned his name, I tried to stay calm and made no comment. At dinner one night, though, I had to put my fork down and ask, "Why couldn't Dave stay with Lora and help her? Didn't he care at all about her anymore?"

"Dave was already married to Lora when we found out about the disease in our family," John reminded me. "Maybe he wanted out then, but felt stuck. And Lora knew how he was before she married him." He shook his head. "I don't blame him. It wasn't all his fault."

Keith's fifth birthday was three weeks after Lora's funeral. Life goes on even when death has stomped on your heart, so we invited five neighborhood boys over. We bought cake and ice cream and organized a few games—Pin the Tail on the Donkey, a beanbag toss—a difficult task with six high-energy boys. Vanessa's head was spinning as she watched them run around the house and wrestle on the floor. When Big John and Lucy arrived with a big box, Keith tore it open, and soon John was putting a tricycle together. Marcia and my sisters and parents were there, too, and I felt thankful for the crowd.

We celebrated Vanessa's second birthday a few months later, in January 1990. Big John had called to say that he and Lucy wouldn't be coming, which wasn't a surprise. Lucy's health had been declining, and they rarely left the house anymore except for doctors' appointments. But once the festivities began, I felt someone was missing and kept turning to the front door. As I watched Marcia play with my daughter, a pain shot through my heart, knowing she would never know her lovely Aunt Lora.

By this time, I was halfway through my master's program, and the two classes I was taking this semester, Organizational Development for Healthcare and Healthcare Ethics, required a lot of research. Since Lora's death, Marcia had driven to our house every Saturday, which worked out well for all of us, because she watched the kids while I went to the library and John worked on chores or a project.

One cool spring afternoon, I arrived home from the library to find Marcia and John sitting in lawn chairs in the front yard. The tulips had bloomed along the fence and the birds were singing a sweet song. Keith was kicking the soccer ball and Vanessa was running after her brother, giggling. As I listened to my children's laughter, the sun warming my body, I felt a sense of well-being.

I took a few deep breaths and gazed into the clear blue sky. Spring, the season of renewal and new beginnings, made me think of Lora, and I hoped with all my heart that she had found the peace she hadn't been able to find on this earth. Watching the two stoic Marins chuckling at the kids, I hoped that they, too, had found serenity in the simple joy of the day and were somehow beginning to accept their tremendous loss. If I knew one thing about Lora, it was that she wouldn't want us to mourn forever.

24

*O*ur beautiful home was finally complete. It had a new roof, new garage, new windows and siding. Every room had been remodeled. John had outdone himself in the kitchen, where he'd refaced the dark, dingy cabinets with oak, added a pantry, tiled the floor and countertops, even put in a breakfast nook overlooking the landscaped yard and beyond, to the countryside. I loved that room.

For the past few months, however, John and I had discussed moving to Auburn, the county seat. His career with Placer County was soaring, and if I could get a job at Auburn Faith Community Hospital, whose small size appealed to me, we could both work where we lived. It was a nice-size community—at the time, the population was approximately twelve thousand—nestled in the western foothills of the Sierra Nevada and edged by the American River Canyon.

Rural Loomis, at that time, had a population of forty-five hundred. Most homes sat on five to ten acres on which cows and horses roamed, with no children nearby. Its downtown consisted of a post office, an old pharmacy, a hardware store, and an old-style Foster Freeze drive-in; to do any shopping or go to a movie or out to eat, you had to drive elsewhere. Auburn had much more to offer: several grocery stores and churches, a police station, a good school system, many artists and galleries, and a quaint downtown, even an historic Old Town and the vintage Old State Theater.

Auburn was a community, a place where the kids could grow up and plant roots. We had decided they would attend St. Joseph Catholic School, which was just three blocks from the hospital I hoped to work in. Keith would be starting kindergarten in the fall, and we didn't want to move him once he was in a school. These were all good reasons to move from our first house, but we had created so many wonderful memories there, it wasn't easy to leave.

In June 1990 a "For Sale" sign went up in our front yard, and in a hot real estate market, we had an offer within a month. On August 1, we closed escrow on our lovely new home: an eleven-year-old ranch-style house that needed very little work, on two and a half acres in the rolling hills of Christian Valley, on the north side of Auburn. It had four bedrooms, two baths, and a huge deck that ran the length of the house. The view from the deck was of dense pin-oak trees and granite outcroppings; there was even a babbling brook at the property's edge.

The Loomis house had been thirty-seven years old when we bought it, and it had needed so much work, a move-in-ready house really appealed to us, especially since the kids were growing up and were our first priority. Barbara Lane, our horseshoe-shaped street, dead-ended into pastureland, and the neighborhood had very little traffic. We quickly met a couple of families with boys Keith's age, and a family with a little girl Vanessa's age had just moved in across the street. Now the kids would have playmates.

We decided to celebrate our new life in Auburn by taking a trip to see Aunt Cindy before school started. She came to California often—every Christmas, during the summer—but we hadn't visited her in a long time. We bought a used Apache pop-up trailer complete with refrigerator, stove, and sink and planned our first camping trip with children.

❧ ❧ ❧

Cindy had been sharing a house with friends in Vancouver since her divorce, three years earlier. The 1890 Queen Anne–

style Victorian reflected the highly ornamented English-aesthetic style known as Picturesque Eclecticism, in that era the most common type of housing in British Columbia. A white wrap-around verandah, gingerbread-style siding, a corner tower, and a domed roof gave it the look of a castle. Keith said it was the biggest house he'd ever seen. Inside, the beautifully carved wooden banisters, footed bathtubs, narrow stairs, and creaky floors added to its charm. Up on the third floor, the kids lay in sleeping bags under a skylight and fell asleep gazing at stars.

Cindy was still working for the same dentist in Surrey, in part because this man embraced life with the same attitude she did: Work hard and play hard, because life is just too short to do otherwise. Each morning around seven, she and John went for a five-mile run, while I sat in the bay window sipping my coffee and watching my children play in the front yard. Cindy usually beat him back and waited on the steps, her body glistening with sweat. Her calves and thighs were so muscular, she looked like a bodybuilder. When John returned the first morning, he bent over, huffing and puffing. "Man, I used to be able to beat you. You are one fit woman, sis."

When the kids had asked their aunt where her TV set was, she told them, "I don't have one, because I'd rather be out with my friends on my bike, or kayaking, or running, or out enjoying Mother Nature."

They looked at each other and shouted, "Yay, can we go on a hike, Aunt Cindy?"

Cindy led us on several day hikes, although one of us usually had to carry Vanessa, who was only two and a half, back to the car. In Stanley Park, we rented bicycles and rode behind Cindy on her five-hundred-dollar bike, John pulling a carrier behind him with our precious cargo. We did our best to keep up with Cindy, but she had to stop and wait patiently for us many times. We ate lunch at Lost Lagoon, the lake in the park I remembered so well. This time, we visited the park's Children's Farmyard, where the children had fun petting the ponies, goats, and llamas.

Now thirty-eight, Cindy was the picture of health. Ever on the prowl, I carefully observed her anyway, thankful I didn't see any odd movements or twitches. Cindy's lifestyle also reassured me; if she had HD, I figured, she would be tripping or falling, unable to do the strenuous activities she so enjoyed. And she was just a few years away from being too old for Huntington's to find her. I played a little game with myself: HD had gotten two of the four siblings—fifty percent—so it won't reach the other two, I told myself.

Since Cindy was scheduled to work the next four days, we headed to the Sunshine Coast, northwest of Vancouver. It was accessible only by air or ferry, so we drove our rig onto a ferry boat and took the forty-minute ride, the children's faces glued to the window as the boat cut through the water. We camped next to a rolling stream in Salty Bay Provincial Park. On our hikes, we marveled at the beauty of the old-growth forests colliding with sandy beaches.

When we got back to Cindy's house that Friday, she was busy packing. "Elizabeth and I got invited to go on a kayaking trip," she told us happily. "We're going to paddle through the Strait of Georgia, which is a channel between the mainland and Vancouver Island. There are a lot of little islands in the strait we can explore, and a couple of them are popular places to camp. We're leaving Monday morning, after you guys take off."

When she suggested spending the weekend at Camp Jubilee, in North Vancouver, just an hour away, she grabbed her stuff—Cindy could always just pick up and go—and we were on the beach by two p.m. The campground was a hidden gem. Situated on majestic Indian Arm, a steep-sided glacial bay, it lay along almost one hundred and thirty acres of oceanfront. Cindy loved playing with the kids, which gave John and me some alone time to sit on the beach with a beer.

It was a great trip, and we were all sorry when we had to leave. It was very hard for John. With Lora and Dave gone from our lives and Marcia struggling with HD, it meant even more to him to spend time with his childhood buddy. Seeing his joy each day had been wonderful. As soon as we pulled out of Cindy's driveway that Monday, his radiant smile disappeared.

❧❧❧

By this time, I had finished the coursework for the master's program, and in January had begun an unpaid internship at Roseville Community Hospital. I shadowed every department director, observing how he or she ran the department, attended meetings, and worked on special projects. I was there twenty to twenty-five hours a week, which worked well with the kids' school schedules.

By May 1991, Keith was finishing kindergarten at St. Joseph Catholic School and Vanessa was attending Tutor Totter Preschool, in Christian Valley about five miles from our house. It was a parent-cooperative school, which meant parents were required to attend monthly meetings, participate in fundraising activities, be active on at least one committee or board, and volunteer in the classroom at least twice a month. Since it was Vanessa's first time away from me, I played "assistant teacher" several times in the first few months.

One Saturday morning in early May, I stood in my new

kitchen, watching my children play tee-ball in the front yard with their dad, and took a moment to be grateful. My love was thirty-six years young and healthy, and we had two darling children. When I thought of not having the three of them in my life, which would have been the case had I chosen not to stay with John, it scared me more than the thought of Huntington's.

Marcia was still living in Sacramento, a forty-five-minute drive away. Now forty-two, she'd been diagnosed five years earlier, though she'd shown signs of HD a couple of years before that. Her chorea, or involuntary movements, one of a group of neurological disorders called dyskinesia, was getting worse, and her driving had deteriorated further. Deep in her basal ganglia, the part of the brain that controls movement, the cells were dying. I felt we'd need to talk to her soon about giving up her car and to try to convince her to move closer to us.

Marcia typically called on Saturday mornings around nine-thirty. "Hi, Therese. How...are...you...?" Because the basal ganglia also controls emotion and cognitive ability, she had begun having difficulty finding words and processing thoughts.

"Hi, Marcia. We're all fine."

I talked about her niece and nephew and a project John was working on around the house, and then I heard a clunk. "Marcia, you still there?" She'd been dropping more and more things lately, too.

After a few minutes, she said, "I'm...here."

She'd always been a private person, never sharing how she felt, but it had become increasingly difficult to decipher whether she was sad, happy, upset, sick, or just having a bad day. Sometimes I wanted to tear my hair out.

I had just about talked myself out when Marcia surprised me. "Me...move...to...Auburn?"

"That's a great idea, Marcia! We could see you more often, and you could go to the kids' games with us. Why don't you come over tomorrow for dinner? We can talk about it then."

Two months later, we moved Marcia into Evergreen Apartments, off Highway 49 about ten minutes from our house and five minutes from John's office. Her ground-floor apartment had been designed for a person with disabilities, with wide doorways, an open floor plan, and a shower with two safety bars. We'd chosen a two-bedroom apartment, anticipating the caregiver she would need eventually.

The chorea was compromising her small motor skills and coordination, so everyday tasks such as getting dressed, brushing her teeth, and combing her hair had become very difficult. Marcia, a woman who'd never stepped out into the world without makeup, who'd always worn the latest fashions and complementing accessories, now looked like a homeless person.

❧❧❧

By August, I had completed my internship and submitted a report on my experience to Dr. Margaret Sorenson, my advisor at California State University, Long Beach. Two weeks later, she approved it. The following week, I mailed her my thesis, "Physician Referral: A Critical Point of Entry for Today's Healthcare Providers." Having revised it a dozen times, I crossed my fingers. Dr. Sorenson called two weeks later to say my thesis had been accepted, and I could now file for graduation.

Since the graduation ceremony would be in Long Beach,

we planned our own festivities. By then, my parents were living nearby—they'd moved to Citrus Heights to be near my sisters and me, since we'd all stayed in the Sacramento area after college—and Mom and Dad brought Marcia to the house. Amy, Jen, and Matt were there, too. I showed off my framed diploma, hanging on a wall, as John barbequed shrimp shish kabobs, my favorite. After ice cream cake from Baskin Robbins, my beloved husband presented me with an anniversary ring, to commemorate my thirty-fifth birthday, our eleven years of marriage, and my master's of science degree in healthcare administration. I couldn't help crying.

Now I had a new mission: securing a job at Auburn Faith Community Hospital.

In the mid-sixties, ten doctors had pooled their money to build this fifty-bed, one-and-a-half-million-dollar hospital. My strategy was to volunteer in the foundation office, the philanthropic arm of the hospital, and get to know people. During my internship at Roseville Community Hospital, the most gratifying work I'd done was in its foundation office. At Auburn Faith, I worked in the foundation office two days a week from eleven to three, when Keith's school let out. I kept my eye on the job board outside the human resources department, and when a position I qualified for was posted, I'd talk to the department head and leave a resume.

Once Marcia was settled in her new apartment, one of us visited each day. John and I both noticed the chorea was escalating; she always had so many bruises, it looked as if someone were beating her. John had the heart-wrenching task of suggesting she not drive anymore, reassuring her that we would take her wherever she needed to go. This was the beginning of many new losses Marcia would suffer as the insidious HD stole her ability to do things the rest of us take for granted. The tasks we helped with then were easy but time-consuming: grocery shopping, washing her clothes, cleaning her apartment. Once I got a job, I'd have less time to help her.

In October, I became the hospital's Lifeline manager. Lifeline is a medical-alert system through which family members can quickly get help to someone at a distance who has fallen down, for example. Subscribers wear a waterproof button that, when activated, calls a pre-programmed phone number. Managing this service to help people stay in their homes and continue to live independently was a perfect fit for me, at a perfect time in my life. It was a part-time job, and I reported to the foundation director. Since the previous manager had already left, I started immediately.

～☙～☙～

The first week on my new job had gone smoothly, and that Thursday evening, after dinner, I went to buy groceries. As I was loading them into my car, I suddenly had a bad feeling about Marcia. To ease my mind, I called John and said I was going to stop by her apartment to check on her, making up some excuse for my late-night visit. I knocked several times and yelled, "Marcia, it's Therese," but she never answered. The door wasn't locked, so I opened it and just about knocked Marcia over. I grabbed her arm, which wasn't easy, with both arms flailing, and steadied her. Blood had run down the side of her face from a cut on her forehead. "What happened?"

"Hit...head."

I grabbed her hand as it jerked wildly. "Don't try to touch it, Marcia." I sat her on the couch and cleaned and put some ointment on it. "Well, you were lucky. I don't think it needs stitches. Are you all right to be left alone, or do you want to come home with me?"

Her head wiggled from side to side. "Doesn't hurt. Don't worry."

I helped her change into her pajamas and brush her teeth. She was so unstable now, and no matter how many times we asked her to lock the door, she couldn't remember to do it.

I knew John had seen her battle scars but, being a Marin, had chosen to ignore them. My biggest fear was that one day Marcia would fall and be unable to get up on her own. The next week, Marcia became a member of Lifeline. I instructed her never to take the button off and fervently hoped she'd remember.

I was so glad to be able to help her. And changing my career to work in healthcare was the best strategy I could have found to calm my OCD. My problem-solving knowledge allowed me to be in control, which lowered my anxiety—and I needed to stay strong and not crumble every time I saw Marcia. I was looking at the face of Huntington's three days a week and every weekend, and it terrified me.

25

Over the next month, we settled into a routine. I'd drop the kids off at their schools, work my four hours, pick them up, and then, three afternoons a week, visit Marcia; on the other two days, John stopped by at lunchtime. On one of our days, the kids and I would take her grocery shopping, which took a lot of time, but I felt it was important for Marcia to get out of the apartment for a few hours. I'd place her hands on the cart and walk beside her. Keith stayed close behind, afraid she might fall; Vanessa walked on the other side of the cart so I could keep an eye on her. I always searched for cans and containers that were easy to open. By then, Marcia could hardly write, so I would make out the check and she'd sign with a scribble.

Back at her place, the kids watched TV with her while I put the groceries away—everything within reach, because climbing on a chair was no longer an option. When we were ready to leave, I made sure Marcia was wearing the Lifeline button. I hated leaving her; she had so many hours alone. I wished her family, especially her father, would visit from time to time, but so far, no one had even inquired how she was doing.

"Your dinner is in the microwave, Marcia. All you have to do is press the start button. And remember, your phone is set to speed-dial us. Come on, guys, say goodbye to Aunt Marcia. Remember, we're only ten minutes away."

It was clear she was struggling. On one of John's visits that December, he found just about everything she'd made since the previous afternoon on the kitchen floor. "She's really having a hard time holding onto things," he sighed.

I nodded. "Honey, she needs help with activities like fixing meals, showering, even eating. I think we'll need to hire someone soon."

"That'll be a delicate subject, Therese. Marcia's lived by herself for so long, and she's such a private person. Having someone in her space is going to be really hard for her."

"I know, and it kills me, but she needs a caregiver, John, if she's going to stay in her apartment. Maybe we can start off with someone four hours a day, to kind of ease her into the idea. How about we take her out for a drive this weekend and talk to her then? It'll be a difficult conversation, but we'll make sure she understands we're doing it because we care."

The following Saturday, John walked Marcia to the car and made sure her seat belt was buckled. The kids were loud and rambunctious in the back of the van with me. I touched Marcia's shoulder and said, "It's such a beautiful day, we thought we'd go to Folsom Lake. The kids love watching the boats. We brought drinks and snacks."

"That…sounds…good."

In the parking lot, John took care of the children, and I focused on Marcia. Our van was pretty high off the ground, so once I unfastened her seat belt, I took her left hand and placed it on the handle to the left of the door, saying, "Let's go slow." When she had both feet on the ground, I held onto the back of her pants and took her right hand. "The ground is very uneven, so we have to be careful."

Keith had carried the picnic basket to a table about a hundred feet from the water, and the kids and their dad were already throwing rocks into the lake. When we got to the table, I gently sat her on the narrow bench. John walked up from the water and said, "That'll keep them busy for a while," sitting down next to his sister as I headed toward the lake. When I looked back, he had his arm around

Marcia and their heads were close together. What a good brother he is, I thought, and how hard this is on them both.

When we left, John picked Marcia up, since at times it was just easier that way, and we all headed for the van. When we got back to her apartment, I changed her into her pajamas and brushed her teeth, and John tucked her into bed.

On the way home, I asked, "How did she take it?"

"Pretty well. She agreed to have someone come for four hours a day."

The following weekend, in her apartment after we'd spent the day together, Marcia touched my arm. "Will... you...pay...bills, Therese?" She shook her wobbly head. "I...can't." She pointed to a huge box full of statements, receipts, and checks.

"Sure, Marcia, I can do that."

Once John and I organized everything and studied her portfolio, we saw that in addition to her disability benefits from the state, she had a good retirement plan. She was on Medicare and had a supplemental healthcare policy through AT&T. When she retired, she'd accrued hundreds of hours of vacation and sick leave and received full pay for a year. She had more than fifty thousand dollars in her savings account and a hundred thousand dollars in stocks.

"You don't know how relieved I am," John said. "With paid help, she can live in her apartment for a long time and, I hope, never have to go into a nursing home. I was afraid we were going to have to ask Dad for money, and you know how that would have gone."

I put my pencil down and took his hand. "At some point, you know, she'll have to go into an assisted-care or residential-care facility, and they're not cheap. Thank goodness she was a saver."

John got up and turned on the TV. It was too scary to think that far down the road.

❧ ❧ ❧

I contacted a long-term-care agency with bonded employees and requested a female caregiver. This agency guaranteed that if the first person was not the right fit, they would send another. The following Monday morning, at Marcia's apartment, we met Debbie, a slight woman about forty with a friendly smile and kind demeanor. A certified home-healthcare aide, she lived in the Grass Valley area, about twenty miles north of Auburn, with her husband and their four children.

I was there to break the ice and fill her in on Marcia's condition, because while Debbie been a caregiver for many years, she'd never had a patient with Huntington's. I had made a list of things she could do for Marcia and proposed that, maybe in a couple of weeks, she suggest helping Marcia with her shower. Debbie asked if we could purchase a gait belt, which would steady Marcia and help prevent falls.

Before I left, Debbie and I sat at the kitchen table. "This is going to be very difficult for Marcia, and she might not accept much from you at first," I told her. "But please be patient. If you take baby steps, she'll come around." I was so nervous, it felt like I had a cotton ball in my mouth. "She's been a professional, independent woman her whole life, so it's not easy for her to accept help."

Each afternoon when John or the kids and I stopped by, Debbie had thoughtfully left a note on how the day had gone, which was a great help. On Saturdays, we continued taking Marcia to the kids' soccer games or on an outing. On Sundays after church, we brought doughnuts and sat with her for a while. The children would get antsy, plus we had chores and homework to do, so we'd leave Marcia alone for the rest of the day and cross our fingers. Every night, we called to check on her before she went to sleep.

When Debbie had been with Marcia for about two weeks, I started feeling less anxious, because Marcia hadn't fired her.

26

After Marcia had been in Auburn for about a year, I found myself referring to HD as a monster. My psyche had changed this menacing disease into a gruesome devil, with pointed ears and razor-sharp fangs. Like a thief in the night, it was sneaking in and stealing her ability to talk, walk, and think. It had dug its claws deep into Marcia and was pulling her away. I often dreamed of beating it to death. Sometimes I'd wake up exhausted after slaying a devil all night.

By now, Marcia was forty-three and had been battling HD for six years. She was allowing Debbie, who spent the whole day with her now, to help her with showers and other personal-care tasks. Debbie was even feeding her, because the chorea was causing her arms to flail so wildly, Marcia was unable to grasp a utensil, scoop up food, and get it to her mouth. My instincts told me that it wouldn't be long before Marcia needed more care than Debbie could provide. Using my contacts at the hospital, I began searching for an independent caregiver, because the cost would be considerably lower than the agency's fee.

Staring into the face of Huntington's constantly reminded me of John's at-risk status for this horrific disease. The medical community didn't know much more than it had when Woody Guthrie died, in 1967. There still was no simple test to determine if Cindy or John had the mutated gene, and no therapy or cure was in sight. My demons were on the prowl again, making me crazy when John dropped his keys or forgot something he needed for work. I couldn't quiet them and was not sleeping well, and whenever I left Marcia's apartment, it was a struggle to hold back my tears.

John was as supportive as he could be, as were my mom and my sisters, but it was not enough; I needed to talk to someone—a professional—on a regular basis. Placer County offered counseling services to employees and their families, so I looked through the list of therapists in Auburn and made an appointment with one.

Pamela Gusland was a clinical psychologist whose office wasn't far from the hospital. She was about forty-five and had been in practice for ten years. Light poured into her office from a huge window; with the rust-colored rug on the hickory floor, it seemed to warm the whole room. A comfortable two-seat couch, probably for couples in counseling, sat against one wall, behind a coffee table with a box of Kleenex and a couple of magazines on it. Pamela's chair faced the couch. The opposite wall had a bookcase with several shelves; children's books and toys were on the bottom shelf.

I immediately felt at ease with Pamela, who I came to know as a down-to-earth woman, completely honest and empathetic. It felt good to talk openly about my feelings, my fears and concerns. Pamela listened, validated my emotions, and offered ways to ease my distress. She suggested I start keeping a journal, writing down how I felt on a daily basis. She recommended making a list of all the good things in my life and keeping it in my pocket, so that I could take it out and read it whenever I felt anxious.

Most important, she offered me a place I could cry. My kids didn't need to see their mother break down, which sometimes happened when we were in the car. With time, she helped me understand that experiencing my feelings, rather than trying to stifle them, was the only clear and direct way to free my heart from pain. Her office became my safe house.

After seeing Pamela once a week for a few months, I felt I was coping better. My demons would never retreat, not until John was at least fifty years old, but knowing that someone was there to listen and corroborate—someone who simply said, Yes, indeed, this is a difficult thing to have in your life—calmed my soul. My heart didn't feel so heavy in my chest all the time, and I was sleeping better. But I couldn't stop the flow of tears. From the moment I stepped into Pamela's office until the moment I left, I cried.

I took a chance around this time and asked John if he'd like to participate in a session with Pamela, or maybe go see her by himself. "No, thanks." He saw the disappointment on my face and added quickly, "I didn't mean to come across so sharply, Therese. It's just that I've lived with so much uncertainty in my life—this disease is just something more. I cope the best I can and have learned not to stress about it."

Driving home from a meeting with Pamela one day, I had another thought. Talking about Huntington's had helped me so much, maybe Marcia could find some comfort in talking with her. I wondered if she might let her guard down and talk to a stranger. At my next session, I asked if Pamela would consider taking Marcia as a patient. She agreed, and even offered to meet Marcia in her apartment.

The next day, on my way to see Marcia, I felt pretty proud of myself, elated to bring such good news. After greeting Debbie, I sat on the couch next to Marcia and turned down the volume on the TV. "You know, Marcia, I've been seeing a wonderful therapist, and it's really helping me to talk about what's going on in my life. You know, juggling work, the kids…Huntington's. I asked if she'd be your therapist also—only if you're comfortable with it—and she'll even come to your apartment." She didn't respond. "So…what do you think?"

Marcia crossed her arms and shouted, "NO!!!!!!!!!!" right in my face.

I left the apartment shaking my head and laughing at myself. What in God's name had I been thinking? The Marins don't talk about their feelings with anyone, not even with each other. What made me think she'd talk to a therapist?

❧❧❧

Managing Marcia's care was a privilege and the greatest gift I could give her. Material items were no longer important to her, but continuing to live in her apartment, with her own things around her, was a priority. My goal was to provide Marcia with anything that could bring joy to her life, along with services to help her stay independent. Protecting her dignity was my utmost concern, along with making sure her life was of the highest quality possible.

Marcia's speech had become very difficult to understand, but trying to talk had become so frustrating, she had pretty much stopped trying. We no longer had conversations, just asked her questions and waited for a nod or shake of her head. But even those replies were hard to decipher. Though she tried to control her limbs by crossing her arms and legs, her flailing was escalating; she continually had welts, bruises, and cuts all over her body. She also had become incontinent. My heart hurt for the suffering she endured.

When Debbie called on Friday nights to give us a weekly report, she'd sometimes cry. At one point, she'd had the gait belt around Marcia and was walking her to the bathroom when they both fell down. On hearing that, I immediately rented a wheelchair and brought it to the apartment. Now Debbie could safely take her out for a walk. They both needed some sun on their faces and a change of scene.

❧❧❧❧

Two weeks before Christmas, we treated Marcia and the kids to a surprise. We loaded everyone into the van and headed to McBurney Christmas Tree Farm, just outside Grass Valley. We slid a Mickey Mouse Christmas cassette into the tape player, and Keith and Vanessa sang "The Twelve Days of Christmas" all the way there. Just as we pulled into the parking lot, snow began falling, setting the stage for a perfect day. John turned around and said, "You guys get to pick out your very own tree this year, and then you can help me cut it down."

Keith's eyes grew big. "Do I really get to help chop it down, Dad?"

"Yes, but you have to mind your father, Keith, and do exactly what he tells you." I bundled the kids up, and they were out of the car in a heartbeat.

John handed a rope to Keith, who was so excited, he could hardly contain himself. John carried a saw and held Vanessa's hand. "Okay, you two. Off we go to find our tree."

"I'm going to go with them," I told Marcia, "but I'll be back in a few minutes. Just sit tight."

It took about fifteen minutes to find the perfect tree. As John and Keith prepared to cut it down, I took Vanessa back to the car. Marcia's eyes were bright, and she was smiling as she watched the snow coming down. "Out, please." I patted her arm and asked her to wait a few minutes. When Vanessa and I returned to her brother and dad, they were carefully sawing the trunk of the tree as snowflakes fell.

As the three of us sat on a wooden bench, watching John and Keith and the other families wrestling with their trees, Vanessa leaned her head back and stuck out her tongue to catch snowflakes, which made Marcia laugh. She laughed again when some children made snowballs and threw them at each other. On the way home, we stopped at the Happy Apple Kitchen and had hot chocolate. The snow was still falling, covering the ground and trees. It looked like a Christmas card.

Once we were home, I sat Marcia in the recliner as John and Keith brought in the tree and attached a stand to its base. The kids clapped when the huge tree stood upright; it was so tall, the top branches brushed the ceiling. Vanessa said, "Aunt Marcia, isn't it a beautiful tree?"

Her aunt got out the word *yes*, and John sat with his sister, his arm around her shoulder, as everyone admired our perfect tree.

"Okay, guys, dinner is ready," I shouted once I had the chicken, mashed potatoes, gravy, and peas on the table. "Please go wash your hands." John put Marcia in her wheelchair, rolled it to the table, and put her bib around her neck. I sat next to her and fed her.

The next day, with so much patience for a three-year-old, Vanessa showed Aunt Marcia every ornament before she hung it on the tree.

❧❧❧

Cindy called a week before Christmas and asked if a friend could come with her for the holiday, because she couldn't drive. When John asked why not, she said she'd tell him when she got there.

That Thursday evening, when a car pulled into the driveway, the kids ran down the hall and flew out the door to greet their colorful aunt. The passenger door opened, and we saw a pair of crutches hit the ground and a bandaged foot swing out of the car. John hugged his sister as her friend came around the car.

208 — Therese Crutcher-Marin

"John, this is Cheryl."

"Nice to meet you, Cheryl. Thanks for driving my sister to California."

"And these are my two favorite kids, Keith and Vanessa."

The children giggled as John handed Keith two bags to carry inside, where he helped his sister into the family room and onto the couch. "So what did you do to yourself, sis?"

"I'm embarrassed to tell you, because it was so dumb."

Her eyes shifted to Cheryl, who said, "Two weeks ago, Cindy was riding my horse Buttercup, and I was riding next to her on my horse, Mable. Buttercup got spooked and took off suddenly. Cindy lost her balance and slipped off, but her foot got caught in the stirrup."

Cindy rubbed her leg. "Yeah, I broke my ankle along with ten bones in my foot. Cheryl felt awful, even though it wasn't her fault, and offered to drive me here for Christmas. Anyway, the doctors operated on my ankle and put a metal rod in it. I have to stay off my foot for six weeks so the bones can heal."

Two days after Christmas, they left to drive to Martinez to see Big John and Lucy. When Cindy asked why we weren't visiting, I said, "Our visits have stopped because they ignore the kids, and Lucy's health is poor, and she makes rude remarks to your dad that she thinks are funny. And they don't even stop smoking while we're there. John and I decided if your dad wants to see his grandkids, he can come to Auburn. If they go to the Marin family picnic, we see them there."

After they were gone, I mentioned to John how I thought it was odd Cindy had had an accident on a horse, since she had ridden as a kid. Naturally, John didn't agree with me. The demons haunted my dreams that night, only this time, they were after Cindy.

As hard as I worked to provide Marcia everything she needed, her quality of life continued to deteriorate. The chorea had gotten so bad that the kids had begun to shy away from her, for fear of being clobbered; Keith got too close soon after the new year and had been kicked pretty hard. Even worse, her swallowing muscles were compromised, a condition called dysphagia, and she frequently choked on clear liquids. My nurse friends suggested adding Thick-It, a food- and beverage-thickening product that had come on the market just six years earlier, to everything Marcia drank.

When John and I explained why their aunt moved the way she did, Keith, then nine, understood; but Vanessa was only six, and couldn't comprehend how a disease would make her aunt move so funny. With a lump in my throat, I added, "Aunt Marcia doesn't hit you on purpose, you know. She can't help it, and she's sorry when she does. Your dad and I appreciate you guys being so patient. And never forget how much she loves to see you."

Marcia hadn't seen a neurologist since she'd been diagnosed, and we both thought it a good idea to have her evaluated again. Controlling her movements was key to maintaining Marcia's independence, because Debbie was struggling to care for her, and I was afraid she might quit. When I asked our primary-care physician to recommend a local neurologist, he said there were only two in Auburn, and they'd probably know little about the disease.

It was a cold, blustery February afternoon when I took Marcia to see one of these men, a Dr. Newman, and we were drenched by the time I got us inside. When I wheeled her into the waiting room, Marcia's arms were flailing out of control, and his staff gawked at her. The room we were ushered into was so small, I had to move the chair into the hallway to fit Marcia's wheelchair in. I climbed up on the examination table and wondered if there was enough room for the doctor.

He entered the room with his eyes glued to a chart. Then he glanced at Marcia and said, "Yup, Huntington's disease is such a bitch."

"Excuse me?" I said. "I'm Therese, her sister-in-law, and we already know that. We're here because of the chorea. It's making her life miserable. Can you prescribe something to calm it down?"

"No, there's no medication specifically for it." He patronized Marcia by patting her leg. "You'd better get your affairs in order, because your future doesn't look too bright." Then he started rambling on about his office's new computer system.

My face grew hot, and I stepped in front of him before he retreated. "You mean to tell us you don't have any suggestions at all?"

"The only thing I can recommend is Valium."

"Well, you're not much help, are you? I think we just wasted our money and time. And you ought to be ashamed of yourself, making a comment like that to her. Where is your compassion?" I wheeled Marcia out the door as fast as I could, running over his toes. As we flew past the desk, I yelled, "Just send us the goddamn bill."

The next day, I made an appointment with the UC Davis Medical Center neurology department, where John and I had gone for genetic counseling.

A month later, John and I left work at noon and treated Marcia to lunch before heading to the medical center, where we waited in a room big enough for all three of us plus the wheelchair. Dr. Hundal, a doctor from India, seemed a kind, patient man. After examining Marcia, asking about her general health, and studying the report by the UCSF Medical Center doctor who had made the HD diagnosis, eight years earlier, he prescribed haloperidol (Haldol), an antipsychotic drug used in treating some symptoms of mental illness, behavior problems, and agitation. It was the only drug he had found, he explained, that would calm the chorea in HD and Parkinson's patients without making them lethargic, as Valium and other sedatives do. Finding the correct dose would take a few weeks of monitoring. The drug, however, might worsen involuntary contractions (dystonia) and muscle rigidity, he warned us.

As John wheeled his sister back into the waiting room, I asked Dr. Hundal what he felt Marcia's life expectancy was. Every HD patient is different, he told me, but he thought she had five to seven years left. I couldn't help praying it would be fewer than that.

It took about three weeks to find the right dose of Haldol, but eventually, we saw the chorea ease. Now only her shoulders jerked regularly; her arms and legs moved sporadically, whenever she tried to reach for something or to get up. I was so thankful we had found Dr. Hundal, because Marcia needed to add something positive to her life, like being able to sit still.

27

*I*n the spring, the Placer County Board of Supervisors and its administrative officer went to Hawaii for a five-day conference on rural counties. John wanted me to go with him, but with my work, the kids' school and activities, and Marcia, it wasn't feasible—which didn't mean I wasn't like a drooling dog around a steak. I mean, who couldn't use five days lying on a white-sand beach?

For the second night, sleep was eluding me, because it felt unnatural not having John by my side. Not long after I did fall asleep, the phone rang. Startled, I turned on the light. "Hello."

"Hello. Is this John and Therese Marin's residence?"

I rubbed my eyes. "Yes, this is Therese."

"This is Lifeline. Marcia Marin pushed her button, and when I called, she didn't answer the phone. Will you go over there and check on her, please?"

"Yes, I'll get there as quickly as I can."

My mind was foggy until I remembered that my parents had moved to Citrus Heights—where Lora and Dave had once lived—not much more than twenty miles away. Soon they were on their way to Auburn. I got to Marcia's place just as the apartment manager was opening the door for two emergency medical technicians.

"I'm Marcia's sister-in-law. Please let me in first." The apartment was so dark, I didn't see Marcia until I turned on a light. She was on the floor in the hallway. I dropped to my knees, cradled her head in my lap, and told them, "She has Huntington's disease."

The EMTs examined her and asked her a couple of questions, and then one said, "We think she may have aspirated some of her vomit. We suggest she be taken to the emergency room to be observed. If she did aspirate, she could develop pneumonia." They gently strapped her onto a backboard, laid her on a gurney, and slid her into the ambulance.

Since it wasn't clear whether Marcia had aspirated into her lungs, the ER doctor wanted to take a chest x-ray to check for pneumonia. I motioned for him to step into the hall. "She can't stay still for a minute. How are you going to get a clear picture of her lungs?"

He nodded. "Then we'll have to observe her and listen to her lungs over the next few hours."

I called Mom, gave her an update, and asked her to take the kids to school.

A nurse entered the room and pulled the curtain around the bed. "Would she like some juice?"

"That would be nice." I stroked Marcia's face and brushed the hair out of her eyes. "Guess we're here for a little while longer. Try to relax."

"Sorrrrrrrry."

"It's okay, Marcia. You didn't do anything wrong." Her arms were flying, crashing into the railings on the bed. I had been in such a hurry to get to the hospital, I'd forgotten to bring her medication. When the nurse came back, I asked if the ER doctor could prescribe ten milligrams of Haldol; I also requested five blankets, to wind around the railings.

Once she took her medication, Marcia's body calmed and she fell asleep. I didn't want to leave her side, so I asked for coffee to help me stay awake while we waited for the doctors to decide that her lungs were clear. As I watched her, my mind wandered to Lora. Though I missed her tremendously, I was glad she hadn't had to endure such a slow, agonizing decline.

It was time for Marcia to have twenty-four-hour care. John proposed another new living arrangement to his sister, and once again, this gentle soul made it easy for him. She looked at her brother and tried to nod.

Finding someone trustworthy to care for a loved one isn't easy. We offered the job to Debbie, out of consideration for all she'd done, and were not surprised when she declined. Finally, we found a young woman named Lynne, twenty-three, who had been a live-in caregiver since she'd moved from Wisconsin to California, three years earlier. She had experience providing care to the elderly, but, like most people, she wasn't familiar with HD. We tried to fully explain the disease process and all the difficulties Marcia was experiencing. We liked Lynne and her references checked out, so we offered her the job: In exchange for room and board and a monthly salary, she would take care of Marcia five days a week. We signed a contract, and then John and I bought a twin bed and dresser and reorganized the second bedroom in Marcia's apartment.

Even with Lynne with her all day, I thought it would be good for Marcia to get out sometimes—to do and see more than she could with Lynne pushing her wheelchair through her neighborhood. Auburn was fortunate to have a licensed community-based daytime healthcare program, Health For All. Its services were available to older people and to adults with chronic medical, cognitive, or mental-health conditions that put them at risk of needing institutional care. The social workers I knew at the hospital and in its hospice program felt this was a good place to send her.

Once John and I saw it, we agreed. The center provided transportation to and from the facility, a nutritious lunch, a shower, recreational activities, and a team consisting of nurses, speech pathologists, social workers, physical therapists, and aides. The healthcare workers would monitor Marcia and try to catch problems such as a urinary-tract infection or a cold before she became very ill. The program ran Monday through Friday from nine a.m. to two p.m., and the cost was a relatively low forty dollars a day. (Insurance didn't cover it unless the patient was on Medi-Cal, which Marcia was not.)

After meeting Marcia, the center's social worker suggested she attend three days a week. On those days—Monday, Wednesday, and Friday—Lynne bought groceries, did errands, baked the goodies Marcia loved, and cleaned the apartment. She called every Friday night to let us know how the week had gone.

Then I found a second caregiver, who took care of another woman three days a week and would live with Marcia on weekends. Kathy was a gracious, kind, motherly type of person. We were spending a ton of Marcia's money to keep her in her own apartment, thankful each day that we didn't have to think about moving her yet.

On our Sunday visits, Keith continued trying to interact with his aunt, but Vanessa began staying close to one of us the whole time. Once the caregivers had settled in, I approached John with my concerns.

"I'm not sure it's healthy for our kids to keep seeing Marcia. I think she frightens Vanessa, and it's only going to get worse." I grabbed a tissue and wiped my eyes. "I'm sorry to say it, but we have to think about them." I turned away from him and stomped my foot. "Goddamn it! She would have been such a great aunt. It's so unfair! Huntington's has stolen another aunt from them."

Knowing Marcia was safe allowed us to sleep better, but

her decline was so upsetting—some days, I just wanted to run away. And watching it firsthand kept me on high alert for symptoms in John. Most days, the demons were pounding on my shoulders, and if John left his agenda for a meeting on the table or dropped his keys, they screamed, "Therese, this may be a sign that he has it!"

Sometimes I could shake the feeling, but when I couldn't, I met with Pamela as often as possible, especially once my anxiety began to affect me physically. I shared my secret only with Pamela. "Last week, I was in the hospital visiting one of my Lifeline patients and replenishing brochures when I started hyperventilating. I didn't know what was happening, so I ran to a bathroom and sat in a stall for a while. When it passed, I went back in the office and talked to one of my nurse friends. She suggested I carry a paper bag with me all the time, and showed me how to breathe into it if it happened again."

Pamela nodded sympathetically. "You've reached a point with your anxiety that I feel warrants exploring the idea of antidepressants." This was hard to hear; it was disappointing to know I couldn't handle things on my own. "Therese, you are under enormous stress every day of your life. Most people don't have this kind of pressure to deal with, and you have been coping with it for fifteen years. The physical symptoms you're exhibiting is your body telling you you're on overload. Antidepressants can help you cope," she assured me.

Since I'd never taken antidepressants, I was hesitant to do so until panic attacks descended on me two or three times a week. I gave in and made an appointment with my primary-care physician, Dr. Cobalt, to request a prescription for Zoloft.

❧❧❧

Cindy came to California twice a year, once in early fall for the annual Marin family picnic—a ritual in this family for more than thirty years—and at Christmas. Her cousins Marie and Ann helped with coordinating and planning the festivities. We always tried to attend this event, because it afforded John time to catch up with his cousins and his remaining aunts and uncle, Christina, Faye, and Jack. (His Aunt Alice had died the previous summer.) By now, Lucy's health had declined to the point where she'd stopped coming to the picnics, and Big John didn't attend every year.

The picnics were happy times for all of us. Marcia's face would light up, and she engaged more with the people around her then. As I watched Cindy tenderly interact with her sister, it always brought tears to my eyes, because, like John, her only concern was for Marcia, never seeming to fear this could be her fate, too.

It had been three years since Lora's funeral, about two since Marcia had moved to Auburn. The 1992 picnic fell on John's thirty-eighth birthday. Cindy had turned forty in July, a milestone for a Cahoon descendant. I clung to the thought that in a few more years, both would be past the age the Cahoons typically began exhibiting symptoms of HD. Her foot and ankle appeared to have healed nicely, and she looked as healthy and fit as ever. The picnic was in Nancy Boyd Park, in Martinez, with its two playground areas, sports fields, and tennis courts. Cindy and Lynne gently pushed Marcia's wheelchair over the bumpy ground to a big covered picnic area as the children ran in circles around them. I was carrying John's birthday cake and had a bounce in my step.

When the Marin aunts, uncles, cousins, and second

cousins greeted us, I could see how shocked they were by Marcia's condition. Some of the cousins visited her occasionally, but she was changing every day, and Lynne was a new addition to Marcia's life. It made me sad to know that one day, Marcia wouldn't be able to come to the picnic anymore—yet another loss she would have to bear.

But that day, Marcia was all smiles, happy to see her family again and to have Cindy nearby. Aunt Faye pulled up a chair and sat with Marcia the entire day. Most of the rest of the family made an effort to spend time with her, and Lynne stayed close, which allowed the rest of us to mingle.

Toward the end of the day, Lynne pushed Marcia to a spot where she could watch the children take turns swinging at a piñata, which always signaled the end of the picnic. Keith and Vanessa carried their haul over to their aunts, sat down next to them, and shared. Around four p.m., Big John made an appearance, even though he was only ten minutes from the park. By that time, some folks had left and others were packing up and leaving. I figured Lucy must have guilted him into not being away from her long, and I didn't even say hello. I was pleased to see him go straight to his daughters—he rarely visited Marcia—but got angry all over again when he didn't seek out his grandchildren.

One-way relationships are hard to nurture. Big John hardly ever called or came to see us, and the last few times we'd visited them, he and Lucy had smoked like chimneys; Vanessa's asthma got so bad, we had to leave. It had been obvious that Lucy was on some heavy-duty drugs, and in her stupor, she said some pretty nasty things to her husband. John and I decided we didn't want the kids around them.

❧❧❧

Cindy had become friends with Marcia's weekend caregiver,

Kathy, who lived in Meadow Vista, one of a dozen small communities adjacent to Interstate 80 east of Auburn. Kathy and her husband owned a home on five acres, with two horses and an open area for training, riding, and exercising. Whenever Cindy came to visit, the three would take off for Kathy's house, where the two women would ride in the corral as Marcia watched.

One Saturday evening, they decided Marcia needed some fun and went to a restaurant. They were waiting at the bar for a table, with Marcia in the middle, of course, when Marcia went down like a wind-toppled tree. John and I were concerned when we saw the huge bruise on her arm; but when she started laughing, we figured, What the heck—she deserves to get out and do something she used to enjoy. It didn't seem that long ago that I was sitting next to her on a bar stool, laughing at Dave's jokes as she smoked a cigarette.

While the arrangement with Kathy and Lynne was going well, Marcia's decline continued to create difficulties. With the death of yet more brain cells, chewing and swallowing had become difficult for her; now all her food had to be puréed, and even then, she often choked and vomited. We asked her caregivers to feed her more slowly, even if it took an hour to finish a meal, and we began putting a high-protein supplement called Boost into ice cream and yogurt to provide more calories.

And it had become very hard to hold onto Marcia, because the flailing, jerky movements had become more fluid, as if she were swimming. After she took a few really bad falls, we insisted she wear a helmet. We could protect her head but could not shield the other parts of her body. In her apartment one day, even with Lynne holding onto her with the gait belt, she fell flat on her face, which left her with raccoon eyes for weeks.

One Saturday in late March, with about an hour until John and the kids came home from Little League practice, I read a headline in the *Sacramento Bee* that I could hardly believe: "Scientists Isolate 'Crown Jewel,' Huntington's Disease Gene."

"Scientists have identified the genetic mutation that causes Huntington's disease (HD), a fatal, neurodegenerative disorder characterized by progressive physical and mental deterioration." The article went on to quote the director of the National Institute of Neurological Disorders and Stroke, Dr. Murray Goldstein: "The Huntington's gene may prove to be the crown jewel of recent neurogenetic discoveries."

Finally, a breakthrough—now a simple blood test could indicate whether a person had the mutated Huntington's gene or not. Though the procedure was easy, the consequences were huge. The information could translate into peace of mind for my children if—and I knew it was a big if—John hadn't inherited the mutated gene from his mother.

Excited, I called my mom, always willing to listen about good times and bad, and we talked until I heard the car door slam. After I got the kids fed and John and I sat down for lunch, I showed him the article. Remembering my promise, I stayed quiet, but my thoughts were racing. Perhaps after seven years and two children, John would have a change of heart about taking the test. His only response to the article was "That's great," and he never brought it up again.

28

*I*n June, Cindy was in Auburn for her forty-first birthday. The children and I made her a cake, and Marcia, Lynne, Kathy, and my folks came to our house to celebrate. Mom sat next to Marcia for a few minutes, and then she got up and went into the kitchen. I followed and put my arm around her as she was wiping away tears. She looked at me and said, "I'm sorry, sugar, that I haven't visited Marcia, but I just can't."

Cindy stayed longer than usual, preparing to meet up with friends for a two-month trip through Thailand. One evening, John was at a night meeting, and we were relaxing in the backyard with a glass of wine. Cindy said, "I've tried to live my life as fully as possible. Whenever there was an opportunity to experience new things or to travel, I'd jump in feet first. But Dad never approved of my lifestyle, and he constantly preached, 'Cindy, you need to settle down and establish yourself. Save your money and buy a house, so you'll have a place when you grow old.' But that wasn't for me."

I said, "I'm glad you did what you wanted and didn't listen to your dad. You know, I have never understood your father. In no way did he ever support any of you, and you never gave him any reason to be treated the way you were, because you were all good kids and became responsible adults. As far as I'm concerned, he missed out on knowing his kids as children and adults. He's also missed out on knowing his only grandchildren."

Cindy looked hesitant, as if she wasn't sure of what she wanted to say. Then she plunged in. "You know, for many years, I looked for ways to heal and find peace. I wanted to shut out the memories of his abusive behavior, and the way I found tranquility was in celebrating nature. The noise in my head goes away when I'm out in the wilderness, on the water, or running a marathon. Also, TM, Transcendental Meditation, calmed me, and I studied the philosophy of Buddhism many years ago. This is where I found harmony." She poured herself another glass of wine. "I hope John has found peace."

"I think he has. He used to turn into this sarcastic person when he was around his dad. He doesn't do that anymore. We have such a strong relationship and positive connection with our kids, I think he realized that not all relationships have to be that way. And life is too short, anyway."

A few months later, John turned thirty-nine, and I rejoiced that both he and Cindy had made it through another year without any symptoms of HD. At the end of the month, we drove to Seattle, where my cousin Polly was getting married. Aunt Mary, my mom's older sister, Uncle Bill, and Polly's three older brothers would be there. Mike, Rick, and Tim were as close as I got to brothers, and they all held a special place in my heart. Since they lived in Kansas, it would be a reunion of sorts, and I couldn't wait for John to meet them.

We camped in Roseburg, Oregon, on our way up, and so did my parents. They had a twenty-five-foot-long fifth-wheeler, and we still had our Apache pop-up tent. It had plenty of room, so Cindy was going to drive the two and a half hours from Vancouver to stay in Seattle with us after the wedding.

It was a small Saturday-afternoon ceremony in the chapel of the University of Washington, where Polly's fiancé was completing his residency and fellowship work. Vanessa couldn't take her eyes off Polly as Uncle Bill walked her down the aisle. The reception was relaxing, and even though it had been eighteen years since I'd seen my cousins, it felt like old times.

Back at the Trailer Inns RV Park, I was making up the beds in the trailer, as the kids changed out of their good clothes and John sat in a lawn chair reading the paper, when wheels crunched on the gravel road in front of our space. A car door opened and slammed shut.

"Hi, there, little brother!"

I opened the screen door and walked down the steps, preparing to embrace my sister-in-law, but was taken aback by what I saw. Cindy was very thin and swaying from side to side. She hugged her brother and then, with a slight dancelike movement, started walking toward me. In her sweet voice, she said, "Hey, Therese."

My eyes were blinking rapidly, and my feet wouldn't move. When Cindy reached me, my arms went around her, and I felt her body twitch slightly. The old anxiety smacked me in the face, and my chest tightened so much, I couldn't breathe.

The kids ran up and plowed into her. "Hi, Aunt Cindy!" Hugging them distracted her for a moment, which allowed me to collect myself.

Finally, my smile reappeared. "We're so glad you could come and visit, Cindy."

John moved close with a worried look and mouthed, "Are you okay?"

I nodded and waited for Cindy's response. "Oh, I am, too. I didn't want to miss an opportunity to spend time with my favorite niece and nephew."

Later that evening, while Cindy showed John and the children photos from her trip to Thailand, I wandered away from where the trailers and RVs were parked. When I knew that I couldn't be heard, the sorrow and anger I'd stuffed into my gut erupted, and I bent over and lost what little I'd managed to eat. Then I covered my mouth with both hands, holding back my sobs and screams the best I could, so that people wouldn't come running, thinking someone was being tortured. My head felt as if it were splitting open, and I almost wished it would, so that I wouldn't have to watch another Marin sister dance the Huntington's dance.

I continued walking, my nails digging deep into my palms. Now I just wanted to hit someone or something, to make he or she or it feel as terrible as I did. Taking big gulps of air to stop the dizziness, I sat atop a deserted picnic table, as hope drained out of me and puddled onto the dirt.

On our way home, John and I had a chance to talk once both kids fell asleep. A true Marin, John would rather ignore the obvious, but that was impossible. Unable to hold back any longer, I let the tears stream down my face. "This is just awful, John. Why is this happening to another one of your sisters? It isn't fair!"

He grabbed my hand. "I know."

We sat in silence for a few minutes, until John turned the radio down and chuckled. "Did I ever tell you about the Vietnam demonstration Cindy took me to when I was thirteen? It's a pretty funny story, now."

"No, I don't think I've heard that one."

"The Vietnam War was in full force, in the newspapers and on TV every day. Many of Cindy's friends were going off to war, and she had a strong opinion and didn't mind sharing it. She attended protest after protest, and one day, she asked if I wanted to go to one in Berkeley with her that afternoon.

"Not wanting to seem uncool, I said yes, of course. We skipped school the rest of the day, and I jumped in the car with her and her friends. When we got to Berkeley, the demonstrators began to march, and I climbed a tree to get out of the way and watch.

"The police showed up with their shields and batons and threw tear gas into the crowd. There was a lot of screaming and swearing, and when I looked down, my eyes started burning. I squeezed the tree and prayed nobody would look up and see me. It was a nightmare. The protestors were arrested, thrown into the police van, and taken to jail to be booked. Cindy was one of them.

"Once it was over, I climbed out of the tree, hitchhiked to Martinez, and acted like nothing had happened. At dinner, Dad asked me where Cindy was. I shrugged my shoulders and said, 'I don't know.'

"Cindy got out of jail, made it home around midnight, and never spoke a word about it to Dad."

What a spitfire, I thought. She is so fearless. How I wished I could be like her.

Over the summer, hope had flourished, and I had grown stronger and was able to push the demons away. And when John turned thirty-nine, I had allowed myself to think he was quite possibly in the clear. But now, with Cindy's symptoms developing so fast and furiously, the picture had changed, and I was thrown into the depths of despair.

❧❧❧❧

In the fall of 1994, St. Joseph's was back in session, and the kids would share their day at dinner each night. Vanessa, a proud first grader, loved her teacher, Mrs. Morris, and her eighth-grade big sister, Joanne, who had helped her acclimate to a full day of school. Now in fourth grade, Keith had Mrs. Smith, who had tutored him over the summer to improve his reading-comprehension skills.

After Grandparents Day, they jabbered for fifteen minutes. I was so glad my parents had been able to share that day with them. John and I smiled at one another across the table, delighted in their enthusiasm and amazed at Keith's increasing appetite. He was only ten; I couldn't imagine what it would be like when he was a teenager. Aunt Mary and Uncle Bill had had three sons to feed, and I wondered how they'd kept their refrigerator full.

Life was busy, to say the least. My every waking moment was filled with work, basketball and soccer practice, Cub Scouts, Vanessa's art class, and managing Marcia's care. John was a very involved dad and shared in the responsibility of getting the children wherever they needed to go.

I'd been managing the Lifeline program at Auburn Faith Community Hospital for three years, and now that both kids were in school all day, I wanted to work full-time. I regularly checked the job board outside the hospital's human resources department, and when a twenty-hour-a-week position opened in the hospice department, I applied and got the job.

Hospice is considered the model for quality, compassionate care that focuses on the symptoms, pain, and emotional and spiritual needs of chronically ill, terminally ill, and seriously ill patients. Usually provided in the patient's home or in a homelike setting, hospice care involves an interdisciplinary-team approach tailored to the patient and extended to his or her loved ones as well. Medicare, private health insurance, and, in most states, Medicaid have a hospice benefit.

The hospice program at Auburn Faith had just received Medicare certification, which meant that it could care for more patients and begin billing for services. The program had been operating solely on donated funds, with a staff of just one full-time nurse and social worker and a part-time clerical worker to support the care of around thirty patients a year. Now the program could hire more staff and offer hospice services to more people.

As hospice support-services supervisor, I was in charge of recruiting, training, and managing hospice volunteers—a required element of a Medicare-certified program— along with marketing, education, and outreach to our community about hospice services. I continued managing the Lifeline program.

We rearranged our schedules so that John visited Marcia at lunchtime on Tuesdays, and I stopped by on Thursdays. She was still attending Health For All on Mondays, Wednesdays, and Fridays, but she'd been struggling with Huntington's for nine years now, and her decline was accelerating. She could no longer walk and had to be strapped into her wheelchair or she would fly out of it. And it took her longer than ever to respond to our questions. While HD is commonly thought of as a motor disorder, its cognitive symptoms can progress to dementia. In the past several months, I had begun to question whether Marcia was still aware of her surroundings.

One Thursday, I took Marcia to see Dr. Cobalt, our primary-care physician, because Lynne thought she had a urinary-tract infection. We were on our way there when I realized I'd forgotten something—I didn't tell her, but it was a DNR (Do Not Resuscitate) Order. John had power of attorney over Marcia's affairs, and after discussing the matter with Dr. Cobalt, I had copies to place in her chart and in her medical records at the hospital.

"Sorry, Marcia, I've got to stop by my office and get something. You've never seen where I work, so I'll show you around." When I introduced her to the nonmedical folks I worked with, her body lurched forward and her arms waved all over; it seemed perfectly normal to me, but their faces told me how shocked they were. You don't see many Huntington's patients, because they are so difficult to manage. That's how they become so isolated.

As I began working in hospice, my fears and demons calmed, and I concluded that I'd been led to this work. Interacting with the dying, working with compassionate colleagues, being reminded daily how precious life is, and assisting patients with the end-of-life issues our society ignores so well—I felt I was being given just what I needed then: knowledge for the future needs of my two dying sisters-in-law and, possibly, of my husband.

29

Not long after that, Cindy called to tell us some news. "I'm leaving my dental-assistant position and returning to school to become a dental hygienist. Since I already have two years completed, the counselor said it would only take one semester to finish the Canadian requirements, and then I can take the test. This is something I've always wanted to do, so I'm just going to do it."

Cindy had a new boyfriend, too. She had met Rob in Stanley Park. Divorced, with two daughters living in Victoria, British Columbia, he was also embarking on a new career path, studying to become a certified RV mechanic. She had moved into his RV with him and was working in a film-developing store part-time. Cindy never mentioned love, and I didn't ask, but I did wonder if Rob knew what lay in store for her five or ten years down the road.

Over the next several months, Cindy called to let us know how her classes were going, always with excitement in her voice. "I'm not even skiing this winter, because I want this so bad!"

She was scheduled to take the written and practical tests in early December. As Christmas approached, John invited her and Rob to our house for the holidays. They could drive the RV to California and park in our driveway.

Since the kids were on Christmas vacation, we let them stay up to greet their lively aunt. Cindy introduced us all to Rob, a tall guy, about forty-five, with sad, vacant-looking eyes. I thought he seemed a little standoffish. After Rob retreated to the RV, Cindy told us, "Well, I have some good news and some bad news. I passed the written test but not the practical test. You are allowed two tries on each test, but

I'm not sure I'll try again, because of the trouble I'm having with my fingers. They're spastic, and my dexterity isn't what it used to be. Guess I should have done this years ago."

"I'm really sorry, Cindy," John said as he hugged his sister. "Don't be so hard on yourself. It's not your fault." He squeezed her hard. "We're so glad you're here. Let's forget about it for a while and enjoy the holidays together."

Her news only reinforced what we suspected. On Christmas morning, after a fitful night, I rose out of bed and had a syncope episode. Syncope is a temporary loss of consciousness, more often thought of as fainting or passing out. It generally occurs when the blood pressure is too low and the heart isn't pumping a normal supply of blood to the brain. Causes can include overheating, dehydration, exhaustion, and emotional stress.

I was out for just a second, woke up on the floor, and wondered how I got there. It scared me so much, I made an appointment with Dr. Cobalt, and he suggested increasing my medication.

Later that day, we all piled into the van and went to my parents' home for dinner. Watching both my sisters-in-law dancing to Huntington's was so disturbing, I had to slip into the kitchen to calm my nerves. Mom understood and gave me a hug. "How're you doing, sugar?"

"I'm fine." I took a deep breath. "It's not about me." I pointed into the living room, where John was sitting between his sisters. "I'm just glad they can be together and live in the moment."

Before Cindy and Rob left to visit her dad and Lucy, John called his father to wish them a Merry Christmas and let them know Cindy was on her way. Before they left, Cindy told John that she wouldn't be continuing in the dental-hygienist program. "I'll find a better-paying job somewhere."

Over the next few weeks, John reacted as he always did, internalizing his emotions, though the tension was apparent in his face. Needless to say, I looked to Pamela for help with my sorrow. She explained that we were both experiencing anticipatory grief; John and I had two impending losses that would not occur soon but would weigh on our hearts for years. Wherever I went, I made sure I had my paper bag, because the panic attacks were becoming more frequent again.

Right after the first of the year, we got a letter from Cindy. "In need of a change of scenery, we have decided to leave the trendy city of East Vancouver and settle in the slow-paced country in Fort Langley, Canada."

Cindy had a unique, upbeat way of writing, and I loved reading her letters. "We found a cozy, charming home to rent. We left the city behind because we both feel the congestion and busy energy are draining for us." She described her beautiful British garden with such passion. "Everywhere you look there are neat little spots to sit and enjoy the garden. It has foxglove, hazelnut trees, white pine trees, wisteria, cosmos, lemon balm, and oregano at least three feet high. I want to sit in the middle of it and enjoy life growing around me. The geraniums are in bloom, vibrant red in color. Some are variegated white and passionate purple. Flowers are the earth's way of smiling and I feel the earth smiling on me when I move through the yard."

I felt she was searching for ways to regenerate, seeking alternative methods to heal her body and mind. Cindy was truly my inspiration—forever positive, finding joy in the simple things in life. I felt she was sending me subtle messages in her letters.

❧❧❧

While Cindy hadn't admitted to herself that she had Huntington's, she sought support from clinicians at the Centre for Huntington's Disease at the University of British Columbia, in Vancouver, and found camaraderie in a Huntington's disease support group. Some of the members were living at risk, like her; others, with a confirmed diagnosis. The group provided Cindy strength, interaction, and connection with people—all vital to her existence. Eventually, she began considering genetic testing and called her brother three times in one week to discuss whether or not to begin the process.

Neither John nor I had been sleeping well, waking up in the middle of the night and talking for hours. During one of those restless nights, John reminisced about his young life with Cindy. I snuggled close to him and listened.

"My happiest childhood memories are the family camping trips to Meeks Bay, at Lake Tahoe. It was an adventure for us kids, because we never got to go anywhere. Dad rented a trailer and slept alone in it at night, because we slept outside, gazing at the stars and watching the moonlight reflect off the water.

"Cindy and I hiked, swam, and played with other kids. Marcia and Lora were teenagers and more interested in spying on boys, working on a suntan, and not getting their hair wet. There was a movie theater nearby, and one year the thriller *Psycho* was playing. Dad told Lora and Marcia they could go, but Cindy and I were forbidden. As usual, Dad didn't know what we were up to, and they took us anyway. After seeing that movie, Cindy and I never went anywhere without each other."

In early 1995, Cindy made up her mind to begin the

testing process. I couldn't find the right words and wound up with the usual platitudes. "Good luck, Cindy. I'll be praying for a good outcome." I hoped she was prepared, because in my opinion, the chance for a negative result was slim.

Before she hung up, she added, "I've also decided to participate in a program that will document and record my journey through the testing. Hopefully, it will help others." Her bravery and generosity didn't surprise me in the least.

❧❧❧

The genetic test for the Huntington's gene had a strict protocol. Because of both ethical and practical concerns, the predictive testing involved a considerable amount of education, counseling, and support. At the University of British Columbia, a consultant geneticist and a genetic counselor were part of the process, which usually took about six weeks from the first of four appointments to learning the results of the test.

John called Cindy once a week to let her vent, feeling that was the best way to support her. "I wish I could be there for her," he told me.

At the end of May, just after the kids got out of school for the summer, we were looking at the family calendar, writing in all the activities they had going on and discussing how we'd get them there, when we realized the six weeks were just about over, and Cindy should be getting her test results.

John looked puzzled. "I'm surprised she didn't talk about it the last time we were on the phone."

We called, left a message, and, when we didn't hear back from her, continued to leave messages over the next few days. On Tuesday evening after Keith's Cub Scouts meeting,

John brought in the mail and threw it on the table, where it was forgotten until the children were in bed. While we were watching the ten o'clock news, I looked through the stack, pulled out a letter, and nudged John apprehensively. "It's from Cindy."

The letter began with a quote from Erich Fromm: "Let your mind start a journey through a strange new world. Leave all thoughts of the world you knew before. Let your soul take you where you long to be.... Close your eyes, let your spirit start to soar, and you'll live as you've never lived before."

Then came a single chilling sentence: "My test result indicates I have the mutated Huntington's gene."

But the Cindy we knew and loved continued to give to others during her time of despair. She wrote, "I'm getting involved in the research project I told you about. It's titled 'The Individual Experiences and Social Meanings of Predictive Testing for Huntington's Disease.' A booklet will be created, and my story will be one of many experiences in predictive testing. It'll be available through the Huntington Society of Canada."

Cindy immersed herself in the Huntington's clinic and support group. She volunteered in the office and helped organize fundraising events. We were so glad she had found a support system to help her cope—unlike Lora, who, even being a part of AA, had never admitted she needed one. There had been no support groups nearby when Marcia was diagnosed, though I doubted she would have taken advantage of one.

For Cindy, writing letters seemed to be therapeutic, and we received many over the next few months. Even with her diagnosis, she never lost hope. She was sure that one day soon, there would be a cure or a therapy.

Forever positive, Cindy wrote, "Me personally, I am doing my best to keep busy doing things that I know I will not be able to enjoy in the future. I've been seeing Christopher Hansard, who is a Tibetan monk [he is a psychotherapist and practitioner of Tibetan Dur Bon Medicine] from London. My good buddy Elizabeth paid for me to see him in August. I cannot say how deep my love and appreciation goes to her for giving me such a gift. When I saw him, he took a look at me and saw a scared rabbit filled with anger and sadness. He said no matter who you are, we don't need to be packing around the skeletons in our closet. He recommended that I have cranial acupuncture, Tibetan-style. I have had ten visits and feel like the weight of the world has been lifted off my shoulders."

In another letter, she told us, "My walk is somewhat wobbly, as if someone has control over my muscles. I think my fingers, thumb, and index in my left hand have some chorea in them. I notice after drinking caffeine the movement is more noticeable. People with HD should not drink alcohol or coffee.

"I remember many nights in my past where I was totally out of control drinking at a café, and now I realize what this monster was on the other side. I can recall feeling like this for ten years. It feels good to be able to put a label on it now. It's interesting how I feel good to be reaching a peak with the demons."

Cindy had found some tranquility in knowing why her body was acting the way it did. Many years later, I was able to see the journal she kept during those years. In her journal, as in her life, she focused on the positive. She'd even written, "When I get the test results, I'll be excited and I'll phone all my friends and have a party. I am quite confident it will not be negative news."

But now I understand why she could not bring herself to call us—or, probably, anyone—when she got the test results. That day, Cindy admitted in her journal, "I was devastated. It was like hitting rock bottom. I did feel like there were certain things happening in my life that hadn't ever really happened before to me yet I felt that I wasn't quite sure where it was coming from. Getting the results was a real blow."

Then she added something that made me so angry, I wanted to scream, though I shouldn't have been the least bit surprised. "When I spoke to my step-mum (Lucy), she said, 'Aw, hell, Cindy, it's not a big deal; I mean, we all have problems. We all have weird genes.' And I wrote my dad this long letter and I didn't hear from him. I ended up phoning him and talking to him myself. He never did really address it. That was before I went down there to visit. It's typical. It's nothing unusual. So I wasn't really overly surprised but I was hurt. Just for my dad or somebody to say they care, just 'How are you doing? Sorry to hear this or that with the results.'"

❧❧❧

At some point, Cindy and Rob went their separate ways; he was negative and temperamental, Cindy told us, which she did not need in her life. She moved in with friends and adopted a little terrier she named Kayla.

It wasn't long before the old wanderlust set in. I'd always felt she would travel until she couldn't walk anymore. When she called one evening in early June, she could hardly contain herself. "I'm going to Africa for five months. I'm so excited! I've always wanted to go there! I'll join a safari tour in Cairo and travel south to Sudan for four weeks; then I'll hop on another tour in Khartoum. I'll actually be on five tours and will end up in Cape Town." She hesitated. "I'm going to ask Dad for some money." Hearing that, my heart sank.

Boldly, she telephoned her dad, only to receive an earful of criticism. Undeterred, she scraped up some of the money and put the rest of the trip on credit cards. Look out, Africa! we thought.

We were happy to care for Kayla while she was gone. Every day when we pulled into the driveway after school, Vanessa would jump out and run to the mailbox, Kayla right behind her, barking. "Mommy, Mommy, here's another card from Aunt Cindy!" Holding the postcard high in the air, she would jump up and down, her face alight. "Look, there are tigers on it."

Both kids would listen closely as their aunt recounted her adventures and described the beauty of the countries she was visiting. Since Cindy's handwriting was barely legible, I improvised.

The 1995 Marin family picnic fell on September 6, John's forty-first birthday. Vanessa decorated the cake we'd made for her dad, though more frosting went into her mouth than onto the cake. I rejoiced again but not too strongly, knowing how quickly Cindy's symptoms had appeared when she was almost forty-two. We were sad and sorry that Marcia couldn't come with us; she had a fever and wasn't well. When relatives asked where she was, I stressed that she was sick and suggested they visit her; I had her telephone number if they wanted it.

When Cindy returned from her African safari, she looked much thinner, almost anorexic, and her gait was far more unsteady. She was her usual upbeat self, however, and we all loved hearing her tales about wild animals and camping in the wilderness. She stayed through Thanksgiving. When she returned to Canada at the beginning of December, she moved in with her friend Elizabeth, returned to the Huntington's support group, and plunged into volunteer work again.

And now, always willing to participate for the cause, she joined a clinical trial for a new medication. "There are two control groups," she explained on the phone, "one takes the real drug and the other takes a placebo. I began a daily regimen last week. I'm not sure which group I'm in, and it doesn't really matter, because I just want to be a part of the research. It seems like a good way for me to help and be involved in something positive.

"I hope the drug slows down symptoms. I haven't noticed any change other than it makes my teeth feel funny. I'm stumbling more, but I'm not in the greatest shape after sitting in a truck for five months. Kayla will get me back into shape with our long-distance walks each day."

30

By Christmas 1995, Lynne and Kathy had been caring for Marcia for three years, and it had worked out well. I'd had to fill in only a few times, when one was ill or something unexpected came up. Kathy, who spent the weekends with Marcia, had become more than a caregiver; she was almost a surrogate mother. She cared deeply for Marcia and was distraught over what was happening to her. Lynne, on the other hand, responded in a sarcastic manner when we asked about Marcia. She had gained a lot of weight and seemed unhappy, and was always on edge when we were around her.

Just after the first of the year, Kathy called to tell us some disturbing news. She had witnessed Lynne become angry with Marcia for not following her instructions. She'd even slapped and verbally abused her.

The next evening, we confronted Lynne. "Why have you become impatient with Marcia?" John asked. Lynne denied doing so, of course. She did say she believed Marcia had gotten lazy and was deliberately ignoring her.

"No, she's not!" I exclaimed. I shut my eyes for a moment to gain control. "It's the disease, Lynne. Her brain cells are dying. She can't make her body move the way she wants it to. She might not even understand what you're telling her."

Speaking more calmly than I could, John said, "Look, Lynne. You can't treat my sister this way. If you don't want to take care of her anymore, tell us right now, and we'll find someone else."

"Okay, I'm giving you my two weeks' notice."

John had had the sense to bring the contract with us. "No,

according to the contract you signed, you have to give us a month's notice."

We couldn't force her to stay, and I wasn't sure we wanted her caring for Marcia a moment longer, but we were in a jam. Lynne just shook her head no, and John gave in. "Okay, Lynne. Two weeks."

This forced us to evaluate Marcia's situation. I really didn't think it was possible to keep her safe at home any longer. I felt a residential-care facility for the elderly (RCFE) could provide the kind of help she required now. Such facilities were becoming more common, and Auburn had several. These facilities provide assistance with personal hygiene, dressing, eating, and walking. In some cases, because of dementia, Alzheimer's, or some other disability, the residents are unable to live by themselves but do not need twenty-four-hour nursing. They are not considered medical facilities and are not covered by insurance. In California, the average number of residents was fifteen.

The following week, with the help of a social worker at the hospital, I learned of a well-managed facility in south Auburn near Placer High School. A rehabilitation nurse, Vickie, who happened to work nights at Auburn Faith, owned and operated it. After a visit, John and I placed Marcia's name on a waiting list and fervently hoped the wait would not be long.

One of us stopped by Marcia's apartment every day, and Lynne was usually very nasty. That Friday, I was just about to leave my office when she called, and I knew whatever she had to say wouldn't be good. "I got a new job that starts on Monday, so I'm leaving tonight. I want my money for this week."

"Thanks a lot, Lynne. Marcia appreciates your sensitivity." After slamming the phone down, I called John and asked him to pick up Keith and Vanessa and meet me at the apartment. Suitcases packed, Lynne stood by the front door, glaring at us, with her hand extended, palm up. "Where's my money? I want to get out of here!" She didn't even say goodbye to Marcia.

After she left, John and I talked quietly at the kitchen table while the kids watched TV with their aunt. I could see the muscles in his jaw twitching. "What are we going to do now?" I said. "We can keep Marcia at our house this weekend, but after that, we don't have anyone to care for her. Kathy said she could help out for a couple of days, but she's got another job during the week."

John rubbed the back of his neck. "I don't know. We can't find a new person that quickly, and besides, the job will only be temporary."

Looking over my shoulder at Marcia, I steeled myself. "Our only choice is to place her in a skilled nursing facility until a space becomes available at Vickie's."

John walked to the kitchen counter and looked out the window. "I don't want to do that to her, Therese!"

I followed him, wrapping my arms around his waist and leaning against his back. "I know, but honey, we don't have another option. At least it's the weekend, and she can stay with us. You'll have time to tell her it's only temporary."

When he turned to face me, the sadness in his eyes just about killed me.

I whipped around to face into the living room. "Okay. Let's see. I'll pack some of her clothes. Why don't you pack up what's in the refrigerator and the medications? Somewhere in the kitchen is a record of when Lynne gave Marcia her meds last."

Marcia perked up a bit when she heard she was going home with us. John was very attentive that weekend, and he broke the news as gently as he could. Kathy stayed with Marcia on Monday while I made the arrangements at Hilltop Manor, off Highway 49 about six blocks from the hospital. I knew enough about the place to have reservations, to say the least, but it was the only local nursing facility that would take her.

The next morning, I had her admitted, and I returned at lunch to see how she was doing. Strapped in a chair with her helmet on, Marcia did not look happy. As I slid a beat-up chair next to her, a dirty bedpan below the bed of her comatose roommate caught my eye. Trying to sound upbeat, I said, "John will bring your TV set tonight and get it working for you."

I really hated that Marcia had had to be admitted into this nursing home, with its awful smells and overworked staff. Though she had enough money to pay a smaller, skilled nursing facility, with a higher staff-to-patient ratio, none of them would take a Huntington's patient. Each said its insurance provider wouldn't allow it, because HD patients are at such high risk of injuring themselves. Hilltop accepted Marcia on the condition she be restrained, in bed or in a chair, at all times. I thought of the words on Phyllis's death certificate: Death due to strangulation; underlying cause, Huntington's disease.

John and I visited together as often as possible: one to sit with her, the other to be her advocate with the staff. The adult Depends we supplied kept disappearing, which meant Marcia had to wear cloth diapers; on every visit, I had to remind the staff to change her. I brought more Depends, but they still didn't change her often enough, and it wasn't long before her skin broke down and bedsores developed on her coccyx.

Marcia had to endure these indignities until the end of

January, when Vickie broke her out of that dreadful place and drove her to her new home. At that time, Vickie's staff was caring for three men and two women—all, of course, elderly. The next weekend, when we took Keith and Vanessa to visit, we explained that older people lived there because it was unsafe for them to live alone any longer. Aunt Marcia also needed help, so she was going to live there, too.

❧❧❧

Not long after Marcia's move, John was due to leave for a weeklong skiing trip he'd planned with his buddies. They were staying at Taos Ski Valley, in Taos, New Mexico, where one of the lifts would take them to Kachina Peak, at 12,481 feet, the highest elevation on the North American continent that could be reached by a triple-chairlift. Two nights before, he'd been gathering his equipment in the garage when he came inside and said, "I've been thinking—with all that's been going on with Marcia, I think I'm going to cancel my ski trip, Therese. It's been hard on both of us, and I don't feel comfortable leaving you and the kids alone."

"Oh, no, John, you know Marcia wouldn't want you to do that. She's in a safe place now, and I'll talk to Vickie every day, since she doesn't know Marcia that well yet. Go and have fun!"

John must have had some kind of premonition, because two days into his vacation, he called me at work. "Therese, I'm in the hospital. I've got an obstruction and may have to have surgery." The strain and pressures of the past month had taken their toll, and for the first time in more than twenty-five years, his Crohn's disease had flared up.

I was soon on the phone with a Dr. Wilson, an internal-medicine and gastroenterology specialist at Holy Cross

Hospital in Taos, who suggested waiting a few days to see if the obstruction resolved on its own. I asked Dr. Cobalt's office to fax John's medical file to Dr. Wilson. Since Mom and Dad were eager to help with the children, I decided to fly out so that John wouldn't have to wait alone.

The next day, I arrived in New Mexico—without luggage, because United had lost my bag—and spent a week at Holy Cross next to John. Fortunately, he didn't need surgery and was discharged, fifteen pounds lighter, with instructions to see his doctor as soon as he got back.

❧❧❧

Now that Marcia was well taken care of, my life was easier and I worried less, because I had nothing to coordinate: All her needs were being met, and there was just one bill to pay each month. But I'd become almost panicky regarding Cindy's diagnosis and John's unknown gene status, which made it difficult to see Marcia now. The only way I could calm down was to limit my visits to about two or three a month. My guilt went into overdrive, but frankly, I had to concentrate on the positives in my life: my children, my work, and John.

One Friday night, after John got off the phone with Vickie, he told me, "Marcia had a bad week. Even though they're puréeing all her food and feeding her slowly, she's aspirated a lot. Vickie thinks she might be getting pneumonia."

I rolled my shoulders up and down in an effort to relieve the stress. "And of course, it's Friday, so if she continues to decline, we'll have to take her to the emergency room." I shook my head vehemently. "No, no. I'm going to be positive and pray she stays well."

"Me, too."

I grabbed the bourbon from the cabinet and made us each a drink. "But you know, her quality of life is so poor." I took a sip and handed him a glass. "I never thought I'd want someone to die, but I do want that for Marcia. My hope is that she can die peacefully and not suffer any longer."

As the year progressed, and the disease, my heart hurt every time I saw Marcia. Because her chorea was so hard to control, Dr. Cobalt was now prescribing Diazepam and Marinol, along with the Haldol she'd been taking, to try to control it. I was glad she was being well cared for, even though she couldn't engage with the people around her.

When I said something to John about his father not visiting, he replied, "I think Lucy doesn't want him to come. Remember, she's always been jealous of my sisters, afraid he would pay more attention to them than to her. That's such a joke, because he never gave us any attention even before he married her. Dad made his choice a long time ago, when he drove to Sacramento every weekend to see her. She always came first."

Knowing how angry their father's lack of concern made me, he added, "You know, Therese, my sisters and I didn't know any different. It really doesn't hurt, because we had no expectation of him ever changing."

Unlike her siblings, Cindy had strong opinions about her dad, and I agreed with her on most points. Once she returned to Canada after the African trip, she was unable to work, mostly because she was deteriorating cognitively, and filed for Canadian disability-retirement benefits. It wasn't enough to live on, and she had no savings and a hefty balance due on her credit card, so she called her father.

"Dad said it's a bad time to ask for help, because he has taxes to pay. I have heard that excuse for forty-four frickin' years! I asked him for a thousand dollars, and he was stunned and stopped talking—boy, that was a first! But it didn't last long. After a minute, he started up again with the criticism. He doesn't get it, so I said it loud and clear. 'Dad, I have Huntington's disease, just like Mom, Aunt Betty, Uncle Dennis and Uncle Ben, Lora, and Marcia. You need to help me.'"

"All right!" I cheered over the phone. "If anyone can put him in his place, it's you." I was elated when a check showed up in her mail a couple of weeks later. In fact, Cindy continued to ask and Big John sent money for the next six months. After that, he cut her off, and she began calling us for help. My usual phrase for Big John was "selfish son of a bitch."

Over the next year, Cindy lived her life as freely and intensely as possible. She drove to Auburn often, spent many weeks with us, and, having stayed close to her cousins Marie and Ann, made an effort to see them. But she devoted most of her time to Marcia. My admiration for Cindy's strength and dedication to her sister, knowing this was her destiny as well, grew exponentially.

Cindy stayed with us for a good part of the summer of 1996. Keith was twelve and Vanessa nine, and though we trusted them, they were still kids. We thought it was great that their vibrant aunt and her lively little dog would be with them while we were at work all day. The three were always up early, eating breakfast and raring to go, to fish in the ponds and explore the wetlands, creeks, pastures, and hidden trails of Christian Valley.

Cindy often shared how Huntington's was affecting her life, and I was grateful to hear the thoughts of at least one Marin. "I feel the disease is progressing slowly," she told me when she arrived that summer. "I'm thankful I don't have any physical pain, like people have with cancer. But I really miss hiking with my friends and riding my bike. Last month, I got on my bike to see how I'd do. I rode around Stanley Park pretty good for a while, but ended up in a ditch. A guy saw me fall and called an ambulance, and the primary-care paramedics patched me up. That was my last bike ride. My friends are all very considerate and I love them for it, but I miss doing stuff with them."

One night in bed, John shared another story about Cindy. "Once, when I was a sophomore and Cindy was a senior and, as usual, we were home alone for the weekend, Cindy decided to throw a party after the next football game. It was all over school that week. All Cindy's friends came over, and boy, did they party. I came home late that night and found a bunch of people sleeping everywhere. The floor was littered with beer cans, and the place reeked of weed.

"But the biggest shock was the peace sign burnt into the carpet in the front room. I panicked, knowing how Dad and Lucy would react. I remember staring at it, wondering what the heck to do. After a few minutes, I had an idea. I moved the couch, which still had people on it, cut a piece of carpet the exact size of the peace sign, and exchanged that piece for the burned one. Lo and behold, the problem was solved—you couldn't tell it was patched, because it was shag carpeting. A few years later, Lucy and Dad replaced the couch. You should have seen the expression on their faces when they saw the peace sign."

That Christmas, Cindy became friends with a professional photographer named Caroline. She had been commissioned by *Sunset* magazine to travel across the country taking pictures, and she invited Cindy to join her in her beat-up old van. Never one to turn down an opportunity to travel, Cindy accepted, under one condition: "Kayla comes along."

Cindy's ability to pick up and go, with only a backpack and a few dollars in her pocket, still amazed me. Their six-month journey began in April 1997, and once again, the mailbox was the chief object of attention each evening when the kids and I got home. Every time another postcard arrived, Keith and Vanessa ran straight for the United States map John had given them, to see where their adventurous aunt was now.

31

Huntington's patients don't die from the disease; they die from complications caused by the disease, such as choking, heart failure, anorexia, or an infection like pneumonia. Huntington's had besieged Marcia's body and mind for twelve years. It had been a brutal battle, and it seemed almost over. But Marcia held fast to life, even though at times I wondered why. The Marins came from strong stock, and if HD hadn't entered her life, she probably would have lived to a very, very old age.

Through the years, I counted it a blessing to have been led into hospice work, where I learned about the physical, psychological, and spiritual struggles that occur when someone is dying. During that time, I'd seen people hang on when their nurses couldn't explain how it was they were still alive. We all have a life force within us, and Marcia's instinct for survival was fierce.

But death cannot be forestalled forever. Marcia was in bed all the time now. Infections caused by using a catheter are common, and since her last infection, which just about did her in, Vickie, John, and I had all noted a sharp decline in her overall health. After one of his visits to monitor Marcia, Dr. Cobalt called to say, "I think Marcia is at end-stage Huntington's disease, Therese. It's time for hospice."

In order for a residential-care facility for the elderly to retain terminally ill residents and get them care from a hospice agency, it must have a facility-hospice-care waiver from the California Department of Social Services. John signed the admitting forms; Janet, the hospice nurse I worked with, evaluated Marcia; and Marcia was immediately admitted to hospice care. The next morning,

Janet came into my office. "I think you and John should know that Marcia has a condition called tachycardia, a rapid heart rate, which puts her at risk for cardiovascular disease. Vickie says that her heart rate has been like this since she moved in. If it continues, Marcia could have a cardio-vascular death."

My thoughts went immediately to my beloved and how he would take this new information.

I, of course, sought solace with my therapist. Constantly whispering in my ears, the demons were chipping away at my sanity. At each session, Pamela reiterated, "They are a manifestation of your fear, Therese."

Pamela had recently offered two techniques to lower my anxiety. The first was to make time each day—in my car, or at one of the kid's games, wherever and whenever—and take ten minutes, say, for worrying. I would worry, worry, worry during that time, and when the ten minutes was up, I wasn't to allow myself to worry anymore.

The second technique involved a folk ritual of Guatemala. Pamela gave me a small yellow wooden box containing four tiny, colorful dolls. In this folk tradition, children are meant to tell a worry to each doll before they go to bed. In the morning, the children feel their worries are gone, because the dolls have removed them. I worked at transferring my worries to the little dolls: The first would worry about Marcia; the second would worry about Cindy; the third would worry about John; and the last would worry about me, since I was about to throw myself in front of the nearest train. Pamela also tried to help me with meditation techniques, but it was difficult to find the time and privacy to use them.

In fact, none of the techniques was working that well. During my last session, I was sobbing with such intensity, I feared the outside world could hear me. Pamela let me cry for a few minutes and then asked gently, "What else is troubling you, Therese?"

Once my tears subsided, I said, "I'm so worried about John. He doesn't want to talk about Marcia's impending death, or the struggles Cindy is experiencing. I just don't know how he can be so stoic all the time. He never tells me how he's feeling."

"Therese, we have talked about this before. That's the way John copes. He internalizes it and detaches himself; he locks the pain away in a compartment of his brain so that he doesn't have to feel or address it."

"You're right, and I know it. But what he says drives me nuts! 'It is what it is, Therese. I can't do anything about it; I can't change it.'" I raised my hands. "Look at me. I'm a mess, and they aren't even my sisters."

❧❧❧

When John had come home from the conference in Hawaii a few years earlier, he'd promised to take us to one of those beautiful islands one day, and we started discussing it in early 1999. I was concerned about being so far away from Marcia, but John reassured me. We had to live our lives, he reminded me, and Marcia would want us to, and besides, she was being well taken care of.

That June, as we were literally packing the car to head to the San Francisco airport, the phone rang. Lucy had had a heart attack, Big John said, and she was undergoing bypass surgery. We stopped by the Kaiser hospital in Walnut Creek on our way to the airport, and John and I thought Lucy looked pretty good for someone who'd just had open-heart surgery. Her doctors felt she would make a full recovery.

We arrived on the big island, picked up our rental car, drove to our beautiful oceanfront condo, changed into our swimsuits, and headed straight to the beach. The temperature was a mild eighty degrees, with a cloudless blue sky and a luscious breeze, palm trees swaying in the wind. It was lovely and peaceful—just what my family needed. The next morning, John rented boogie boards for the week, and he and the kids went back to the beach. My job was to fill the condo's refrigerator with food for four, including a fifteen-year-old boy with a hollow leg.

That evening, Big John called, and we were shocked to hear that Lucy had died. John wanted to be with his father, so the next morning, we canceled our excursions, changed our return flight, and packed our bags. The kids understood that their grandfather needed his son, and John promised them we'd come back.

In Martinez, we found a despondent old man, utterly confused by this unexpected outcome. Over the next week, John's compassion toward his father was extraordinary. He notified Lucy's relatives in Texas, because his dad just couldn't make those calls. He helped make the funeral arrangements, at Oakmont Memorial Park & Mortuary, in Lafayette, where Lora was buried. Lucy hadn't wanted any kind of service, so the five of us and her son, Matthew, were the only people at the funeral home. Through all this, Keith and Vanessa were so thoughtful, never complaining, truly showing their grandfather what fine children they were. I hoped he noticed.

John was very concerned, because this man whom he'd never seen shed a tear was breaking down and crying every other minute. "I can tell Dad's going to have a hard time," he told me after the funeral. "Poor guy has lost two wives. It just doesn't seem fair."

This man whom I'd despised and loathed for years was crumbling before my eyes. There was a chink in his armor after all, and much to my surprise, seeing how much he'd loved Lucy made the ice around my heart soften just a bit.

We did all we could to support Big John that week. Carrying our bags to the car, John said, "Our door is always open, Dad, and we have an extra bedroom. You can come and stay as long as you like."

Two hours later, we drove into our garage, and everyone grabbed a suitcase and threw it into the family room with a thud. When I walked into the kitchen, the first thing I saw was the number thirteen flashing on the phone-message machine. John watched over my shoulder as I wrote the messages down. With only one left, we breathed a sigh of relief, only to gasp when we heard it. It was Vickie, and the call had come in that day. It was already ten p.m., so we agreed to call back first thing in the morning. I knew it couldn't be good news.

As soon as I opened my office door, I picked up the phone and called Vickie. "Oh, Therese, I'm so glad you guys are back. I hate to tell you this, but Marcia had a cardiovascular event yesterday, and the left side of her body is weak. I called hospice, and the weekend nurse came out. Dr. Cobalt said he would make a visit today. Can you and John come over?"

I knocked on my boss's door and explained the situation, telephoned John, and flew out the door and into my car. Feeling lightheaded, I found a paper bag in the glove compartment and breathed into it.

John and I pulled into the driveway at the same time, and as we walked up to the door, I slipped my hand in his and pulled him back. "Before we go inside, let's take a deep breath. We don't know what we'll find, and we need to be strong for Marcia."

That was easier said than done. Marcia was strapped into her wheelchair wearing a bib, as usual, but the left side of her face was drooping, and her left shoulder was lower than her right but continued to move involuntarily. My hand went over my mouth, and I had to turn away. Marcia was on the precipice of her humanity, whether she knew it or not, and I prayed for a painless transition. But Huntington's pushed on, destroying everything in its path, including Marcia's dignity and my hope that she could retain a vestige of it. All we could do was pray that her mind had shut down and she wasn't aware of the destruction of her body.

Day and night, the staff continued to lovingly care for Marcia. If there are angels on this earth, they were among them, holding her hand and encouraging her to leave this world. If anyone deserved a special place in heaven, it was Marcia.

❧❧❧

Three months later, John woke up with a gasp at two a.m. He sat straight up in bed, trying to catch his breath. Awakened by this swift, unexpected movement, I asked groggily, "What is it, hon? Are you all right?"

"Yeah, I think so. Sorry I woke you up." He slid out of bed and went into the bathroom.

A half-hour later, I found him sitting in the darkened living room, drinking a glass of water. Sometimes when John woke up in the middle of the night and couldn't go back to sleep, he'd watch TV for a while. But the television set wasn't on. I sat next to him, and he took my hand and rubbed it, smiling at me. "I had a dream about Marcia. We were in San Francisco, walking along Market Street, and she was smiling and laughing. It was like old times. She told me she was all right now."

Just as we lay our heads back on our pillows, the phone rang. It was Vickie, crying. "Marcia died a little while ago. She finally let go."

John said, "We'll be right over. Please call hospice and Dr. Cobalt." We woke Keith, told him where we were going, and assured him we would be home before six.

Once Marcia had been taken to the funeral home, we hugged Vickie and the others who had taken such good care of her and thanked them. We were just about to leave when a thought occurred to me. "What time did Marcia die?"

"It was around two," Vickie replied. "I checked on her at one-forty-five, and she was alive."

John's eyes met mine as we realized Marcia had come to say goodbye to her brother before her soul took flight.

Marcia Louise died at two a.m. on September 8, 1999, two days after John's forty-fifth birthday. The main cause of death was cardiopulmonary failure, with Huntington's as the underlying factor. She was forty-nine years old.

Marcia gave John an extraordinary present, and I was grateful to have been witness to it. With all my being, I believed this powerful experience was a gift, because it renewed the hope I thought I had lost.

❧❧❧

I drove Keith and Vanessa to school, then stopped by my office and took the rest of the week off. As soon as I got home, I called Lassila Funeral Chapels, in Auburn, with instructions not to cremate Marcia until I could arrange for a pathologist to take a brain-tissue sample to send to the Harvard Brain Tissue Resource Center, at McLean Hospital, affiliated with Harvard Medical School. Research over the past decade had shown that studying human brain tissue was essential to increasing our understanding of how the nervous system functions. Most recently, postmortem human brain research had played a significant role in the development of the genetic test for Huntington's disease, as well as in a treatment for Parkinson's disease.

Years earlier, I'd read an article about the center in the Huntington's Disease Society newsletter, and when I'd shown it to Marcia, she hadn't hesitated when asked if she wanted to participate. Carrying out her wishes provided a measure of comfort, knowing that something positive could come out of this tragedy.

That afternoon, John made the dreaded phone calls to his family, and soon Cindy was on a plane. His father, now seventy-nine years old, showed up at our door that evening with a suitcase, food, and boxes in hand.

John had made it clear to me that he didn't want to share Marcia's goodbye gift with anyone in the family. I respected his wishes but told my hospice coworkers about it at our next interdisciplinary-team meeting. This amazing experience, I felt, was important to share.

Our children had grown up watching us care for their aunt, so it was doubly important to include them in our preparations to celebrate Marcia's life. We designed a storyboard with the photographs their grandfather had brought, and Vanessa added an artist's flare. The sound of laughter filled the room as Big John and the kids heard their father's stories about Marcia and the mischief she'd gotten into. Lucy had been dead just a couple of months, and I was glad that despite his heartbreak, Big John could laugh at John's tales.

Marcia's celebration of life was held three days after her death, at Lassila Funeral Chapels; she would be interred at a later date at Oakmont Memorial Park & Mortuary, in one of the four spaces Big John had purchased, next to Lucy. Fifty folding chairs sat in the middle of the small room we'd reserved; a little waterfall provided a peaceful backdrop.

A friend and coworker, Thomas Nadelin, our chaplain, led the service. Tom had been the hospice chaplain for five years, providing spiritual guidance to terminally ill patients, in their homes if they desired. As bereavement-services coordinator, he communicated with the families of our hospice patients for a year after their death. An excellent writer, Tom wrote a book, *Griefland*, which he self-published in 2011. One Amazon reviewer called it "the best book I've read so far about the grieving process."

In his positive way, Tom began with kind words and encouragement. I started crying the minute the ceremony began, knowing in my heart they were not tears of sorrow. I was determined to speak and had asked John to help me through it. When it was my turn, he lovingly took my hand and walked with me to the podium. Knowing my husband's love for his sister, I also spoke for him, since he was unable to verbalize his feelings.

Looking out at the familiar faces of my parents, my sisters, my children, and so many members of the Marin family, I pushed through my tears. John continued to hold my hand, and his body trembled with emotion.

"Marcia was one of the sweetest people I've ever known. How I wish her life had been different. We supported her through the years, dealing with delicate subjects and situations. She was such a sweetheart, always giving us a look of gratitude that tugged at our hearts. I watched her with awe and wonder, because she never complained or uttered words of anger. She never cursed God for her fate and accepted her destiny.

"It's amazing, the strength she had, day after day, year

after year. Huntington's slowly took control of her body and mind, but Marcia kept up the fight to the very end. She was so brave, with the strength and tenacity of a thousand people. I'm a better person for having known her; I'm blessed to have had her in my life. She taught me many lessons about love, acceptance, and courage."

After I spoke, her cousin Marie shared stories of her relationship with Marcia over the years. Cindy stood up and told the story of John and Marcia visiting her in 1976, when she lived in a rustic cabin and her stylish sister had to wear tennis shoes and make coffee on a wood stove. She didn't shed tears until she sat down and then quickly wiped them away.

I looked at Big John, sitting next to her, and saw a broken man. When I considered the magnitude of the losses he'd suffered—first Phyllis, then Lora, now Lucy and, so soon after, Marcia—my anger subsided and compassion entered my heart again. Maybe it had just been too hard to visit Marcia after watching Phyllis's terrible decline, and he simply couldn't muster the strength to face Huntington's again. In my hospice work, I'd interacted with many families after the death of a loved one, and it made me wonder how much grief and loss one person could bear.

All were invited to our house for lunch, and I was glad to be busy, arranging the lasagna, garlic bread, Caesar salad, and brownies on the dining room table and making sure everyone had something to drink. Mom could see how my shoulders sagged from the heavy loss, how interacting with everyone exhausted me. She made sure everyone had food and drink and pushed me into my bedroom to relax for a few minutes.

When the doorbell rang, I knew it was Janet, owner of Doves of White, in Colfax, delivering a cage full of beautiful birds. I had used doves in bereavement events that Tom and I organized and loved the peaceful feeling they created as they took flight. I sat the cage on the living room floor and listened to their soothing sound for a while.

Once everyone had finished eating, I carried the doves into the backyard, and John said a few words. "We are going to miss you, Marcia. But we're happy you're finally free." Slowly, I opened the cage and released these divine white creatures into the clear blue sky. They circled several times, flying in formation, and then took off toward their home.

I closed my eyes, thinking of Marcia and praying her homecoming in heaven was sweet, with relatives surrounding and welcoming her. The atmosphere in the yard changed—became peaceful, hopeful—and my family embraced.

Later that day, I watched my husband and his remaining sister, and my mind reeled. Unlike John and Cindy, I'd cried a river, and I knew my river was nowhere near dry.

32

*E*ach time we saw Cindy, she had lost more weight and muscle mass. The eternal optimist, Cindy always said, "I think losing weight was a good thing." Though I dearly loved her, I was thankful she lived in Canada; whenever she told us she was coming to visit, the demons assaulted my dreams.

Just after the new century began, we got a call from Elizabeth, Cindy's best friend for twenty-five years. She was a strong and independent woman who loved life and adventure as much as Cindy did. Cindy had been living with her for the past three years, paying no rent, and when Elizabeth telephoned, crying, we knew it was serious.

When John got off the phone, he was rubbing the back of his neck, always a sign of distress. "What's going on, John?"

"She's really worried about Cindy," he said, and his face told me that things were getting very bad very quickly. "She can't fix her meals any longer. Elizabeth has to help her shower, and she has a lot of bruises and cuts from the falls she's taken. And every day when she goes out with Kayla, she's afraid Cindy's going to get hit by a car, or something worse." He took a deep breath. "She thinks we should move her back here."

John talked with his father, explaining how it made sense for Cindy to live with him, now that he was alone in a four-bedroom house. After several heated discussions, Big John conceded.

John made an unannounced visit to British Columbia and convinced his sister she should move back to California. He and Elizabeth packed up Cindy's belongings and shipped them to Martinez; Elizabeth hugged her faithful friend, said a tearful goodbye, and promised to visit; and John, his sister, and Kayla flew home. I believe Cindy left without a fight because it was her loving brother and childhood pal who had come to her rescue.

Over the next few weeks, we waited to hear about the new living arrangements, unsure they would work out. Much to our surprise, the once-neglectful father not only accepted Kayla, he doted on his daughter and tried to make her life as comfortable as possible. Big John bought his rebel daughter new clothes and shoes and stocked the refrigerator with the foods she enjoyed. He had a second cable-TV outlet installed in Cindy's room. They saw Aunt Faye and Uncle Jack, who still lived in Martinez, and went for drives; her cousins Marie and Ann came to visit. Now that Lucy was gone, it appeared, Big John's heart had room to embrace and love the daughter he had asked his sister Jessica to care for so long ago.

I believe Cindy was as happy as she could be considering the circumstances. Once she settled in, she reconnected with a high school girlfriend with whom she had stayed in touch over the years. Divorced, with two preteen daughters, Maria lived in Lafayette and owned a beauty salon. The two got together once a month, and Maria cut and styled Cindy's hair.

The next thing we knew, Cindy called to tell us, "I'm going to France with Maria next month! She has to take her girls to France each year to visit their father and invited me to tag along. Isn't it great?"

Then Big John called. I wanted to hang up on him, because yelling accomplished nothing and he was furious. "She's got no money. What is she thinking? I swear to God, she never changes. She's always been like this, irresponsible!"

We decided it was best to stay out of it, and by the end of the week, Cindy let us know her dad was paying for the trip.

❧❧❧

Big John and Cindy visited us often, and each time, we noticed a little more deterioration in Cindy's speech and cognition. It was truly painful seeing this once buff, active woman reduced to a frail-looking, hundred-pound being who couldn't walk in a straight line. They always arrived early on Saturdays. Keith, now in eleventh grade, and Vanessa, in eighth, loved seeing them with their Grandma and Grandpa Crutcher in the stands, cheering them on as their teams competed. Aunt Cindy's movements were reminiscent of Marcia's, and Vanessa shied away from her, so we let her spend as much time as she wanted with her best friend, who lived across the street. On Sundays, John raked leaves and fixed things around the house with his dad. Cindy sat at the kitchen table and talked as I fixed meals and baked goodies.

During those times, I saw a change in Big John. He was not as talkative; he listened more and even tenderly touched my arm when he spoke to me. John smiled a lot when his dad and Cindy stayed with us.

But in 2002, Big John was diagnosed with bladder cancer. Smoking causes about half of all bladder cancer in both men and women—smokers are at least three times as likely to develop the disease as nonsmokers—and Big John had smoked for sixty-seven years. The tumor was surgically removed; Big John endured a round of intravesical chemo-therapy; and his cancer went into remission.

Thanksgiving 2003 was truly a day for giving thanks. In

September, John had turned forty-nine and, as Dr. Cobalt had explained to me years earlier, was now on the down side of the bell curve; at this point, the chance of his developing symptoms of Huntington's was very low. Big John's cancer was still in remission. I'd let go of my anger at him for rarely seeing his grandchildren when they were young and appreciated that he was here now, witnessing them grow into kind, loving, generous, talented young people whom he could be proud of.

Keith was a freshman at Menlo College, on the San Francisco Peninsula in Atherton, studying business management and a tight end on the collegiate football team. Our son now stood six-foot-three and weighed two hundred forty-five pounds. Vanessa, a high school sophomore, loved her art, calculus, and physics classes at Bear River High School, in Grass Valley. John had been administrative officer to the county board of supervisors for fourteen years; I considered him a walking encyclopedia on Placer County. I'd been at Auburn Faith Community Hospital (now owned by Sutter Health) for twelve years, and had become the face of hospice in our community.

The Sunday after Thanksgiving, Keith and Vanessa were in the front yard with their grandfather, raking up piles of fallen leaves—John was hauling wheelbarrels full of them down to the creek—as Cindy sat in the garage with Kayla, watching the activity. I was inside making turkey soup.

Hearing laughter, I peeked out the kitchen window, then put on a sweater and stepped outside. "Lunch is ready!" I yelled.

I stopped short at the chair in which Cindy had been sitting. "Hey, guys, where are Cindy and Kayla?" Everyone shrugged, and my heart skipped a beat. "We have to start looking for her!"

John said, "We'd better split up. Keith, you go with Grandpa, and Vanessa, you come with Mom and me."

I was really upset, because the roads around our house were very hilly; Cindy could easily lose her balance and roll off the road into some brush. Just as I was turning to run inside and turn off the stove, a sheriff's car pulled into our driveway, with Cindy and Kayla in the back seat. The sheriff got out and asked, "Does this woman live here?"

John quickly opened the back door and helped Cindy out. "Yes, she's my sister."

"We got a call from a resident in the area complaining a drunk, homeless woman was wandering the streets of Christian Valley." Unfortunately, Cindy did look drunk when she walked, because she weaved and tripped so often, and she had obviously fallen, because her clothes, now way too big for her, were torn and dirty.

Even so, I muttered, "How insensitive can people be?" as I put my arm around her. "She has Huntington's disease. She's not going to hurt anyone. If anything, I'd be worried someone would take advantage of her."

"Ma'am, I'm just responding to a citizen's request to look into a possible homeless person walking around this neighborhood."

I looked over at my children, sorry they had to witness this.

The incident set off a conversation that night between John and his father. Big John was already concerned, because Cindy was unable to feed herself anymore, which had been apparent at Thanksgiving dinner, and was having bouts of incontinence. With the constant moving of her body, she couldn't keep weight on. He'd been feeding her Boost with ice cream, but she was exhibiting the same swallowing problems Marcia had and choked often.

Cindy had been living with her father for more than three

years, and I gave him a lot of credit, because he had come through when she needed him. But the assistance she required now was too much for an eighty-two-year-old man, in part because it involved very personal tasks. The inevitable was becoming a reality. Big John wanted to move her into the residential-care facility for the elderly that Marcia had lived in, saying he would pay for her care. He had never visited Marcia when she lived there, but he promised he would not ignore Cindy.

The next day, I called Vickie and put Cindy on the waiting list. Another nightmare had begun: John's precious sister, the only one left, was entering a turbulent time, and the momentum couldn't be stopped. Knowing Vickie and her staff would tenderly care for Cindy until her death was the only comfort we would gain from placing her there.

❧❧❧

By spring 2004, when Vickie called with an opening, Cindy had been dealing with HD for almost ten years. The plan was for Big John to bring her to Auburn without telling her she'd be moving. It would be heartrending news, of course, and to top it all off, her beloved Kayla couldn't go with her. I prepared a nice dinner, and John explained the situation as gently as he could.

Cindy was not happy but didn't argue. We all drove her to her new home, where Vickie welcomed her with open arms. As we were about to leave, she grabbed her brother's hand and pulled on it. "John, when do I get to go back to Dad's?" She swallowed hard. "Or is this going to be permanent?"

None of us had the nerve to tell her the truth. John hesitated and then said, "Let's see how it goes."

John visited regularly, usually at lunchtime, although it

was difficult to see his much-loved sister continue to decline. I visited once a week, but slowly had to back off. Even though John would soon turn fifty, the demons were deep in my psyche, and I could not dismiss them. It seemed to me that my body had gotten used to functioning on high alert, adrenaline pumping through my veins. It was stuck in high gear. Peggy suggested we meet twice a week.

Cindy was still ambulatory and used to being active, not cooped up in a house all day, so she accompanied Vickie on errands a few times a week. One day, Vickie took Cindy to Curves, an exercise franchise in Auburn, while she worked out, and it wasn't long before she asked John if Cindy could join. "She really wants to exercise. I'll be right next to her the whole time, and we'll work out together. I think it will make her feel better. She's told me she hates the fact that she's lost so much muscle mass."

John and I wanted Cindy's life to have the highest quality possible, and we paid for her membership.

When Marcia had lived at Vickie's, we knew not to visit at three o'clock, because that's when her favorite TV program, *The Oprah Winfrey Show*, was on. At three o'clock, if the television wasn't set on the right channel, she'd make a lot of noise. Vickie had talked of taking Marcia to Chicago to watch a taping of the show, but it never happened. Cindy was just as enthusiastic about Oprah, and Vickie wanted to take her. I guess the wanderlust sister was destined to go on one more adventure, because once again, Big John surprised us and agreed to finance the trip. Marie went along to help, and that fall, the three flew off to Chicago for three days.

When they returned, Vickie told us how giddy Cindy had been on the plane. In the studio, they'd been allowed to sit in the front row, and after the show, Cindy got to shake Oprah's hand.

Big John was still smoking two packs a day, and in the fall of 2004, his cancer returned with a vengeance.

"Well, John," his oncologist said, "I told you last year if you stopped smoking, you could have a few more years. Since you haven't done that, the cancer has recurred. We can try chemo again, but I'd rather remove your bladder. That way, the cancer can't spread."

"No way!" Big John barked. "I'll be damned if I'm going to carry a bag of piss around with me. You just give me something to manage the pain, and let's do the chemo again."

After the appointment, Big John was leaning against the car, smoking a cigarette, when John caught up to us. "Dad, come on. What did the doctor just say?"

His father dropped the cigarette on the asphalt and stepped on it. "Oh, to hell with him. I'm not going to quit cold turkey. Maybe I'll cut down."

The side effects of the chemotherapy treatments he'd had two years earlier had been troublesome, and he did not want to go through it again. Even so, Big John had the chemo treatments, and the cancer went into remission again. But the side effects didn't allow him to venture far from home.

With all this, John's stomach started bothering him, and one morning in early December, his color looked bad. I made our usual egg sandwiches and handed him one. "Thanks, hon, I'm not hungry."

I hadn't been at work long and was in a meeting when the office receptionist entered the conference room and whispered in my ear. I excused myself and answered the phone. "Therese, I'm in the Auburn Faith emergency room."

That's where I found John lying on a gurney, doubled over

in pain and sweating profusely. "Oh, my God!"

When Dr. Cobalt entered, he pressed on John's belly as John stomped his foot hard on the gurney. "I'm going to give you some morphine, then we need to get Dr. Smith in here right away. I'm sure it's the Crohn's flaring up."

To watch the man I love in this state was almost more than I could bear. The morphine helped a little, and after Dr. Smith, John's internal-medicine physician, ordered an x-ray, he examined him again. "You know, John, when I did your colonoscopy last month, I couldn't get through the site of the surgery area. I'm afraid there's lots of scar tissue in that spot, and it's created a blockage. We're going to have to cut it out and reattach the intestines. I'm going to call Dr. Acosta and get him over here for a surgical consultation."

Dr. Acosta didn't waste any time, and John had surgery that night. Even though I'd worked at this hospital for thirteen years, I'd never spent any time in one of our waiting rooms. Three hours later, I was pacing up and down a cold, sterile room and wringing my hands when Dr. Acosta, still in his surgical gown, came to tell me all had gone well. Keith and Vanessa appeared just as I collapsed into a chair.

For the next few days, my mornings began with a visit to John's room. I checked on him at lunchtime and again before heading home; Vanessa stopped by most afternoons. On the fourth morning, Dr. Acosta was examining the surgery site when I arrived, John wincing with every touch. "I'm afraid you have an infection, John. We've got to clean it out and put you on stronger antibiotics. I'm sorry, but you're going to have to stay a few more days."

After twenty-four years, sleep did not come easily without John lying next to me. I drifted off thinking that watching his father dying and Cindy wasting away had been too much for him—too much for any human to bear. Internalizing his emotions all his life had compounded the damage that fear was doing to his body.

John remained upbeat and, naturally, did not want to discuss why his Crohn's had escalated to the point of necessitating surgery. Once he was released, Virginia, a home-health nurse I worked with, was scheduled to come to the house to pack and dress the wound. Since she wouldn't be coming every day, she taught me how to do it. "Ew, Mom," Vanessa said, observing me perform the task. "I could never be a nurse or a doctor."

A few days after he returned home, a flat-screen television was delivered to our front door. "It's from Dad!" John exclaimed. "Can you believe it?"

❧❧❧

It's funny how things work out sometimes. When Cindy had moved to Auburn, Kayla had had to stay behind with Big John. He wasn't too happy about it, but he'd come to love that dog. She was a great companion to him, just as she'd been to Cindy. But one day, Kayla died, and when Big John called to tell us, he was more upset than we'd ever dreamed he would be.

John knew the news would break his sister's heart. Indeed, she sobbed when he told her, and her reaction left me confused. "You know, John, in all the years I've known Cindy, this is only the second time I've seen her cry. The first was when she divorced Brad. Now it's over a dog." After all this time, I still didn't understand.

33

In the spring of 2005, Placer County built a modern new building and created the Community Development Resource Agency, which would regulate land use and development in the unincorporated area of Placer County and had offices in both Auburn and the Tahoe area. John was asked to be its director. It meant a huge increase in salary, because he'd be overseeing divisions that covered building services, code enforcement, engineering and surveying, environmental coordination, geographic-information systems, and planning services. The hot new electronic device then was the BlackBerry, and John had his with him at all times, even texting and answering calls at Vanessa's high school water polo games.

My job was changing, too; I'd added eight hours dedicated to Auburn Faith Foundation philanthropic events to my busy week and had already planned two events a year for the hospice program. I told John I didn't know how I could get everything done, but I persevered.

Big John didn't get out much anymore, due to incontinence and pain, but he talked to Vickie often on the phone. John and I visited Cindy during the week, usually at lunch, because we were involved in the college-admission process with Vanessa and touring college campuses in California on weekends.

In December, my heart experienced another assault: My mother was diagnosed with brain cancer, which had metastasized from her lungs. She had never smoked, so Dad and my sisters and I were shocked to learn this. According to her doctor, she had twelve tumors floating around in her brain and had, at most, six months to live.

Mom was so important to me, and I wanted to support my father and help with her care, so I requested a leave of absence. She was admitted into the Roseville hospice program, and we got a hospital bed set up in her living room, from which she could participate in everyday life. The following May, we had another blow: My father received a diagnosis of advanced prostrate cancer.

Though I struggled with these impending losses, the time off allowed me to be involved in many of Vanessa's senior-year activities. I found it difficult, however, to switch modes: one minute with my dying mother, the next watching my daughter play soccer or try on her graduation gown. Most of the time, I just felt numb. Recognizing my struggle, especially since most days I was in Citrus Heights with my mother, my wonderful daughter was a great help at home. And her excitement about graduating and heading off to college lightened my spirits.

As graduation day approached, Mom declined dramatically, so I planned Vanessa's graduation party from her house. It was good for both of us. The day of the party promised to be warm and clear. John, Vanessa, and I were up early to decorate around the pool and set up. When my parents arrived, Mom was in her wheelchair, with deep, dark circles that looked as if they'd been painted on under her eyes, and bald as an eagle, with a bow around her head. She hugged Vanessa as hard as she could.

"Congratulations, sugar. I'm sorry I didn't make the graduation ceremony last night. I wanted to get here before everyone arrived to tell you I love you." She wiped away a tear. "I'll probably have to leave in about an hour. Enjoy your day."

I was so glad she was able to sit on the deck and watch the festivities, with my father at her side. Three days after the party, Mom slipped into a coma. We thought this was it, until she opened her eyes two days later and said, "I'm hungry."

But the disease continued stealing her from us, until by the first of July, she was paralyzed and having grand mal seizures. After a few more days, she drifted back into a coma, and we took turns staying with her. Cleo Rita (McKibben) Crutcher died, with her family by her side, at five p.m. on July 19, 2006. She was seventy-six years old. My father, who was to start eight weeks of radiation treatments the following month, cried as he held my mother's hand.

❧❧❧

Vanessa had been accepted into California State University, San Diego, where she planned to major in engineering. Both our children were excellent at math, and Vanessa excelled in the sciences and was good with a hammer and nails, so we weren't surprised when she showed an interest in civil engineering. SDSU is the third-oldest state university in the twenty-three-member California State University system. Founded in 1897, it is the largest institution of higher education in San Diego County. It was a long way from home, but she'd long dreamed of attending a college near the beach. In mid-August, the three of us took a road trip to move her into the dorm, and in many ways, it was a wonderful distraction.

With the complicated grief I was experiencing, though, I felt mired in the land of sorrow. While we were immensely proud of our daughter, her leaving for college meant another kind of loss for John and me, one for which the term "empty-nest syndrome" is completely inadequate. It was yet another layer of heartache.

Complicated grief is different from general grief. Most of the time, we figure out how to live our lives without our loved one—a way that makes it possible to experience joy and satisfaction again, to find purpose and meaning. Our grief hasn't vanished, but it is reshaped, transformed, and integrated, so it becomes part of the background of our lives. Complicated grief entails certain kinds of thoughts, feelings, and behavior that derail this natural healing process. People with complicated grief often feel stuck, their pain as intense as it was at the beginning.

I tried to see my return to work as a good thing. I never regretted being intimately involved in my mother's care for six months, nor having taken so much time off, but the experience left me feeling like a different person. My job had meant so much to me, and now I questioned whether I could work in hospice any longer.

I was due to return to work on Monday, September 9, 2006. I'd called my boss to ask her to lunch, a way of thanking her for letting me take the leave of absence. She never returned my phone call. When I arrived that morning, carrying photographs for my desk, she informed me that my position had been eliminated. The hospital needed to tighten up on spending, she told me, and was eliminating twenty-five middle-management positions. Although I'd had mixed feelings about returning to work, it was a blow to learn, and in such a cold, abrupt way, that the job I'd loved and done diligently for fifteen years had vanished.

I'm not sure how I made it home. I sat in the driveway staring over the steering wheel for a long time; just opening the car door and walking into the house seemed impossible. This loss, on top of the rest, took me to a depth of despair I'd never reached before.

A colleague of mine had seen me leaving the hospital,

crying, my arms full of stuff I'd just carried in. She had telephoned John, and he came home to find me on the bed in a fetal position, sobbing. I felt trapped in what my friend Tom called Griefland, and I'd lost the map that would show me the way out. I stared blankly at my best friend, husband, and lover as his arms wound tightly around me.

Over the next few months, John encouraged me to retire, reminding me that I'd worked since I was sixteen years old. Before I could even consider it, I reviewed our finances. Thanks to my diligent saving all these years, and the fact that John would have a fine retirement plan whenever he stopped working for Placer County, I felt secure enough to take his advice.

By then, Cindy had been living in Vickie's residential-care facility for the elderly for two years. She was seriously anorexic, bedbound with a catheter; she couldn't communicate and didn't engage with people anymore. One evening in late November, John said, "I hate seeing her like this. She's living her worst nightmare! She wouldn't want to live this way if she could have any say in it. I wish she could die right now, this minute."

I remembered a comment Cindy had made years earlier, telling me that when she could no longer do the things she loved to do, she would climb a mountain and jump off, because she didn't want to be a burden and die like Marcia had. Secretly, I wished she had followed through.

No matter what was going on in our lives, I was always happy when I was with my children. Christmas came and went, and my kids went back to college. After the first of the year, Dr. Cobalt suggested it was time for Cindy to have hospice care: Another sister had reached end-stage Huntington's disease. I was bracing myself for another loss, and I knew John was, too.

❧❧❧❧

I had been struggling with pain in my left hip for four years. I'd been only forty-six—young, by most standards, for a hip problem—when it began. Four orthopedic surgeons had been unable to offer more than a few guesses as to what was wrong. During my last two years of work, the pain had been so horrendous when I put weight on that leg that I'd resorted to using a cane and then crutches. Now I could hardly walk.

Finally, I was diagnosed with hip impingement, a malformation of the ball-and-socket joint that I'd had since birth. The ball-like top of the thighbone fits into a cuplike area in the pelvis, much like a ball fits into a baseball glove; normally, the ball glides smoothly within the socket, but in my case, either the ball or the socket rim had long interfered with a smooth motion. This caused early osteoarthritis of the hip, and now it was my turn for surgery. That January, I had a total hip replacement.

Less than a week later, Vickie called to inform us that state auditors had shown up unannounced and said they needed to talk to one of us that day. I pushed for more information, but all Vickie told me was that they were focused on Cindy. John went as soon as he could, as I sat in the house, worrying.

He was terribly upset when he got home. The auditors had informed him that Cindy didn't meet the criteria required to live in a residential-care facility for the elderly, and we had seven days to move her out. "We made it perfectly clear to Vickie last November," one of the auditors told him, "that your sister didn't meet the criteria and the facility didn't have a hospice waiver."

John and I worked fast. Even though I was still recuperating, I contacted the Auburn Faith hospice program and talked with the social worker there, Jean, a former colleague of mine. I called Dr. Cobalt to request a letter describing Cindy's medical condition and a copy of his referral to hospice. Then I prepared a letter for the state licensing board, explaining Cindy's situation and asking for approval of the hospice waiver Vickie had requested. Jean agreed to write a letter stating that Cindy was under hospice care.

John and I didn't want to think about moving Cindy, but we had to be realistic and find a place to take her if our plea was unsuccessful. Jean began searching for a skilled nursing home nearby but had bad news. "Therese, no facility in Auburn will take Cindy. Nursing homes will take only so many Medi-Cal patients, because of the low reimbursement, and she's such a high-risk patient. I'm looking in the greater Sacramento area right now, but it doesn't look good."

John gathered the letters from Dr. Cobalt and Jean and a copy of Vickie's application for the hospice waiver. He sent the package via overnight mail, and the auditor called him the next day. "We are still denying her approval to stay there, because they allowed your sister to live there without a hospice waiver. We'll grant your family a thirty-day extension to place her somewhere else."

Meanwhile, the only skilled nursing facility willing to admit Cindy was in Lodi, in San Joaquin County, some seventy miles away. Jean thought the state auditors might reconsider if they knew that Cindy's immediate family lived in Auburn and that she was dying, so John called the auditor handling the case. In the end, they approved the hospice waiver and allowed Cindy to stay so long as she was receiving hospice care.

John and I were very angry with Vickie and the position she had put Cindy in. After we cooled off, John had a talk with her. "We need to know when there's an issue concerning Cindy," John told her. "We pay you to take care of her and trust your facility is following all the rules."

In a few months, I was back on my feet, and I started visiting Cindy in the morning, after my Pilates class. The kids were my favorite topic. Sometimes I'd sit in silence, reading a book while I held her hand. Huntington's affects people in diverse ways. Cindy's symptoms were very different from her sister's. Marcia's body had been moving constantly, and no drug on this planet could stop it. Cindy lay motionless in her bed; only when she tried to move did her body respond with a spastic motion. There was no interaction between us. I desperately searched for a glimmer in her eyes, but they remained vacant and lifeless.

Surprisingly, there was a calmness about her, and when I was with her, a tranquil mood filled the room. I believe positive, cheerful Cindy continued to give to those she loved.

❦❦❦

In May, Keith graduated from Menlo College with a bachelor of science degree in business management. He moved into an apartment with a college buddy, worked two part-time jobs, and waited to hear from the University of San Francisco, where he'd applied to study for a master's degree in its sport-management program. After Vanessa's first year of college, she came home for the summer and worked as an engineering intern with the Community Development Resource Agency, where her dad was director.

John was fifty-two years old and my demons had abated, so when he talked about purchasing a fifth-wheel trailer and new truck, I didn't flinch. A fifth-wheel trailer is a towable RV that connects to a truck by way of a special fifth-wheel hitch. My parents had had one for years and traveled all over the country in it. John took me to a RV show, and when I walked into one, I was amazed. Campers now had slide-outs, sometimes referred to as expanding rooms, and it created twice the space. It was like pulling a little house behind you. We invited the kids on our first adventure, to Graeagle, surrounded by the majestic Sierras about a three-hour drive from Auburn.

Despite the joy in our lives, it was hard watching both Cindy and Big John decline: Cindy confined to a hospital bed, the TV constantly blaring, and Big John housebound. Big John called Vickie often, and Vickie would place the phone at Cindy's ear so that she could listen to her father's voice.

By Thanksgiving, Big John's cancer had progressed, and he now suffered from colon cancer. Again, he declined surgery. John and I began going to Martinez at least two weekends a month. While John and his dad talked, I'd clean the house when he wasn't looking, careful not to hurt his pride, or cook. Big John shared many stories his children had never heard. I even found him open to questions about Phyllis and their early years together.

I loved hearing how a justice of the peace in Carmel had married them, in November 1947. Big John spoke to his son in a small voice, his eyes glistening with tears, as he proclaimed the love he had felt for John's mother and wished their lives could have been different. He bent over as if in pain when he recalled what he now knew were early symptoms of HD. "It wasn't too long after we got married that I'd come home from work and she'd be crying, because she'd dropped and broken several plates that day. When she couldn't remember where she'd put things in the house, she'd become terribly agitated. I didn't know what was happening to her or why."

At Christmas, when Keith was home from the Bay Area and Vanessa from San Diego, we took Christmas dinner to their grandfather. On that happy occasion, he shared black-and-white photographs of his time in the Philippines. I'd never seen photographs of Big John as a young man. In one, he was holding a mango the size of a small watermelon; he remembered eating it while the men were awaiting new orders. Some of the photos were gruesome: Filipino men holding the severed heads of their Japanese enemies. And the general conditions he described were terrible. Their wool uniforms, for instance, were made for fighting in Europe, not in the tropics, and their wool socks led to fungal infection or foot rot. The kids were properly impressed.

On every visit, Big John reinforced his wish to remain independent in his own home as long as he could. He also made it clear he wanted no heroic measures taken. "I've got two cancers that cannot be cured. I'm eighty-four years old and made the decision not to have surgery. So don't let them cut on me when it's the end."

❧❧❧

Hospice was keeping Cindy as comfortable as possible, but her gag reflexes were impaired and she was choking often, as Marcia had. She couldn't have weighed more than eighty pounds by then; she looked like a skeleton.

Having worked in hospice for ten years, I'd learned that as one's metabolism starts shutting down, the body no longer builds tissues and organs. This is called an anabolic state of metabolism. When the tissues and organs begin to break down, it's a catabolic state of metabolism. In this state, food cannot be absorbed; tissues no long heal well; infections are difficult to cure; and an irreversible downward spiral is set in motion. Whatever nutrients Cindy was taking in would not stop the catabolic process. Thank God, it was not a painful one.

We set up a meeting with Stephanie, the hospice nurse, and sat outside on the patio, where John could be perfectly honest and the staff couldn't hear.

"I know my sister, and she wouldn't want to be living this way. She's stuck in bed with the TV on all the time, alone in a room with one tiny window, with no quality to her life at all." He looked at Stephanie sternly. "You know, she never owned a TV. In your best estimation, how long can she go on like this?"

"We don't really know, but she's severely anorexic, and it puts a strain on her heart. My best guess is she'll last maybe a couple more months."

I took John's hand. "I've noticed something when I feed Cindy. She doesn't acknowledge the food when you show it to her, but when I touch her lips with the spoon, she opens her mouth like a little bird. It almost seems like a primal reflex. I wonder if we should stop trying to provide nutrition? We can all see it is not making one bit of difference."

"This is a tough place to be with a loved one, and I can't tell you what to do," Stephanie replied. "My suggestion is for the two of you to talk with Jean, the social worker, and our medical director. If you decide to stop feeding Cindy, we can keep her comfortable."

Even though John understood catabolic metabolism, he had to ask, for his own peace of mind, "Is starvation painful? That's what we'd be doing to her, right?"

Stephanie shook her head. "No—she's emaciated now,

even though she's being fed. During the final months of life, the body's ability to process and utilize food changes. People do not die because they are not eating; they do not eat because they are dying." I glanced at John as she said this. "Complications due to forced feeding and the use of tube feedings can actually hasten dying. Cindy will be more comfortable when not taking in nutrition. One reason is that endorphins, the body's natural painkillers, which promote a sense of well-being and comfort, are released then."

I listened intently to her explanation and thought how our world seems to revolve around food. Denying nutrition to someone seemed cruel, but surely it would be more cruel to continue trying to feed Cindy. Later that evening, John called his father to ask his opinion. He didn't judge John; he supported him. "Do what you think is best for Cindy. I don't want her to suffer anymore either."

John asked Jean to meet us in his office the next day, and when she arrived, he got right to the point. "We've talked a lot about it, and we want to stop feeding Cindy. My father agrees with me. She's not going to get any better, and the nutrition is not benefiting her. We want to let her go."

Jean tapped her pencil on the table. "This doesn't happen very often, but if that's what you want to do, we'll support you. I just want to warn you that you may have some resistance from the caregivers."

"Do you really think it will be a problem?"

"It could be. Stephanie and I can work with the staff and help them understand your reasoning. Hopefully, we can assure them she won't have any pain."

Over the years, Marie had continued to visit Cindy, so John decided to call his cousin. "I want her to know what we're doing, because she and Cindy have always been close. She sees Cindy often, and I appreciate it."

He invited Marie and her husband to our house for dinner that weekend. John and I tried our best to explain the importance of quality of life, to clarify how little difference nutrition makes to a dying patient, to stress how Cindy would not have wanted to continue in this state. I was skeptical she got it. As they left, Marie said, "I've never gotten over my mother's death. I don't know how I'll ever get over Cindy's."

When they were gone, I asked, "Didn't your Aunt Jessica die over forty years ago?"

Two nights later, the telephone rang, and Marie began chastising John. "It's not about you, Marie. It's about Cindy! She's my sister, and I don't want her suffering any longer." He ran his hand through his hair in frustration. "I know her better than you—that's why she gave me power of attorney. She trusted me to make the right decisions, not you!"

I could tell she kept cutting John off. Finally, he told her, "I disagree, Marie. I'm going to hang up now, since you haven't heard a word I've said."

I was on the edge of my seat. "What did she say?"

John rubbed the back of his neck. "She's going to take us to court if we don't feed Cindy. She says we're murdering a vibrant person, and they are going to do everything they can to stop us."

John asked a good friend of ours, an estate lawyer, for advice. He considered it a no-win situation: If we went to court, he told us, Marie would petition to be put in charge of Cindy's care, and the conservatorship proceeding would probably involve a fight over whether it had been Cindy's desire not to have her life continued when she was able to state that desire, that is, when she'd signed the power of attorney form. He said both sides would spend a lot of money, and the case could go on for years. His advice was to keep feeding her.

"So what's the use in having the power of attorney?" I asked. "It doesn't serve any purpose if someone like Marie can come along and take away the power Cindy gave you. She knew you would have her best interests in mind."

"It all changes when you go to court," John said. "This is really bullshit."

Needless to say, we didn't sleep much that night. John kept repeating, "I know my sister! She would not want to live this way." Around five a.m., John decided to call Marie and set up a time and place to talk.

The kids were still home for the holidays, and John and I glued smiles on our faces. Marie had agreed to drive to Auburn and meet at a coffee shop at noon. My anger was still raging, so I thought it best for John to go alone. At this point, with the loss of his last two family members approaching, John's energy was depleted, and he admitted that Cindy wouldn't want her brother and cousin to be arguing this way. Not wanting to fight any longer, he agreed to continue feeding his sister.

34

By the first of the year, our weekend treks to Martinez had become imperative, because Big John was weak, unable to eat much, and wished to have his son near. During the week, he called often, and I listened patiently. His pain was unpredictable, and he was working to manage it the best he could, but it was escalating out of control. At the end of the conversation, he always said, "Don't give John all the details. He doesn't need to know."

In early March, I headed home one morning after my workout and visit to Cindy. The phone was ringing as I opened the door, and my gym bag and purse hit the ground. Any phone call made me jumpy these days. "Therese, I need to go to the hospital!" Big John whispered. "My pain is terrible. I didn't sleep a wink last night."

"John, take a pain pill. And call 911 if it's that bad."

"No, they don't work. Could you and John come and take me to the hospital?"

Still in my gym clothes, I called John. "Something is really wrong if he wants to go to the hospital. Maybe this is it." In thirty minutes, we were on the road to Martinez. Big John was standing in his garage, smoking a cigarette and talking with his neighbor Randy. His shoulders were sagging, and his face was gray.

"How're you doing, Dad?"

Big John's brow furrowed. "Not too good. Can we go to the hospital?"

"Sure. What do you need to take with you?"

"Nothing. Let's go." He handed me his keys and said, "I've paid all my bills, and my paperwork is organized on the kitchen table. I've cleaned up the house and watered my garden."

Then he handed John his wallet and slowly turned back to look at his house, as if he were saying goodbye. John and I looked at one another, each grabbed one of his father's arms, and we headed for the car. Once we were on our way, it wasn't five minutes before the pain returned, and it never stopped.

I held onto the armrest and prayed we wouldn't get into an accident. John got off the freeway at Walnut Creek, weaving in and out of cars, and soon the car screeched to a stop in front of the Kaiser Permanente emergency room. Big John moaned, and if not for the seat belt, I would have hit my head on the dashboard. I jumped out of the car and retrieved a wheelchair, and we raced to the triage area. Big John's color had gone from gray to white, and he was about to lose consciousness.

Through the night, we watched over him, held his hand, and prayed for his pain to subside. When the tests were complete, a doctor told us, "He has a huge tumor in his belly that's wrapped around his intestines. It's inoperable."

Hearing that, John slipped into shock; the doctor waited while I guided him to a chair and walked back to the nurses' station. "He is my father-in-law, and I've known him for over thirty years. He's eighty-five and has been battling cancer for five years. His wish was to stay in his home tending his garden, making his own decisions, for as long as possible. He doesn't want any heroic measures, and most of all, he doesn't want to end up in a nursing home with no quality to his life, just to die at a later time. His son and I request comfort care. John has power of attorney." I choked on my words. "This man deserves to die with dignity, without pain or suffering."

Just then, a nurse yelled, "Doctor, we need you." The doctor ran into the room and read the tape spewing from the heart-monitoring machine near Big John's bed. Something registered in John's brain, and he was suddenly by my side, observing the chaos in the room. We kept asking, "What's happening?"

The doctor motioned to the nurse, and she pushed us out of the room. "Your father just experienced a massive heart attack. We're going to take him to ICU." A couple of hospital workers kicked the locks off the bed and wheeled him out and into an elevator. I asked what floor the intensive-care unit was on, and John and I got there just as they were hooking his father up to a multitude of machines. John looked at me, sad and upset. "Why are they doing this? He doesn't want this."

There was so much commotion in the room, I didn't know who to talk to. I grabbed a nurse as she was leaving and said, "This man's son wants to talk to the doctor in charge right now!"

She pushed us to the waiting room, and we paced until the doctor came in. John was livid. "Look. My dad doesn't want any heroic measures. I want him off these machines right now. He knew he was dying. He doesn't want to be kept alive."

We followed him back into the room, where I couldn't help shaking my head and muttering, "He should never have been brought up here."

It seemed like hours before Big John was unhooked from the monitors and wheeled into a regular hospital room. He was unconscious, and his breathing was labored. John sat on the bed; I dropped into a chair next to it. I felt as if I'd been run over by a truck.

About an hour later, someone entered the room and introduced himself as the hospitalist—a physician whose primary professional focus is the general medical care of hospitalized patients. John asked him, "How much time do you think he has?"

"It's hard to tell. It could be hours or a few days."

We walked outside to clear our heads, since we hadn't slept or eaten in thirty-six hours. As we stared at our coffee cups, I said to John, "Maybe we should call everyone and suggest they come. They'll want to see him before he dies."

Back in Big John's room, John called his Uncle Jack and his father's neighbors, Kelly and Randy, and I called Keith. Big John was so quiet and still; it just wasn't like him. I pulled the blanket up under his chin, and when I tucked it in at the foot of the bed, his feet were ice cold. Big John's circulation hadn't been good for years; he wore long underwear under his pants all year round. I asked the nurse for a couple of warm blankets, and when she brought two fresh out of a microwave, I wrapped his feet and legs with them, praying the blankets made him more comfortable.

Not long after that, people started arriving. Kelly and Randy had picked up Aunt Faye and Uncle Jack, and soon Keith and his girlfriend, Fran, walked in. The two-patient room was so small, I suggested going to a waiting area to talk. John looked at these folks who were important to his father and turned his head away, unable to speak.

"The doctor said John is in a coma and probably won't wake up," I told them. "You are welcome to go into his room and spend some time with him." No one spoke. "Uncle Jack and Aunt Faye, why don't you go first, then John and Keith?" Kelly and Randy seemed hesitant. "John would want to see you. You've lived across the street from him for more than thirty years and have been such good friends," I reassured them. "Please go in and take your time."

Once his family and friends had been with Big John, we gathered in the waiting area again. "The doctors can't tell us how long he has, so why don't you all go home for now? You can come back tomorrow if you like. We promise to call when anything happens."

John didn't want his father to be alone; the bed chairs looked uncomfortable, but we were determined to stay and watch over him. I went to the head of the bed to check on him. His breathing pattern had changed; each exhalation was longer than the inhalation. He was Cheyne-Stoking, a pattern of breathing characterized by progressively deeper, sometimes faster, breaths followed by a gradual decrease until the breathing temporarily stops; this is called apnea. As the pattern repeats, each cycle takes from thirty seconds to two minutes.

This type of breathing indicates that death is near. Indeed, Big John's lips, hands, and feet had become a pasty-looking gray. My pulse quickened, and I motioned to John. "Come here," I said gently. "Your dad is going right now."

John raced to the other side of the bed, and we watched his father take his last breath. John gasped. "I can't believe how quick it was."

John Marin died at eleven p.m. on March 11, 2008. He was eighty-five years old.

Big John's breathing had been loud and labored; now the room was quiet. John sat down heavily at the foot of the bed. "Are you all right, honey?"

He nodded. "I'm going to let the nurses know he's gone."

A few minutes later, a nurse entered the room to tell us a doctor would be in soon. As we waited for him, I asked John, "Did you see that smoke, mist—I don't know what to call it—drift up out of your dad when he died?"

John said, "Yes. What do you think that was?"

I hesitated, trying to find the right words. "I think it was his soul or his spirit leaving his body."

❧❧❧

We returned to Big John's house around three a.m., exhausted and in need of sleep. John was up at six, his usual time, and let me sleep until I woke up at eight. He started calling family at nine. Kelly and Randy saw our car in the driveway and rang the doorbell. When we told them Big John was gone, Kelly cried.

At the funeral home that afternoon, we discovered his policy called for cremation, with a viewing the night before. I did not look forward to an open casket, but this was Big John's wish. We were still wiped out, so we slept twelve hours in Martinez and drove back to Auburn the next day. On the way home, we talked about telling Cindy. John was beside himself. "I don't think I can tell my dying sister our father is dead." He decided to ask Marie to do it.

Since John had no siblings to help plan the funeral, he asked his godfather, one of his cousins, to lead the service, because he didn't have the strength to do it alone.

We flew Vanessa from San Diego to Oakland, and Keith and Fran picked her up at the airport and drove to Martinez. As a family, we designed a storyboard of John Marin's life with photos we found in the house that the kids and I had never seen. They learned some things about their grandfather and the life he'd led, and once again, I wished they'd had more time with him.

Since Big John was a World War II veteran with an honorable discharge, he qualified for a military funeral. Once again, family and friends gathered in Lafayette at Oakmont Memorial Park & Mortuary. The ceremony began with "Taps," which all recognized the moment the trumpet began to play. John bowed his head and then looked up, teary-eyed, as the color guard presented him with a United

States flag to honor his father. The kids and I stood together at the podium to pay tribute. I read Big John's favorite psalm, Psalm 23, until I was overcome with emotion. Keith read the final line.

Afterward, everyone gathered at Big John's house, and we laid out all the food the family had brought: fried chicken, pasta, potato salad, fruit salad; I'd made blueberry, chocolate, and apple pies. John interacted with his cousins and seemed most drawn to his Uncle Jack—the second-oldest of the Marin siblings, now the last of that generation.

Keith and Vanessa returned to their lives, and once back in Auburn, John and I went to see Cindy. Though her eyes appeared vacant, she understood on some level, because when John told her about the funeral, a tear slid down her cheek.

35

I thought getting away for a few weeks would be good for us, so later that month, we drove to Zion National Park, in southern Utah, in our fifth-wheel camper. We'd taken it out only once since we'd purchased it, because John didn't want to be too far from home.

Once we were in the park with the trailer set up, it felt so good to relax, enjoy a beer, and drink in the beauty of this exceptional place. The colors—the massive sandstone cliffs of cream, vermilion, and rose soaring into a brilliant blue sky—took our breath away. Each day, the Zion Canyon Shuttle took us to a new hiking trail. Rambling in this park, with nature hugging us on every trail, truly soothed our souls.

Two weeks later, we were on Highway 50 heading home. Known as "the loneliest highway," it is a two-lane adventure through the heart of Nevada. We'd filled the truck with gas before we got on the highway, because, the cashier informed us, it was two hundred miles to the next little town. After the most boring two hundred miles of my life, during which we passed only six cars, we stopped in Ely, Nevada, which had been a Pony Express station and a stagecoach stop on the Central Overland Route, which ran between Salt Lake City, Utah, and Carson City, Nevada.

As we were eating breakfast, my cell phone rang, but the call was dropped. When I recognized the number on my phone, my breath caught in my throat. "It's from Vickie. I'm going outside to see if I can get better reception." I crossed the street and dialed nervously. "Hi, Vickie, did you call?"

"Oh, thank goodness you called back, Therese." She paused and began to cry. "Cindy died a few minutes ago. Your cousins and Stephanie are here. Do you want to talk to her?"

Stephanie, the hospice nurse, came on the line and told me how sorry she was. It had been a peaceful death, she said. I began to shake uncontrollably. By then, John was walking toward me, and he ran and caught me before I fell. "Cindy," I said, and I handed him the phone.

I turned my head away so that he couldn't see the tears. He listened for a few minutes, said thank you and goodbye, then sat next to me, and I buried my head in his chest.

Once we were back on the road, my brain started working and I called Stephanie back. "Cindy wanted to donate to the Harvard Brain Tissue Center, like her sister, so I'll arrange for a pathologist to perform the procedure. Would you please call Lassila Funeral Chapels and tell them not to cremate her until that has been done?"

Cynthia Ann died quietly, a month after her father, in the early morning of April 14, 2008, three months after John and I had wanted to withdraw nutrition. Her death certificate named Huntington's chorea as the underlying cause of death. The main cause of death was cachexia, the general ill health and malnutrition, marked by weakness and emaciation, usually associated with severe disease. She was fifty-four years old.

After finishing the call, I sobbed again, having lost my beloved friend and third sister-in-law to this terrible disease. Then, as my tears abated, I thought of Cindy, and rejoiced in her release from her battered body. Her soul now resided with her sisters'.

❧❧❧

We drove six hundred miles, which made for a very long day, to get home as soon as we could. Yet again, we met with the people at Lassila Funeral Chapels. Yet again, John called his relatives with sorrowful news. That afternoon, we talked with Tricia, Cindy's main caregiver, who told us, "Two days before Cindy died, her eyes were fixed on the ceiling above the TV. She smiled and stared. So I asked her, 'Cindy, do you see something that makes you happy?' Of course, she couldn't answer me, so I encouraged her. 'Go to them.'"

I had heard similar stories many times, from hospice patients and their families, and I'd come to believe they were seeing loved ones already gone from our sight, reassuring them they would not be alone on their passage. It soothed my soul knowing that Lora, Marcia, and their father, seen only by Cindy, were encouraging her to join them. I could hear Big John saying, "Come on, babe; let's go together."

Once again, Keith and Fran drove up from San Jose and picked Vanessa up at the airport. We made the storyboards about their aunt's life on the back of the poster boards we'd used just a month earlier for their grandfather's celebration of life.

Once again, we were at Lassila Funeral Chapels. This time, John led the ceremony with the help of the new hospice chaplain, someone I didn't know. John was strong and pushed through his grief. "Cindy was my buddy, and I loved her. I'm here to honor her today."

Sitting next to me, Vanessa held my hand as, once again, I unleashed a river of tears. How I prayed that one day, my tears would run dry or I could find the strength to build a dam to hold them back.

When the celebration of Cindy's life was over and people were looking at the storyboards we'd made, a woman approached me. Staring at an older version of Lora, I felt chills run up my spine. She said, "Hi, I'm Eleanor, John's cousin from Galt"—Aunt Evelyn's daughter. Aunt Evelyn, one of just two of Phyllis's siblings to escape Huntington's, the woman who'd told the Marin sisters about their risk of

HD all those years ago, was still alive. We'd called her twice in the last month. She was ill and couldn't make the trips to the funeral home, and I thought it was very sweet of Eleanor to come to Cindy's service.

Once again, everyone gathered at our house for the ritual of eating comfort food: Chinese chicken salad, angel hair pasta with scallops, corn bread with honey. This time, we congregated in the yard to release white balloons, each one containing private words. Before Vanessa released hers, she showed me the picture of Kayla she'd drawn on it.

While the balloons were being released, John read a poem written by a friend in Cindy's Huntington's support group, in British Columbia.

CINDY'S TRAVELING SHOES

Wander lust really describes
The state of her mind through and through
Thru the world with her great heart
Photos bearing witness true
She's walked in Argentina
Colombia, Chile, and Peru
She's visited half the world by now
In Cindy's traveling shoes.
Long before she had H.D.
She had the walking blues
She loves the world...all of it
...and all its creatures too

> She was born in California
> It's a fine place to be
> But her soul found its home
> Right here in B.C.
> She's looked on the pyramids

And they looked back at her
She's seen half the world by now
You know her next trip is sure
Long before she had H.D.
She had the walking blues
She loves the world...all of it
...and all its creatures too
Her feet know the trails
In Alaska and B.C.
She's walked in Southeast Asia
...and in Zimbabwe....
She's traveled half the world by now
And there's still half to see.

The deaths of Big John and Cindy, barely a month apart, had stolen energy from our bodies and clouded our minds. The only way I could make sense of these turbulent times was to believe that darkness occurred before the dawn. John and I were strong people—we'd had to be—and I was certain that light would seep slowly back into our lives.

So I lovingly watched and supported my beloved as he fought the aloneness he felt after his accumulated losses. Patiently, I stood by him, ready to listen; but the Marin siblings had their own way of dealing with pain, and even as John's wife, I couldn't replace his sisters and the silent strength they had drawn from one another.

Over the past twenty-eight years, this man, my love— who'd had such a difficult childhood, no mother, a neglectful father, who had learned to bury his feelings—had become, like his sisters, a gentle, forgiving, considerate, loving adult, as well as a loving husband and excellent father. Despite his anger and frustration, John had worked hard to develop a good relationship with his father, with forgiveness in his heart, and through the years came a special rapport that I believe brought him a good measure of consolation.

❧❧❧❧

Having Big John's house empty that summer was a blessing for the three daughters of Aunt Faye and Uncle Jack, who were now living in the Chateau Retirement Community in Pleasant Hill. Aunt Faye was terminally ill, and when her daughters were in town, caring for their mother with the help of Kaiser hospice, they were able to stay in their Uncle John's house.

This was another significant loss for John. After Faye died, John started talking about retiring, after working for Placer County for thirty-four years, and attended classes offered by the county department of human resources to calculate his retirement benefits. After much contemplation, his decision didn't surprise me. "I'm going to retire at the end of the year."

In 2005, we had planned a trip for our twenty-fifth wedding anniversary, but the past two years had been so tumultuous, we'd put it on hold. In September, on John's fifty-fourth birthday and celebrating our twenty-eighth anniversary, we boarded a Royal Caribbean cruise ship and enjoyed a three-week tour through Europe. The beauty we discovered in Venice, Rome, and Paris rejuvenated our spirits and pushed the darkness away. We drank in the history, the culture, the sights, and, of course, the wine and food.

Big John's house awaited us. In all the years he and Lucy had lived there, it had never changed, inside or out, except for a new roof. The thought of emptying this big house was daunting. After returning from our trip, we felt strong and ready to face the memories we would uncover.

I approached John with a plan. "Why don't I drive the truck to Martinez on Wednesday morning and start working on the house? I can pick you up at the Martinez Amtrak station on Friday night, and we can work over the weekend together."

As I parked in the driveway and pushed the electric garage-door opener, I imagined Big John in his usual stance, smoking a cigarette by the shrubbery, awaiting our arrival. I gathered the papers thrown on the doorstep and opened the squeaky front door. An overpowering odor of cigarette smoke seemed to cling to everything. Standing in the hallway, I wholeheartedly believed Big John would appear from his bedroom and walk down the hall. Once I mustered the courage to move on, I wandered into every room, looking at its contents, opening and closing closet doors. Where to begin?

I retrieved the food, overnight bag, and numerous boxes from the truck, opened a bottle of water, and stepped through the sliding-glass door into the backyard. After taking many deep breaths of fresh air, I thought I was ready to tackle the house; but suddenly, I felt like a burglar, invading someone's privacy and taking things that weren't mine. Rummaging through Big John's personal items felt faintly sinister. I stepped back inside and sat in the recliner Big John always relaxed in, cigarette butts still piled in the ashtray on the table next to it. I realized this was the feeling I'd experienced so many years earlier when we'd closed up Marcia and Lora's apartments.

The pungent smoky smell started giving me a headache, so I opened every window in the house. The back bedroom seemed a good place to start, until I discovered all of Cindy's stuff was there. Curiosity took me into the master bedroom, opening dressers and drawers, and sure enough, there were

Lucy's clothes, shoes, makeup, and other items. She'd been dead for more than nine years.

After discovering what the house had in store for us, I sat in the living room for a while, staring out the picture window into the backyard and blinking my eyes, because scenes of Christmases with the four Marin siblings were dancing vividly across the glass. Tears threatened, but I quickly realized I should be glad, because those were happy times. With each framed photograph I took off the wall, I smiled.

We were able to have an estate sale in the front yard early in the new year. By then, we'd gone through everything but the garage and the walk-in closet in the master bedroom. One Saturday morning, while John sifted through his father's tools in the garage, I started taking Lucy's clothes from the built-in dresser. The dust generated by items that had been on the shelves for years tickled my nose, and I sneezed and sneezed again.

By four p.m., the end was in sight. I climbed a stepladder to reach the shelf in the very back of the closet, pulled everything forward, and tossed ancient shoes and purses onto the floor. Finally, I found an old shoebox tucked way back in a corner. The tape around it was yellow and brittle and crumbled in my hands; clearly, the box hadn't been touched in decades. The writing on the box top was in pencil and very faint. Looking closely, I could see it said "Phyllis."

I went into the living room, calling, "John, come look what I found. It has your mother's name on it."

His brow furrowed as he said, "Huh, I've never seen this box." We sat together on the couch as John carefully lifted out the box's faded treasures: photographs of his father and mother, a card certifying that Phyllis Marin had trained to work in some Martinez dry cleaners, a ring from Berkeley High School, more photographs.

My heart beat fast as I watched John shake out the rest of the contents. A little ring box tumbled out last. John picked it up and opened it slowly. Inside were a diamond ring and a narrow silver wedding band. A tiny, yellowed piece of paper slipped out, and John read it to me: "Phyllis's engagement and wedding band."

He closed the box, and we looked at the rest of the pictures without uttering a word.

Later than evening, we were in the backyard drinking a beer, pondering the day's events. Big John's grapevines were overgrown and hanging low from the arbor. His fruit trees looked healthy, even though no one had been tending them.

"He loved his garden, didn't he?" I remarked as John turned the chicken on his dad's Weber grill.

"He sure did. But you have to remember my dad was a farmer at heart. He loved working with soil and tending what he grew, and he had a green thumb." John went into the house and came out with a platter for the chicken. "I wonder how Phyllis ended up going to Berkeley High?" He shook his head. "I guess I'll never know the real story of my mom and dad."

John carried the chicken over to the table, and I retrieved the beans and salad from the refrigerator. About halfway through the meal, I said, "You know, John, maybe your dad planned it this way—I mean, keeping the ring and the pictures with your mother hidden all these years. They were the only personal things he brought here from the ranch! And knowing Lucy, he wouldn't have let her know they were here. Obviously, those items were precious to your father, because he'd kept them all these years. I don't know—perhaps he wanted you to discover them during a difficult time, hoping they would bring you some joy."

Even though John was not convinced, I saw it as a gift.

❧

Epilogue

In the summer of 2015, my son, Keith, married Frances Sorenson at the historic Rengstorff House, on the banks of Shoreline Lake, in the San Francisco Peninsula town of Mountain View. The manicured lawns, aromatic Victorian flower garden, and gorgeous views of the mountains made it a romantic spot in which to proclaim their vows. And in the fall of 2016, my daughter, Vanessa, married Scott Garrett in her hometown of Auburn, in the elegant garden overlooking the lush vineyard at Mount Vernon Winery. John and I could not be more delighted about these marriages, about the fine young people our children have become and the lives they are beginning. I am so happy to be experiencing this joy with my strong, healthy husband.

And after forty years, this man can still surprise me—shock me. Knowing that both our son and daughter want children of their own, he decided toward the end of 2015 to take the test for Huntington's—something we hadn't discussed in decades. He's long past the age range when symptoms manifest, which would seem to indicate he doesn't carry the mutated gene, but he wanted to give our children a definitive answer. So once again, we drove to Sacramento and met Dr. Vicki Wheelock, a neurologist at the HDSA Center of Excellence at the University of California, Davis, Medical Center.

The testing process began with a two-hour session that included meetings with a genetic counselor and a psychiatrist, then a physical examination by a neurologist and having blood drawn. All this was done anonymously, not involving an insurance company; it cost about a thousand dollars for the lab work and consultation. It was impossible for me not to feel worried and distracted until we got the results, which took around six weeks. They were negative! We were both so elated to finally know, without a doubt, that John does not carry the mutated Huntington's gene. My heart felt lighter than it had in forty years. Now we know that Huntington's will never again affect a member of the Marin family.

But we still think of those it affected, and John and I still miss his sisters terribly. How I wish all three could have been with us at Keith and Vanessa's weddings. How I wish they were still on this earth, so that we could enjoy one another, have the good times we used to, and grow old together.

And yet, the lives of Lora, Marcia, and Cindy are tightly woven into my own. It's a strong, warm fabric that provides comfort; I keep it close and draw strength from it. How they loved one another, John and me, and, even with all they'd endured as children, their father. How I admired each of them.

Lora was the sweetest, most generous person I have ever known. Through her caring, nonjudgmental character, I learned to love myself with all my shortcomings, and to accept others for who they are.

Marcia, the unassuming sibling, had the strength of an army in a subtle way. She never complained when compromise was her only option; she exemplifies the words *gentle* and *brave*. Her patience, grace, and courage motivated me to apply these qualities to my life. She is my hero.

Cindy was the most positive individual I have ever met. She embraced life and all it had to offer. Material things were unimportant to her; she drew joy from simple pleasures. She inspired me to live my life with John and our children as fully as possible.

My dream is to see this book on bookshelves and in libraries throughout the country, where their story will endure beyond my lifetime. I find contentment knowing that Lora, Marcia, and Cindy will be remembered each time this book is read, because there is nothing I want more than for others to know these three amazing Marin women.

Afterword

Inspired by Bruce Springsteen's
"A Land of Hope and Dreams"

We're all riders on a train traveling through life. The choices we make on the journey determine the weight of our load. When confronted with tough times, many folks discover they must lighten the load.

John Anthony Marin, my key rider, willingly disembarked in 1978, while I struggled with the direction my train would go. Eventually, I circled back to find him waiting patiently for me. He boarded my train again, and together, we rolled through the fields of life where sunshine streams and set a new destination, a land of hope and dreams.

My sisters-in-law—Lora, Marcia, and Cindy—sat next to us on my train for as long as fate allowed. As each sister disembarked, my emotions ran high; their departures came much too soon.

As my journey unfolded, other key passengers—Keith and Vanessa—came aboard, enriched my life, and encouraged my train to forge into the unknown. This was precious cargo and deserved every comfort and all the safety possible.

At times, my train hurled down such deep, dark ravines, into such deep, dark tunnels, that I feared it would not be able to climb out again. But my faith in a higher power fueled my train, and I traveled in and out of those ravines and tunnels with hope as my guiding light.

Long ago, I learned it is not the destination but the journey that is significant. We reach the final station soon enough, so I slowed the pace of my train to enjoy the passengers and the scenery, to learn patience, pray, meditate, and reflect on my life.

As the stops on my life's journey became longer, I could

enjoy, explore, and appreciate each place, each one unique, with a beauty and wisdom of its own. Each stop had a purpose, filled a need, conveyed a lesson. When the stop seemed to have no rationale, I waited, because I don't believe in coincidences, and its significance became apparent over time.

My train paused patiently as I watched for those who had fallen behind and assisted those struggling to come aboard. Delaying my train's departure for those passengers was essential, as they shared wisdom gathered during their travels and added joy to my journey.

The train has traveled through the seasons of my life, and as passengers boarded and disembarked, I came to understand the words *forgiveness* and *acceptance*. The human condition encompasses both peace and turmoil; they are interwoven. I have learned that peace is not the absence of conflict but the ability to cope. Now my train has begun taking long, relaxing breaks from its journey, pulling under the awning of tranquility. The relationships with my passengers, those still on my train and those sweet souls departed, still resonate within me and soothe my soul.

John, my soul mate, has been my companion on my train for thirty-six years. We have left our sorrows behind; we have made the journey through the darkness into the light together. And on January 8, 2016, our train sounded the bell of freedom, when John's test for Huntington's disease proved negative. Liberated at last from the threat of this disease, John and I now travel peacefully into the winter of our lives.

Huntington's Disease Update

While there's still no treatment or cure for this fatal progressive disease, scientists worldwide continue their research into Huntington's and other neurodegenerative diseases, including amyotrophic lateral sclerosis (ALS), Parkinson's, and Alzheimer's. At present, all are incurable, but researchers have found many similarities that relate these diseases to one another on a subcellular level. These similarities offer hope for therapeutic advances that could benefit many diseases simultaneously.

In terms of finding a treatment or cure, researchers say that Huntington's has an advantage over the other neurological diseases, because it's already known what causes HD, as well as who is at risk of developing it.

The first and largest HD clinical-research network, the Huntington Study Group, consists of more than four hundred active investigators, coordinators, scientists, and HD experts working at more than a hundred HGS-credentialed research sites around the globe, seeking treatments that can improve the quality of life and disease outcome for people affected by HD. (For more information, see huntingtonstudygroup.org.)

Many researchers believe the most exciting thing happening in HD research is a treatment approach called gene silencing. The Huntingtin [sic] gene—also called the HTT or HD gene—provides instructions for creating a protein called the huntingtin protein. This protein is what slowly kills the brain cells in HD sufferers. Gene silencing uses targeted molecules that, in layman's terms, tell the cells not to produce the harmful protein.

Ionis Pharmaceuticals, which has the most advanced HD-gene-silencing program, has developed a drug that targets the HD gene in mice, delivering a harmless virus through an injection into the blood. Mice treated with the drug have shown remarkable improvement in HD-like symptoms. Because running a clinical trial is expensive, Ionis has partnered with the pharmaceutical giant Roche to test the drug, which they call IONIS-HTTRx, as quickly and competently as possible. Clinical trials of the HTTRx drug are being conducted in Canada, the United Kingdom, and Germany. (To find out more about the clinical trials, see the website en.hdbuzz.net.)

The Huntington's Disease Society of America (HDSA), the premier nonprofit organization dedicated to improving the lives of those affected by HD, has a wealth of information on its website (hdsa.org). With the fundraising component to this book, I hope to generate thousands of dollars to donate to this fine group.

The Huntington Society of Canada is a not-for-profit charitable organization that raises money to fund medical research to delay or stop the progression of the disease, and to deliver counseling services to individuals and families living with HD. Its informative website is at huntingtonsociety.ca.

Acknowledgments

I began writing this story at our cabin at Lake Tahoe in March 2010, two years after the death of my third sister-in-law, Cindy, John's childhood buddy. Huntington's disease had already stolen Lora and Marcia, John's other sisters and my dear friends. Pamela Gusland, a doctor of psychology whom I saw for years, told me that studies have shown how writing influences the process of healing. I'm grateful she suggested writing a book to honor my sisters-in-law and acknowledge the twenty-eight years of watching these women I loved die protracted deaths.

Many thanks to the Sacramento Suburban Writers Club for sharing invaluable information and providing continuous encouragement to aspiring writers. I am deeply grateful to April Edsberg and Brit Lord, who listened with empathic hearts and read early first drafts of this story.

To Pamela Feinsilber, my editor, thank you for being the queen of questions, and for your gentle manner in explaining the "why" behind the suggestions that guided me to write a more compelling story. Your skill, enthusiasm, and encouragement have fueled my desire to become a better writer and forge ahead with my second book.

Many thanks to Book Passage, the renowned independent bookstore in Corte Madera, California, for creating the Path to Publishing program and helping first-time authors like me navigate the writing and publishing process. I appreciate the many workshops, classes, and more than eight hundred author events the store offers each year, too.

This book would not exist without my husband, John Marin, who brought me many glasses of wine and a variety of cocktails, pulled me out of my office to go on walks, and prepared hundreds of dinners while I wrote or stared out the window as day drifted into dusk. I'm indebted to him for sharing difficult stories of his childhood so that I could write an honest story to celebrate his three beloved sisters. Reliving their deaths is so painful, I know he will never read this book. But he has been my steadfast advocate, and I'm so grateful for his unending support.

And to my children, Keith and Vanessa, and their partners in life, Fran and Scott: You are my presents today and my gifts for tomorrow.

About the Author

Therese Crutcher-Marin lives with her husband, John Marin, in Auburn, California. They are involved in social issues close to their hearts. The eradication of Huntington's disease is of utmost importance, so Therese is donating the proceeds from sales of *Watching Their Dance*, her first book, to the Huntington's Disease Society of America (HDSA). John and Therese volunteer to help the homeless in their community, and John is a board member of two nonprofit organizations, PlacerArts and Placer County Land Trust. Therese has been a board member of the HDSA Northern California chapter since January 2017. She has not given up her love of writing and is now working on a novel. With the working title *Forever Young: Life with Thirteen Siblings in the Breadbasket State of Kansas*, the novel is based on the lives of her paternal grandmother, Christine Mary (Mages) Crutcher, who died in 2014 at age 102, and her 87-year-old father, James Crutcher, who resides in Citrus Heights, California.

47353926R00175

Made in the USA
San Bernardino, CA
28 March 2017